WITHDRAWN

Wagner's *Ring* and German Drama

Recent Titles in
Contributions to the Study of Music and Dance

Music of the Repressed Russian Avant-Garde, 1900–1929
Larry Sitsky

The Voice of Nations: European National Anthems and Their Authors
F. Gunther Eyck

Communities in Motion: Dance, Community, and Tradition in America's Southwest and Beyond
Susan Eike Spalding and Jane Harris Woodside

The Music of Stuart Saunders Smith
John P. Welsh

The Music of Morton Feldman
Thomas DeLio

Dancing Spirits: Rhythms and Rituals of Haitian Vodun, the Rada Rite
Gerdès Fleurant

Wiser Than Despair: The Evolution of Ideas in the Relationship of Music and the Christian Church
Quentin Faulkner

The Music of Anthony Braxton
Mike Heffley

Jazz Poetry: From the 1920s to the Present
Sascha Feinstein

Whose Master's Voice?: The Development of Popular Music in Thirteen Cultures
Alison J. Ewbank and Fouli T. Papageorgiou, editors

The Piece as a Whole: Studies in Holistic Musical Analysis
Hugh Aitken

Mythology as Metaphor: Romantic Irony, Critical Theory, and Wagner's *Ring*
Mary A. Cicora

Wagner's *Ring* and German Drama

❖ Comparative Studies in Mythology and History in Drama

MARY A. CICORA

Contributions to the Study of Music and Dance, Number 52

Greenwood Press
Westport, Connecticut • London

Library of Congress Cataloging-in-Publication Data

Cicora, Mary A., 1957–
    Wagner's Ring and German drama : comparative studies in mythology
and history in drama / Mary A. Cicora.
        p. cm. — (Contributions to the study of music and dance,
    ISSN 0193-9041 ; no. 52)
    Includes bibliographical references (p.   ) and index.
    ISBN 0–313–30529–3 (alk. paper)
    1. Wagner, Richard, 1813–1883. Ring des Nibelungen. 2. Drama.
I. Title. II. Series.
ML410.W15C54 1999
    782.1'092—dc21   98–37782
                                 MN

British Library Cataloguing in Publication Data is available.

Library of Congress Catalog Card Number: 98–37782
ISBN: 0–313–30529–3
ISSN: 0193–9041

First published in 1999

Greenwood Press, 88 Post Road West, Westport, CT 06881
An imprint of Greenwood Publishing Group, Inc.

Printed in the United States of America

The paper used in this book complies with the
Permanent Paper Standard issued by the National
Information Standards Organization (Z39.48–1984).

10 9 8 7 6 5 4 3 2

Contents

Preface

This comparative study of Wagner's *Ring* and selected German dramas gradually grew from a larger project that attempted to place the drama theory presented in the second part of *Oper und Drama* and demonstrated by the *Ring* within the context of German tragedy theory from Schiller to Brecht. My intent was to focus not on poetics, such as "open" and "closed" form or Aristotelian unities, but, rather, on the notion of mythology in drama, which would become the organizing principle for my comparisons. The chapter on *Oper und Drama* and the *Ring* dissociated itself from the rest and begged for expansion, magnetically bringing with it the observations about the affinities between the *Ring* and German Romantic drama, which had originally belonged to a chapter on Wagner and Kleist. Thus, this new interpretation of the *Ring* completely split away from the remainder of the project, grew to a four-chapter study, and became a separate publication.[1]

Four of the other chapters subsequently became, in altered form, the present collection. My desire here is to indicate some ways of analyzing Wagner's dramas in conjunction with the works that are more traditionally included in German drama history, and thus transcend some boundaries between disciplines that are often regarded in isolation from each other. Thus, the two books are still somehow related. This one builds on the other one. I have kept the theme of the interrelationship of mythology and history as a unifying focus, using the analysis of the *Ring* that I previously evolved as a basis for the comparisons. Some of the insights presented in more detail elsewhere will be repeated when necessary.

❖

This study was one of several written during my stay as a Visiting Scholar at Stanford University. I would like to thank the German Studies Department at Stanford University for allowing me access to the library facilities. The staff of Green Library made the technical aspects of my research much easier by giving me special borrowing privileges, and they made the library work a real pleasure in other ways as well. I have a special thanks for Paul Robinson of the History Department at Stanford, who patiently read, reread, and criticized these manuscripts. The interest that he took in this project, and his feedback on the manuscripts, were of enormous help to me in completing these books.

All translations from the German into English, unless otherwise noted, are my own.

NOTE

1. See *Mythology as Metaphor: Romantic Irony, Critical Theory, and Wagner's* Ring (Westport, CT: Greenwood Press, 1998).

Introduction: On Finding Mythical-Historical Parallels between Music-Drama, Spoken Drama, and Opera

*R*ichard Wagner clearly saw and consciously placed his works within the German drama tradition. The second part of *Oper und Drama* presents a selective survey and slanted analysis of the history of German drama. His pronouncements are controversial, his method highly suspect. However, it is not evading the issue to say that the question of factual validity or interpretative integrity according to modern philological standards is not of chief importance. Inconsistencies and misinterpretations can often be telling to the utmost. The text must be taken as it is, Wagner's purposes taken into consideration and respected. What is crucial to this text is Wagner's intent to ground, that is, to legitimate and validate, his own music-drama within the tradition and vis-à-vis earlier works of the canon. This is just one instance of what Bryan Magee refers to as Wagner's incessant historicism, the constant desire to show where each phenomenon under discussion originated, and what function and significance it has within the teleology of history.[1] Wagner was, all would agree, a multifaceted talent. He needs to be critically regarded as such.

Furthermore, *Oper und Drama* also demonstrates an ambivalent stance toward the German drama tradition. Wagner begins the second part of *Oper und Drama* with polemic against Lessing, and he revises Lessing in a way that is fully consistent when understood in the light of his other concerns. He devastates the German dramatic tradition with the bold statement that Lessing has been misread and misunderstood. Wagner writes that when Lessing, in *Laokoon*, forbids the mixing of genres, he is not referring to drama but, rather, only to narrative literature, that is, literature that appeals solely to the imagination, not to the senses. In this manner, Wagner justifies his use of music in drama. For Wagner, mixing genres meant reuniting the art forms that with the decline of Greek tragedy had become separated, this disintegration of the unity of the arts being a symptom of the basic fragmentation that afflicts modern culture in general. Moreover, Wagner felt that bringing the arts back together would actually lead to the regeneration of modern culture. In Wagner's theory, art can affect politics, and the inner can revolutionize the outer.

In particular, Wagner's thought belongs to the stream of nineteenth-century redefinitions of tragedy. He explicitly placed his works within the tradition of Greek tragedy, and many Wagner scholars have variously investigated this topic. For instance, the influence of Greek tragedy upon Wagner's works has best been outlined by Wolfgang Schadewaldt.[2] The three main aspects of Wagner's work that show, according to Schadewaldt, the influence of Greek tragedy are, first, the notion of Greek tragedy as a religious celebration; second, the raw material of Greek tragedy as myth and legend, that is, indigenous products of the "Volk"; and, third, Greek tragedy as a "Gesamtkunstwerk," that is, as a union of the arts of poetry, music, and dance.

An analysis of Wagner's theory with regard to only the use of music in drama thus neglects this important aspect of his thought. Wagner was, of course, first and foremost a composer, but to regard his works as purely musical phenomena does a great injustice to their complexity, in fact, their very nature as a synthesis of art forms, as Wagner prescribed, of which music is just one, regardless of the almost overwhelming importance it assumes in his theory and dramas. In *Oper und Drama*, Wagner made a point to describe music as a means to an end, and not an end in itself. Not only does this treatise contain an elaborate theory about how to synthesize words and music in the art-work of the future, which is presented mostly in the third part of the treatise, but in the second part, Wagner discusses German drama at great length. In this manner, Wagner embeds the theory about words and music in a broader framework. He makes it clear that the work he sketches out is drama, not opera. In particular, it is a modern German rebirth of tragedy.

Wagner never advocated a simple return to the form of Greek tragedy. He felt that it needed to be redefined for the modern age, which is what he does in the second part of *Oper und Drama*. He essentially deconstructs Greek tragedy, and in doing so he presents a theory that describes the rebirth of Greek tragedy on the stage of reflection. Thus, when one simply compares the plots of his dramas with the myths of Greek tragedy by drawing parallels between the *Ring* and plays by, for instance, Sophocles or Aeschylus, one completely ignores Wagner's insistence that Greek tragedy cannot be revived in its previous form but, rather, that it needs to be tailored to the problems of modern times.

Considering, then, that Wagner distinctly opposed previous styles of opera to drama, thus classifying his works as the latter type of art form, it seems highly ironic that his theoretical and dramatic output is treated primarily in music histories and music departments. Of course, there is no dearth of interdisciplinary works about Wagner's theoretical and dramatic output. Wagner, probably more so than any other composer, is frequently discussed by scholars of disciplines other than music. For instance, it is all too clear that Wagner was a political phenomenon. His influence on the plastic arts and painting has also been investigated. There is, in fact, a veritable plethora of studies that present treatments of Wagner's work in relation to the German literary tradition.

For example, the thematically organized studies of Othmar Fries[3] and Paul Arthur Loos[4] treat the topic of Wagner and German Romanticism, which is, as they have shown, a rich field for scholarly investigation. Dieter Borchmeyer offers much of value for the literary scholar in his general, tripartite "Germanistik" approach to Wagner's work.[5] I will be building upon some of his work. He notes, for instance, affinities between Wagner's theories and the aesthetics of Weimar Classicism, and he repeatedly places Wagner in the tradition of Schiller. He shows that the dramas by Wagner can be treated in the tradition of German literature. In a chapter of the "influence" section of his study, Borchmeyer gives an overview of Wagner's possible influence on the Hofmannsthal-Strauss works.

Most common are literary studies of how Wagner used his source material and, conversely, inquiries into Wagner's impact on particular German writers. For this reason, investigations of Wagner's works by literary scholars often discuss medieval literature and modern prose works. When comparative studies of Wagner's dramas with specific works of German literature are undertaken, these investigations are usually "genetic." One finds an allusion to, or use of, one in another. For instance, one compares a scene or element of the *Ring* with the corresponding analogue from, say, one of the *Edda*s or the *Volsunga Saga*, that is, the source material that gave rise to it.[6] Considering how well read Wagner was and the various literary, philosophical, and political influences on his thought, it seems clear that his works need to be studied within the German tradition and with regard to the broader history of ideas. Because his sources were primarily medieval and not dramatic, Wagner's works, though, are rarely treated extensively and exclusively in relation to German drama.

Furthermore, because scholars can easily find explicit allusions to Wagner's works in stories and novels of such writers as Thomas Mann and Theodore Fontane, studies of Wagner influence on German writers often focus on narrative literature.[7] The allusions in Mann's prose to Wagner's music or music-dramas, conversely, always raise the question of how the Wagner works function in the specific narratives of Mann, that is, how Mann has used the Wagner works as sources. Scholars have repeatedly discussed Mann's ambivalent feelings toward Wagner and his works, as documented in his many essayistic treatments of Wagner from all different times of his life. However, aside from occasional discussions of the obvious pairing of Wagner's and Hebbel's respective versions of the Nibelung legend, one rarely sees detailed comparisons of Wagnerian dramas with specific works from the more traditional canon of German drama.

Moreover, attempts to discuss Wagner and his works in German drama histories tend toward theoretical generalization. Including Wagner and his works in a history of German drama seems to pose large theoretical and methodological problems that need to be addressed in a small space, and that therefore deflect attention from a discussion of the Wagnerian music-dramas themselves. Therefore, one does not get beyond broad statements about genre that ignore the singularity of the music-dramas themselves and any interrelationships that the plots and characters of these dramas might have with similar or analogous ones from the German drama tradition. Wagner does not seem to fit into the German drama tradition. Rather, his works, probably because they use music as well as words, seem instead to stand outside of it.

Helmut Schanze, for instance, in his work on German drama in the age of Realism, includes a section on opera, explicitly raising the issue that Wagner tackled in his Zurich trilogy, that is, what the difference between "opera" and "drama" is, and to which genre Wagner's works really belong.[8] Schanze stresses the contradiction that Wagner's works are indeed received as "opera," and notes that in this respect Wagner's utopian strivings failed, considering the care that Wagner took to differentiate his later works from the genre of traditional "opera." Schanze also questions the validity of discussing opera in a history of drama, pointing out that in opera, as Wagner pointed out in *Oper und Drama*, the language and the libretto are often regarded as mere pretexts for the music, which is usually the dominant medium in this form. Thus, the discussion that he presents remains theoretical; close analysis or further discussion of Wagner's music-dramas is also precluded.

In a different section, Schanze places *Oper und Drama* at the center of his discussion.[9] As his work is a survey, Schanze is concerned with situating Wagner's thought in relation to the major nineteenth-century currents of thought and in relation to the dates around which he orients his discussion. Using 1848/50 as a political and social caesura, Schanze notes the affinity of Wagner's theories with those of the Romantics (in particular, the "Gesamtkunstwerk" and "progressive Universalpoesie"), his theoretical rejection of the novel and the purely verbal drama, and his dual opposition to the trends represented by Lessing and Shakespeare. Schanze notes the conflation of art and social revolution in Bayreuth, and the eventual irony of the whole Bayreuth project, that Wagner's art in Bayreuth was originally intended to be a revolutionary and utopian work aimed at the "Volk," but it in fact became the exclusive possession of a small, select circle.

Schanze centers his analysis of *Oper und Drama* and his discussion of Bayreuth on a rough contrast between Wagner's emphasis at different times of his life. He outlines a shift in Wagner's theory of art from "drama" to "music," attributing Wagner's later emphasis on the dominance of music to the failure of the revolution, and the resultant necessity of communicating with the contemporary public by catering to its demands. The influences upon Wagner's thought were, however, literary as well as philosophical and political, the ones on which Schanze focuses. In the present study, moreover, I intend to show how various currents of German thought find expression in both German dramas and Wagner's *Ring* tetralogy. Furthermore, the interrelationship of aesthetics and politics in Wagner's thought was not a simple one, and politics cannot adequately explicate works of art. Though the contemporary political context must be taken into consideration, I feel it cannot replace textual analysis of individual works of drama and music-drama.

In his history of German drama in the age of Realism, Fritz Martini stresses Wagner's theoretical opposition to spoken drama.[10] He feels that Wagner's art is important in relation to the history of German drama only insofar as it represents an opposition to a purely verbal kind of drama. Paradoxically, though, his discussion of Wagner is aimed at explaining why a discussion of Wagner has no place in a history of German drama. He opens his discussion of Wagner and his works by stating that they have no place in a literary history. Because his music-drama attempted to fuse the word with the tone, it impoverished, Martini asserts, both language and music.

That music was an essential part of Wagner's theory and art is beyond dispute. However, I differ with Martini in his conclusion, and argue that it does not necessarily follow from this that his works have no place in a history of German drama. Though my approach differs from his, I will build upon and apply Martini's idea. Thus I will show the similarities as well as the differences between Wagner's music-dramas and selected spoken dramas. While still taking the words/music problem into consideration and taking into account the differences between purely spoken drama and music-drama, I will also point to specific affinities and parallels, rather than general differences and oppositions, between Wagner's music-dramas and spoken German dramas. Such an analysis can indeed be interesting, as music-drama is such a vastly different medium from spoken drama; one can ask in what way the different constraints of each type of drama may actually determine the plot of a work.

Benno von Wiese, in his work on German tragedy from Lessing to Hebbel, discusses the contradiction inherent in Wagner's work, the unity of the arts or "Gesamtkunstwerk," as a nineteenth-century synthetic rebirth of Greek (mythological) tragedy.[11] Wagner is typical of his age, von Wiese notes, in showing a mixture of pessimism and utopianism. One can observe this dichotomy in Wagner's dramas, I would argue, particularly in the contradictory nature of myth in them. In the present study, I will also expand on von Wiese's theme and explore how Wagner's modern reworking of Greek tragedy is manifest in his music-dramas themselves. Wagner's work as a kind of modern mythical drama that consciously opposes the modern technical age is a complex phenomenon indeed. It defies reduction to the usual genre and medium classifications. Wagner's theoretical writings deal, to a great extent, with the redefinition of genres. Wagner did what Hans Sachs instructs Walther to do. He made his own rules.

In the present study, I propose a way in which Wagner's works can be situated in and discussed with reference to German drama history. To this end, I make Wagner the focal point of the comparisons that I present, rather than trying to fit him into a preconceived plan or discussing him within the boundaries of traditional forms and disciplines, which he took special pains to redefine and the rules of which he violated. Wagner is, of course, a singular phenomenon. A section on Wagner in a history of nineteenth-century German drama, which is by its very nature and function limited in size and scope, cannot possibly do justice to these complex issues.

German drama history as conventionally considered and understood is, in fact, simply too broad in scope to leave enough room for the complex phenomenon that is Richard Wagner to be treated in detail. Wagner's music-dramas are complex and influential enough that they really need to be made the focus of a study, as I have done here. My treatment of German drama history in this book does not approach the panoramic scope of the surveys I have been discussing. My intent is to write an analysis of Wagner's works with reference to German drama history, rather than just including him in a history of German drama. Wagner, and not German drama history, is, accordingly, the center of my discussion.

The present study is an attempt to place Wagner's *Ring* within the context of the German drama tradition. It proceeds through a series of comparative studies, treating dramas (or, in some cases, as in those of the Hofmannsthal/Strauss or Brecht/Weill works, operas) of Schiller, Hebbel, Hofmannsthal, and Brecht. Thus, I work primarily from the dramas themselves, rather than from their theoretical foundations. The main idea of the book, the focal point of my comparisons, is the notion of mythology or mythological drama.[12] I could also state this thesis in the converse, working from the other part of the dichotomy, and consider Wagner's work as a revolt against the hegemony of the historical drama in Germany.[13] Several of the texts that I analyze can be broadly classified as historical dramas, though, as I show, they are also mythological or antimythological in other respects as well.

Although I do not undertake a close analysis of the complex mythical nature of the *Ring* in this study, any treatment of the *Ring* and selected German dramas with regard to the use of history and myth in drama must be preceded by some preliminary remarks concerning the *Ring* as a mythological work of art, and the dialectic of myth and history that the work represents. The brief summary of the basic problematic of history and myth in the *Ring* that I will now present shows that using this theme does not merely draw some coincidental and meaningless parallels between selected pairs of works, but, rather, that it is one way of penetrating to the core of these works themselves.

A cursory discussion of the mythical nature of the *Ring* shows that my pairing of history and myth is anything but contrived or forced. In Wagner's theory, history and myth actually imply each other. From the evidence of the spoken dramas and the operas that I consider in relation to the *Ring*, using myth in drama is often a problematic undertaking, for artificial myth resulting from modern consciousness is by definition not genuinely mythical. Furthermore, one can well suspect that the historical dramas under discussion are historical dramas because the authors disdained the use of mythical subject matter. What seems simple is often exceedingly complex. Myth is not necessarily mythical when used with a modern historical consciousness. Similarly, historical drama can be analyzed as displaying some kind of critical stance toward myth. In short, the texts under consideration all have a tension between history and myth.

My choice of unifying theme needs no justification. When asked about Wagner's contribution to the history of drama, most would agree with Thomas Mann that he discovered the use of myth for drama/opera. My choice of dramas (or operas) with which to compare Wagner's *Ring* thus facilitates this approach. Although not all of the dramas I discuss are mythological, the topic of mythological refabrication in drama, and the dichotomy and interrelationship of mythology and history, will nevertheless provide the points of comparison between each of these individual works and the aesthetic program upon which each drama or opera is based, on one hand, and on the other hand, the *Ring* and its aesthetic presuppositions.

The treatise *Oper und Drama*, the theoretical counterpart of the *Ring* tetralogy, is evidence enough that myth was, after all, a central point of Wagner's aesthetics. In *Oper und Drama*, he expounds at length on the origin and secondary use of myth. In doing so, he outlines a dialectic of history and myth, with one affecting the other. He even gives a sort of (Wagnerian, i.e., pseudoscientific) history of mythology, recounting the collision of various currents of mythology through history, and the demise of myth in the modern world. A major theme of this treatise, to which these historical explanations lead, is naturally a formulation of why music-drama should use mythology as its raw material.

The topic of myth is, of course, not a new one for Wagner scholarship. It is common knowledge that myth was an essential part of Wagner's theory. Scholars have discussed at length the use of myth as raw material for Wagner's music-dramas. Stefan Kunze, for instance, discusses Wagner's use of myth in relation to the aesthetics of German Idealism in the nineteenth century.[14] The Romantics considered art a substratum for symbolic revelations, for in representing a synthesis of the real and the ideal, it could thus constitute a sensual revelation of the Idea. Myth was deemed the appropriate vehicle for such symbolic revelations, for it was general and symbolic, and thus it legitimated the work of art.

It would not be an exaggeration to say that myth is probably the most essential element and main feature of the modern reworking of tragedy. Anette Ingenhoff has discussed how Wagner defines form (tragedy) with regard to raw material (myth).[15] Wagner's music-drama, as a modern version of tragedy, is thus a mythological drama by definition. Jean-Jacques Nattiez points out that Wagner's thinking was essentially metaphorical, and how Wagner, in his theoretical writings, often illustrates a theoretical point by means of a myth, in this manner placing an equals sign between two patterns of thought.[16] Nattiez discusses the *Ring* as a mythic account of the history of music.[17] One could take Nattiez' ideas further and suggest that, by positing an equation between history and myth, Wagner considers myth as a metaphor for history. Wagner did say, in a letter to Franz Liszt (11 February 1853), that his *Ring* was an image of world-history; he wrote that his *Ring* told the story of the beginning of the world and its destruction. In this manner I build upon Nattiez' ideas and apply them to my discussion of Wagner's work and that of other German dramatists. Myth as a metaphor for history is, it seems, interestingly enough, basically contradictory. The equation is intrinsically flawed.

To understand Wagner's use of myth in the *Ring*, one must first consider why he saw myth as essential to his music-drama. Myth, Wagner felt, was an explanatory model that presented a condensed, primal world-view that was thus readily comprehensible to the senses. Lengthy parts of *Oper und Drama* are devoted to discussions of how myth is formed. According to Wagner, myth expresses one's perceptions of one's surroundings, and it allows one to explain the world, and thus it communicates this world-view with other members of the "Volk." Wagner's theory of myth has an important regressive tendency. His use of myth as raw material for his music-dramas clearly places him within the Romantic tradition. Myth was, for this age of patriotic sentiments, a product of the German "Volk," and as such it was thought to have therapeutic value. Friedrich Schlegel, for instance, in his *Gespräch über die Poesie*, appealed for a "new mythology" to help unify society and thus mend the fragmentation of modern times.

Wagner's own works, however, though they use myth as raw material, are different kinds of myths from their primal source materials. One could say that they represent a higher level of myth. Wagner stressed the mythological nature of his own works. He was fond of drawing analogies between his works and Greek myth, as shown by his "Mitteilung an meine Freunde," in which he likens Lohengrin and Elsa to Zeus and Semele, and the Flying Dutchman to Odysseus. Scholars often discuss his abandonment of a drama plan based on Friedrich Barbarossa in favor of one about Siegfried, as recounted in his "Mitteilung," as a turn from history to myth. This turn from history to myth, though, was not a simple about-face, nor are the two terms of the dichotomy of history and myth mutually exclusive. Wagner views history in relation to myth, and vice versa.

Dagmar Ingenschay-Goch observes that Wagner sees myth as a product of the historical period in which it arose, and that he distinguishes between the structure and the manifestation of myths.[18] In this manner, he acknowledges the historicity of myth, for he theorizes that, depending on historical circumstances, myths appear different. In showing that Wagner acknowledges how myth changes with history, his theory, in fact, outlines complex multileveled processes of mythological refabrication. In discussing the use of myth in drama, *Oper und Drama* presents an elaborate theory of mythological reconstruction. In the modern age, Wagner felt, myth should be reworked from the standpoint of modern consciousness.

Throughout the treatise Wagner shows a historical consciousness concerning myth, and thus a self-consciousness of his own perspectivism. Wagner clearly realized that history affects myth. That is, he felt that myths appear differently at various periods of time depending on present external (i.e., historical) circumstances. In other words, myth fluctuates with and thus reflects history. According to Wagner, though, not only is myth historically conditioned, but it should be reworked to, in turn, change, that is, revolutionize history. Using myth in modern music-drama is, according to the theory presented in *Oper und Drama*, no simple undertaking but, rather, a complex and paradoxical project.

The *Ring*, for instance, is a synthetic mythology, a nineteenth-century artistic myth that gives a quasi-mythological explanation of world-history. However, the use of mythology in the nineteenth century was also, as Kunze remarks, an attempt to escape historicity. The *Ring* is a strange and fundamentally paradoxical work, indeed. A myth written by a nineteenth-century composer is a contradiction, an oxymoron of sorts. It is synthetic, fake, and inconsistent. Thus, the mythological nature of the *Ring* is not only complex, secondhand, and reflective, but also ambiguous and contradictory. Herbert Schnädelbach notes the paradox of an individual reconstitution of myth, which is, after all, by definition a product of a collective.[19] Accordingly, the mythological nature of the *Ring* cosmos is neither pure nor unproblematic. In other words, the work is not totally mythical in the sense that conventional mythology is. It has other, more modern characteristics.

Thus, mythological music-drama is not true for all time. Rather, it comments on the modern world; that is, it is historically conditioned. Dieter Borchmeyer, for instance, cites Wagner's statement from *Oper und Drama* about myth being true for all time, as a weapon with which to take issue against modern productions of Wagner's works, which Borchmeyer feels violate the mythological nature of these dramas.[20] However, in doing so, he overlooks the fact that Wagner goes on to say in the next line that it is the task of the poet to *interpret* mythology and thus formulate works that are at some remove from actual myth. Wagner's dramas are myths on the stage of reflection. It is not superfluous or trite, in this regard, to repeat the simple fact that the *Ring* was written by a nineteenth-century composer. Mythology is ancient and of anonymous, collective origin.

Studies of *how* Wagner used specific elements of myth abound.[21] Scholars have discussed at length how he recombined these fragments and elements to form new myths. What is most interesting, though, is what happens to the mythical nature of the works when these originally mythical elements are used in a nineteenth-century drama. Wagner wrote myths, that is, nineteenth-century synthetic reworkings of mythological stories or recombinations of mythological elements, that are thus not genuine myths. The *Ring* is actually a myth in two senses. One could say that its mythical nature is overdetermined.

In the sense in which Roland Barthes uses the term, "myth" designates a type of speech, a system of communication, a mode of signification. Everything can be a myth, he explains. There are formal limits to myth, but no substantial ones. To Barthes, myth is not defined by the object of its message, but rather by the way in which it utters this message.[22] Similarly, Friedrich Schlegel uses the word "myth" in two senses when he writes in his *Gespräch über die Poesie* that the world needs a new mythology, that is, a set of fictions, to be just what mythology was to the ancient world. A new myth is not the same as genuine myth. Kunze notes that the demand for a new, artistic myth is an admission that a binding mythology is lacking.

Wagner, moreover, sketches in his theoretical treatises a complex dialectical relationship between myth and history. Not only does history affect myth, but vice versa. According to Wagner, myth should affect history. Besides seeing myth as a metaphor for history, Wagner also establishes a causal relationship between the experience of his (quasi-) mythological drama and the resultant social revolution. Thus Wagner presents a reciprocal, revolutionary dialectic of myth and history. The aesthetic system of *Oper und Drama*, the poetics of the music-drama, is embedded into a "frame" that outlines the revolutionary function and societal purpose of art. The first two of the Zurich writings provide a context for *Oper und Drama*, which is thus political, though only in an indirect way. Wagner places his theory of myth in a larger framework that concerns the function of art (especially, of course, drama) in society. Myth had an important place in Wagner's aesthetics of audience reception. According to Wagner, not only could myth explain history; it could also change history.

Wagner felt that myth, when used in modern music-drama, could be revolutionary. Thus the Zurich writings present a utopian program. *Oper und Drama* is not a political tract; it is mostly concerned with operatic history, drama through the ages, and the poetics of the art-work of the future. "Die Kunst und die Revolution" forms a revolutionary "frame" for the elaborate theory of words and music, myth and tragedy, that Wagner presents in *Oper und Drama*. There can be no doubt, though, that Wagner wanted to change society with his music-drama. Myth, in his theory, though not directly political in its otherworldly unreality, is paradoxically highly politicized in what one could consider a specifically Romantic, Wagnerian way.

He demonstrates his linking of myth and revolution by giving, in *Oper und Drama*, a revolutionary, subversive interpretation of the myth of Oedipus. Wagner interprets this myth as portraying the conflict of the "state" and the free individual. Through the experience of such a drama that interprets this myth, the audience was to become wise through feeling. For Wagner at this time of his life, the topic of aesthetics was closely bound up with that of politics. Wagner was engaged in revolutionary activities at the time he was writing the Zurich treatises, and the *Ring* is, in form and content, undeniably a revolutionary work.[23] Paradoxically, the aim of Wagner's use of mythology, a main characteristic of which is its unreality and remove from normal bourgeois existence, is the reform or revolution of modern society or, in other words, the mythicization of history.

Wagner even states the usual tripartite model so common to the German tradition, the Romantics especially, in terms of history and myth. One of his ways of formulating this triad is to say that myth is the beginning and end of history. By defining tragedy as a mythological work of art and reworking mythology on a modern level of self-consciousness, Wagner can transcend tragedy and the dissonance of modern existence and thus redeem history through myth by, ironically enough, destroying myth. The *Ring* tetralogy, accordingly, reflects upon, and in doing so unworks, the form of tragedy. In this respect, too, Wagner belongs in the Romantic tradition. Wagnerian music-drama does seem very unlike the drama form that the Romantics were known for, the comedy or "Lustspiel." However, deeper affinities between these forms can be found. The Romantics were intent on repairing the dissonances of earthly existence. They therefore wanted to transcend tragedy in some kind of utopian reconciliation or ultimate redemption. Surprisingly, Wagner's work can be grouped with the dramatic production of such writers as Ludwig Tieck, as Wagner, too, in the cataclysmic redemption at the conclusion of the *Ring*, represents the Romantic transcendence of tragedy.[24]

Scholars have used traditional terms of drama analysis to demonstrate the complexity of Wagner's music-dramas. Anette Ingenhoff, in a study I cited earlier, and Reinhold Brinkmann[25] both discuss Wagner's drama theory, and the *Ring* in particular, with reference to the concepts of epic and drama. Carl Dahlhaus uses the oppositions of opera and drama, investigating if and how Wagner's dramas use the conventions of traditional opera, as well as the terms of Volker Klotz, the polarity of "closed" or Classical form and "open" form, the extreme of which is epic drama.[26] Rather than focusing on form, which, like genre, can be a problematic term when applied to Wagner's work, the present investigation goes into content and themes of particular texts in more depth than has previously been done.

These ideas about, or themes of, drama, history, myth, and tragedy, as presented in Wagner's theory and demonstrated in the *Ring*, provide points of comparison of his *Ring* with the works and thought of selected German dramatists. In the course of this study I point out how several of the dramas that I discuss implicitly raise doubts as to the validity of using myth as a metaphor for history, or else destroy any productive interchange between history and myth. For instance, I argue that with *Elektra*, Hofmannsthal portrays the irony that is inherent in the project of a modern rebirth of myth that will supposedly change history. This reworking of a Greek myth on the modern level of consciousness is actually doomed from the start, and thus the play is inevitably tragic. In analyzing the Hofmannsthal/Strauss opera *Ariadne auf Naxos*, I show how the idea of myth as metaphor occurs, in a comic, parodistic way that overcomes tragedy, on the linguistic level.

Thus the present study actually combines two organizing principles. It is, first of all, oriented toward a specific genre of art, that of drama. This huge field of investigation is, in turn, narrowed down through a theme. I explore the affinities of Wagner's works with selected texts of German literature by analyzing these dramas as embodying an interrelation of myth and history. This theme, in turn, specifies the kind of drama that I discuss, in particular, tragedy. There is nothing contrived about this dual kind of organization. In fact, it seems almost a necessity when analyzing Wagner's theory and works. It should be obvious that these two principles imply each other reciprocally. I investigate the works under scrutiny as revisions of a specific kind of drama. I ask how each revises the form (or, rather, mythological content) of tragedy.

By virtue of being mythological, Wagner's music-dramas somehow belong in the German tradition of the reworking and redefinition of Greek tragedy. This, then, opens up new doors to scholarship and links works that may seem too dissimilar for such comparisons. To parallel the *Ring* and *Wallenstein* or *Mahagonny* does, it is true, seem unlikely. Structurally, thematically, and historically-mythologically, though, these comparisons can make sense, as I will show. Therefore, the present study is novel in that it not only offers some preliminary steps toward a history of Wagner and

German drama but also deals with in-depth comparisons of Wagner dramas and other German dramas, some of which would occur to few people as fitting analogues to the *Ring*.

I intend, through my selection of a small number of texts, to discuss more extensively, and investigate in more detail, topics that literary studies of Wagner's works, in tending to deal with the interrelationships between Wagner's works and those of the rest of the German tradition in broad terms, merely skim the surface of. There is some repetition in this study, which will hopefully not seem tiresome to the reader, to the end of making each chapter a self-contained entity that can be read separately from the others. In particular, some assertions about the relationship between history and myth in Wagner's *Ring* and his theory of myth and tragedy in *Oper und Drama* may be repeated from one chapter to the next.

The comparison of Wagner's and Hebbel's treatments of the Nibelung legend, of course, seems a reasonable one, as do contrastive investigations of Mann's narrative Wagner allusions. The Schiller, Hofmannsthal, and Brecht comparisons that I draw to the *Ring* will doubtlessly appear less obvious, but they may be no less revealing. I actually propose the Schiller parallel as possibly a genetic one. We know that Wagner was well acquainted with the *Wallenstein* trilogy. Though I am not ignoring form, the more thematic orientation of my study allows me to compare formally disparate works, such as music-dramas with spoken dramas. Using the basic theme of history versus myth enables me to compare such seemingly dissimilar works as the *Ring* and *Mahagonny*, or the *Ring* and *Wallenstein*. This, in fact, places Wagner's works more firmly within the German drama tradition than a tautological comparative analysis of drama versus opera, or words versus music, such as I mentioned earlier, ever could.

One would think that the main difference between Wagner's dramas and those of, say, Schiller or Hebbel, is that the former, being a composer, uses music in his dramas, whereas the latter two, being playwrights, deal exclusively with spoken language. There is, of course, a crucial difference between music and language. This difference, however, can be subsumed under a broader one, that is, Wagner's choice of myth (as opposed to history) as his subject matter. After all, he felt that only music could properly communicate the multifaceted nature of myth, and only music was the appropriate means of expression for myth, which is a condensed worldview, for music appeals to the feeling, whereas spoken language addresses only the capacity of understanding.

The present study is, of course, by no means exhaustive. My choice of texts does not pretend to be comprehensive. I have chosen to center this book on the *Ring* because of its central position in the composer's output, and its exemplification of the theory of *Oper und Drama*. The other dramas to which I compare the *Ring* all, accordingly, represent some kind of interrelationship between history and myth, and thus they seem to invite this comparison. Two of the spoken dramas that I discuss, those by Schiller and Hebbel, are, interestingly enough, historical dramas that show a critical, negative stance toward myth. The outwardly semimythical work by Hofmannsthal-Strauss and the historical work by Brecht use music in a non-Wagnerian way. I have termed *Ariadne auf Naxos* "semimythical," for it shows myth with Romantic irony as mythical opera that is relativized by the historical prologue and the low art form of the commedia dell'arte. Accordingly, the work uses Wagnerian music to purposes that are definitely not totally Wagnerian.

Not only do the texts I have chosen all represent some kind of interrelation of myth and history. Furthermore, they all stand in some more specific relation to the *Ring*. In the case of Schiller, for instance, I propose the *Wallenstein* dramas as a covert source for the *Ring*. The analogy of the *Ring* with the *Nibelungen* trilogy of Hebbel is self-evident, as both are nineteenth-century reworkings of the Nibelung legend. The last two chapters, those on the Hofmannsthal-Strauss and Brecht-Weill collaborations, investigate the influence of Wagner's works, the *Ring* specifically, on twentieth-century drama and opera. In these last chapters, I discuss, first of all, Hofmannsthal's play *Elektra* back-to-back with the opera *Ariadne auf Naxos*, a product of the Hofmannsthal-Strauss collaboration. Finally, I analyze the Brecht-Weill *Mahagonny* and the accompanying essay by Brecht as parodistically playing off of the *Ring* and *Oper und Drama*.

My method can probably best be described as structural. I am primarily interested in literary criticism, literary and dramatic history, and the history of ideas. My aim is an interpretation and thus a better understanding of these works as complete entities. Though I make reference to the music and take into consideration, of course, the interrelation of music and myth, and music and literary-dramatic form, in the operatic works, giving a broad outline of how the music of each musical work echoes the drama theory upon which the work is built, I do not propose any kind of detailed treatment of the influence of Wagner on Richard Strauss or Kurt Weill. I will leave this to the musicologists and deal here with the music in much broader terms. My discussions of the music of these music-dramas or operas should be accessible to the literary scholar familiar with the works who has little or no formal musical expertise but a perceptive ear.

The literary analyses that I provide can, on the other hand, offer musicologists a literary-historical context within which they can analyze the music of the works under discussion. Hopefully these last two chapters of this study will inspire musicologists to expand the parallels that I have presented and seek new ways of linking Wagner's works with the tradition that is, after all, commonly known as "post-Wagnerian." At best, the present study will further the collaboration of literary critics and musicologists or an exchange of ideas between these two realms of study to the end of better understanding the complex phenomena of Wagner's dramas, which are too often unjustly and narrow-mindedly regarded from only one aspect, that is, as purely musical phenomena unapproachable by scholars from other disciplines.

NOTES

1. Bryan Magee, *Aspects of Wagner*, rev. ed. (Oxford: Oxford University Press, 1988), p. 14.

2. Wolfgang Schadewaldt, "Richard Wagner und die Griechen," in *Richard Wagner und das neue Bayreuth*, ed. Wieland Wagner (Munich: Paul List, 1962), pp. 149–74.

3. Othmar Fries, *Richard Wagner und die deutsche Romantik: Versuch einer Einordnung* (Zurich: Atlantis, 1952).

4. Paul Arthur Loos, *Richard Wagner: Vollendung und Tragik der deutschen Romantik* (Munich: Leo Lehnen, 1952).

5. Dieter Borchmeyer, *Das Theater Richard Wagners: Idee, Dichtung, Wirkung* (Stuttgart: Reclam, 1982).

6. See: Peter Wapnewski, *Der traurige Gott: Richard Wagner in seinen Helden* (Munich: C.H. Beck, 1978; Deutscher Taschenbuch Verlag, 1982).

7. See, for example: Erwin Koppen, *Dekadenter Wagnerismus. Studien zur europäischen Literatur des Fin de siècle*, Komparatistische Studien, vol. 2 (Berlin and New York: Walter de Gruyter, 1973).

8. Helmut Schanze, *Drama im Bürgerlichen Realismus (1850–1890): Theorie und Praxis*, Studien zur Philosophie und Literatur des neunzehnten Jahrhunderts, vol. 21 (Frankfurt am Main: Vittorio Klostermann, 1973), pp. 145–48.

9. Schanze, pp. 56–59.

10. Fritz Martini, *Deutsche Literatur im bürgerlichen Realismus 1848–1898*, 4th ed. (Stuttgart: Metzler, 1962, 1981), pp. 186–92.

11. Benno von Wiese, *Die Deutsche Tragödie von Lessing bis Hebbel* (Hamburg: Hoffmann und Campe, 1948; 6th ed., 1964), pp. 547-50.

12. For a close analysis of the second part of *Oper und Drama* and a more extensive discussion of how the *Ring* exemplifies Wagner's theory of myth presented therein, I direct the reader to my previous study: *Mythology as Metaphor: Romantic Irony, Critical Theory, and Wagner's* Ring (Westport, CT: Greenwood Press, 1998).

13. On the historical drama in Germany, see: Friedrich Sengle, *Das historische Drama in Deutschland. Geschichte eines literarischen Mythos*, 2d ed. (Stuttgart: Metzler, 1969).

14. The following summary is based on: Stefan Kunze, *Der Kunstbegriff Richard Wagners: Voraussetzungen und Folgerungen* (Regensburg: Gustav Bosse, 1983), pp. 65–78.

15. On Wagner's theory of myth, see: Anette Ingenhoff, *Drama oder Epos? Richard Wagners Gattungstheorie des musikalischen Dramas*, Untersuchungen zur deutschen Literaturgeschichte, vol. 41 (Tübingen: Max Niemeyer, 1987), pp. 101–16 (here cited from p. 104).

16. Jean-Jacques Nattiez, *Wagner Androgyne*, trans. Stewart Spencer (Princeton, NJ: Princeton University Press, 1993), pp. 91–96.

17. Nattiez, pp. 53–90.

18. See: Dagmar Ingenschay-Goch, *Richard Wagners neu erfundener Mythos: Zur Rezeption und Reproduktion des germanischen Mythos in seinen Operntexten*, Abhandlungen zur Kunst-, Musik- und Literaturwissenschaft, vol. 311 (Bonn: Bouvier Verlag Herbert Grundmann, 1982), pp. 17–20.

19. Herbert Schnädelbach, " 'Ring' und Mythos," in *In den Trümmern der eignen Welt: Richard Wagners "Der Ring des Nibelungen"*, ed. Udo Bermbach, Hamburger Beiträge zur öffentlichen Wissenschaft, vol. 7 (Berlin: Dietrich Reimer, 1989), pp. 145–61.

20. Dieter Borchmeyer, "Vom Anfang und Ende der Geschichte. Richard Wagners mythisches Drama. Idee und Inszenierung," in *Macht des Mythos—Ohnmacht der Vernunft?*, ed. Peter Kemper (Frankfurt am Main: Fischer, 1989), pp. 176–200.

21. See, for instance: Deryck Cooke, *I Saw the World End: A Study of Wagner's "Ring"* (London: Oxford University Press, 1979); see also: the work of Dagmar Ingenschay-Goch, referred to in note 18.

22. Roland Barthes, *Mythologies*, trans. Annette Lavers (New York: Hill and Wang, 1972).

23. On Wagner's revolutionary activities, see: Martin Gregor-Dellin, *Richard Wagner: Sein Leben, Sein Werk, Sein Jahrhundert* (Munich: Piper, 1980), pp. 242–76; "Beziehungen zum Sozialismus," in *Richard Wagner—die Revolution als Oper*, Reihe Hanser 129 (Munich: Carl Hanser, 1973), pp. 20–41; Rüdiger Krohn, "Richard Wagner und die Revolution von 1848/49," in *Richard-Wagner-Handbuch*, ed. Ulrich Müller and Peter Wapnewski (Stuttgart: Alfred Kröner, 1986), pp. 86–100; Udo Bermbach, "Die Destruktion der Institutionen. Zum politischen Gehalt des 'Ring'," in *In den Trümmern der eignen Welt: Richard Wagners "Der Ring des Nibelungen"*, Hamburger Beiträge zur öffentlichen Wissenschaft, vol. 7 (Berlin: Dietrich Reimer, 1989), pp. 111–44.

24. On Romantic drama, see: Peter Schmidt, "Romantisches Drama: Zur Theorie eines Paradoxons," in *Deutsche Dramentheorien. Beiträge zu einer historischen Poetik des Dramas in Deutschland*, ed. Reinhold Grimm (Frankfurt am Main: Athenäum, 1971), vol. 1, pp. 245–69; Otto Mann, *Geschichte des deutschen Dramas*, 3d ed., Kröners Taschenausgabe, vol. 296 (Stuttgart: Alfred Kröner, 1969), pp. 322–27; George Steiner, *The Death of Tragedy* (New York: Alfred A. Knopf, 1961), pp. 106–50.

25. Reinhold Brinkmann, "Szenische Epik. Marginalien zu Wagners Dramenkonzeption im *Ring des Nibelungen*," in *Richard Wagner: Werk und Wirkung*, ed. Carl Dahlhaus, Studien zur Musikgeschichte des 19. Jahrhunderts, vol. 26 (Regensburg: Gustav Bosse, 1971), pp. 85–96.

26. Carl Dahlhaus, *Wagners Konzeption des musikalischen Dramas* (Regensburg: Gustav Bosse, 1971); Ingenhoff (pp. 117–20) also uses these terms and lists the elements of "open" form in the *Ring*.

Chapter 1

Wagner and the Eighteenth Century: History and Myth, Tasso and Tannhäuser, Wotan and Wallenstein

To assert that Wagner is an heir to the tradition of German Classicism should surprise nobody. Dieter Borchmeyer, for example, notes that Wagner's thought is anchored in the Classic-Romantic tradition, above all, in the aesthetics of Goethe and Schiller.[1] At first glance, of course, there does seem to be a discrepancy between the Classical ideals and Wagner's style which, most would agree with Thomas Mann, is typical of nineteenth-century Romanticism. What appears incongruous, however, is a deep affinity, even if the correspondences are not strict. If Wagner, I would argue, clearly saw himself as heir to Weimar Classicism, as Borchmeyer points out,[2] one wonders how this could not be reflected somehow in his dramas as well as his aesthetics.

It is common knowledge that the writers of the nineteenth century were clearly working within the Classic-Romantic tradition, and there is no reason to exclude Wagner, as he was, after all, a dramatist, from this generalization. Furthermore, one is fully justified in seeking particularly Schillerian influence on the Wagnerian music-dramas. In his work on nineteenth-century drama, Schanze discusses the important position that the figure of Schiller held for writers of the nineteenth century.[3] The proponents of Young Germany had criticized Goethe, but when their revolutionary hopes were disappointed, the writers tried a different, more positive approach. The figure of Schiller held up some hope for national unity. The problems of the day were projected into Schiller's dramas, which came to signify an ideal unity, an ideal freedom.

The interest in Schiller, furthermore, flourished around the middle of the century. The year 1859 was a Schiller year, and the celebration became,

Schanze explains, a profession of spiritual unity. In other words, Schiller was a major topic of conversation at the time that Wagner was working on the *Ring*. Just how, though, does this influence manifest itself in Wagner's dramas? Can one find Schillerian elements and structures in Wagner's Romantic tetralogy? By comparing two sets of dramas, I would like to ask in what relation Wagner's works really stand to those of Schiller.

Although others, too, have discussed the affinities of Wagner's thought with that of Schiller, critics seem to focus on the theory of the two men. Some of these parallels are striking, and thus they present themselves with no trouble. That Wagner was an heir to the Classical tradition seems, at least with regard to his theoretical writings, an obvious fact. Brinkmann and Ingenhoff, for instance, both discuss Wagner's reception of the aesthetics that Goethe and Schiller devised in their correspondence of 1797 (the essay "Über epische und dramatische Dichtung").[4]

Wagner and Schiller also share the basic tripartite model of human history common to German thought in the eighteenth and nineteenth centuries. The similarity in this regard between the Zurich writings and "Über naive und sentimentalische Dichtung" is obvious. Furthermore, the "Gesamtkunstwerk" is, curiously enough, based in Classical aesthetics in a way. Both Wagner and Schiller looked back to Greek tragedy as their model, they saw Greek culture as exemplifying some kind of unity of art and public life, and they envisioned a kind of societal-artistic utopia, an aesthetic organization of society. The symbol of this aesthetic state, this unity of art and public life, was for Wagner, Borchmeyer notes, the "Gesamt-kunstwerk."[5]

Borchmeyer, moreover, writes that Wagner can be placed in the context of the "German movement" of the eighteenth century, which sought an art form that was universal and thus that transcended nationality.[6] Wagner propounds the notion, held time and again since Schiller, of the universality of the German spirit ("Deutscher Geist"), which synthesizes and transcends the spirits of all other nations. However, this ideal form of art, according to Wagner, could not be found in literature. Wagner felt that it necessitated the use of music, the universal form of art comprehensible to all. Borchmeyer explains that the music-drama was, for Wagner, the culmination and fulfillment of the "German movement" and thus the aesthetic strivings of Goethe and Schiller. That Wagner was a composer and that Schiller dealt exclusively with words are as obvious from a comparison of their aesthetic systems as are the parallels between these systems.

Despite all that has been written about their aesthetics, though, one rarely sees detailed comparisons of Wagner's and Schiller's dramas. In this chapter, I will discuss the dramas of Schiller and Wagner in more depth by analyzing and contrasting, in particular, one major dramatic work of each of them. Wagner's views on Schiller pose in many ways a paradox. Cosima's diaries are full of praise for Schiller; the poet was a kind of god in

Haus Wahnfried, with the composer and Cosima celebrating his birthday every year.[7] Yet at the same time Wagner the artist and aesthetician had severe criticisms of Schiller's works. This chapter will therefore explore Wagner's ambivalent relationship to Schiller.

In the case of *Wallenstein*, which I investigate in this chapter, one finds negative evaluations of these dramas in *Oper und Drama*, and then praise of the same works in Cosima's diaries. I aim to present some solutions to this puzzle. I explain Wagner's position with regard to *Wallenstein* and also, in doing so, propose a way of reconciling the contradiction. I turn Wagner's words against him by showing what the *Ring* and *Wallenstein* really do have in common. The negative comments that he made must be understood with reference to his own views of what a drama should be.

The divergences of the theoretical viewpoints of Wagner and Schiller are inevitably, I would argue, illustrated by their dramas, which cannot help but embody these ideas in some way. Thus, I wish to proceed by scrutinizing what Wagner wrote about *Wallenstein* and where he wrote or said it, and why, and then analyzing the drama texts under discussion with these considerations in mind. Thus the apparent contradictions can somehow be seen as demonstrating, in a roundabout sort of way, some kind of consistency.

After discussing Wagner's critique of *Wallenstein* in *Oper und Drama*, I then turn to these dramas themselves and show how Wagner's views concerning *Wallenstein* are reflected in his *Ring* cycle. I not only compare Schiller's trilogy to Wagner's *Ring*, but I also argue genetically and point out influence, and show that, despite what Wagner says about *Wallenstein* in *Oper und Drama*, it must have influenced his composition and the structure of the *Ring*. As befits Wagner's ambivalence toward Schiller, I will discuss similarities and differences between the *Ring* cycle and the *Wallenstein* trilogy. These correspond to what Wagner praised and criticized about Schiller's trilogy.

My thesis in this chapter falls into two basic though overlapping parts. First, I make the unlikely suggestion of *Wallenstein* as a covert source for the *Ring*, as evidenced among other features by, in particular, a comparison of the protagonists, Wotan and Wallenstein. Next, I present a more general argument concerning the differences between the two works under discussion, centering on their difference in subject matter, that is, whether history or myth was used, and the complementary nature of the works. Both theses concern an unworking and redefinition of Greek tragedy, which was the common goal of Wagner and German Classicism, and therefore, in connection with this, the notion of fate in each of the dramatic works under discussion.

WALLENSTEIN IN OPER UND DRAMA

Wagner's treatment of Schiller in *Oper und Drama* is a totally negative one. The treatise is, after all, a theoretical justification of Wagnerian music-drama, and thus it is Wagner's intent in writing this treatise to illustrate how the teleology of musical and dramatic history somehow leads up to Wagnerian music-drama, and to show that everything that was not Wagnerian music-drama was something that must be superseded. Wagner's drama history in *Oper und Drama* is thus highly selective. Wagner was most interested in those dramas that allowed him to demonstrate his theoretical schema of musical and dramatic history. It seems understandable, therefore, that Wagner, in the second part of *Oper und Drama*, chose to discuss *Braut von Messina* and *Wallenstein*. Wagner argues that Schiller's work was a vacillation between the history and the novel, on one hand, and, on the other hand, Greek drama.[8] Neither option, the way Schiller exercised it, won Wagner's praise.

Schiller's essay on the chorus in drama, the prologue to *Braut von Messina*, presents itself as a forerunner to Wagner's and Nietzsche's ideas about the Greek chorus and its counterpart in the modern rebirth of tragedy.[9] Wagner explicitly drew this analogy between the chorus of Greek tragedy and the orchestra of modern music-drama in *Oper und Drama*. The notions of using music in drama and thereby working on the model of Greek drama, fundamental ideas of Wagner's theory, can easily be traced back to Schiller's essay. But Wagner, according to Cosima's diary, considered *Braut von Messina* a document of an unproductive age.[10] Furthermore, in *Oper und Drama*, Wagner brutally criticizes Schiller's revival and reworking of Greek tragedy.

Wagner rejected a mere external, superficial imitation of Greek tragedy. In addition, he felt that in the modern age, one should not portray a collective on the stage; rather, individuals should be shown. Instead of advocating a reintroduction of the chorus, Wagner felt that the orchestra of music-drama would fulfill a function similar or analogous to that which the chorus of Greek tragedy served. Furthermore, Schiller felt that the chorus destroyed the illusion of the drama and tempered the passions by introducing reflection into the reception of the drama, so that the spectator would retain his or her freedom. This is the opposite of what Wagner and Nietzsche felt the orchestra of nineteenth-century music-drama, the modern equivalent of the chorus of ancient Greek tragedy, should do. They felt it should appeal to the feeling.

Schiller's interest in and imitation of Greek tragedy was, according to Wagner, the necessary consequence of his preoccupation with form. Wagner says that Schiller made form into content. Wagner had the reverse priorities, it seems. He did the opposite by, according to his definitions, making content (i.e., myth) into form (tragedy). One can see Wagner's views of *Wallenstein* as in some roundabout way, paradoxically, reflecting his criticism of *Braut von Messina*. In the case of *Wallenstein*, Wagner criticizes not mainly an overemphasis on form but, rather, the choice of the wrong content or subject matter. In fact, *Wallenstein* is the only other work of Schiller besides *Braut von Messina* that Wagner discusses in *Oper und Drama*. The topic of Wagner's views on *Wallenstein* raises a major issue. One could even go so far as to say that this point is the main difference between Wagner and Schiller. According to Wagner, a proponent of mythological music-drama, the fallacy exemplified by *Wallenstein* was the use of history as raw material for drama.

One of the dichotomies that Wagner uses in the second part of *Oper und Drama* is that of the novel and the drama.[11] According to Wagner, the drama of the modern age originates from two sources, the Greek drama (which led to the tradition of Racine) and the medieval romance (from which, in Wagner's system, evolves the drama of Shakespeare). Like the Romantics, Wagner theorizes that the novel is the genre of the modern age. Because he was also influenced by Feuerbachian materialism, he argues, though, at the same time, that the novel, which appeals solely to the imagination, must be superseded and transcended by the genre of music-drama. Wagner felt that a work of art that appealed to the imagination without also addressing the senses was deficient, decadent. He grounds his (basically untenable) thesis of the evolution of Shakespearean drama from the medieval romance with a structural affinity of the two forms. The medieval romance was rich with plots and locales. Medieval mystery plays and other festival plays (the "Volksschaubühne") were, Wagner argued, the beginnings of the "translation" of the romance into the terms of the stage.

In Wagner's schema, Shakespeare, working within this tradition, failed to realize that there was a formal limit to how far the romance could be adapted to the stage.[12] The romance, Wagner felt, was irreconcilable with the drama. According to Wagner, Shakespeare did not feel the necessity of a literal portrayal of the scenario; therefore, his plays appealed to the imagination, and thus he began a fallacy in drama history, which Wagner states continued into the time in which he was writing *Oper und Drama*. The romance, Wagner felt, needed to be condensed ("verdichtet") to the drama form, which must be unified. History, as far as Wagner was concerned, could not be adequately represented on the modern stage.

Wagner argues that Schiller, like Goethe, mainly dramatized the romance form, the novel. History, Wagner felt, was the proper subject matter for the novel, but not for the drama. Thus Schiller's *Wallenstein*, according to Wagner, is based on the fallacy of using historical material for drama. Wagner writes, "Dieses 'dramatische Gedicht'—wie Schiller selbst es nennt—war dennoch der redlichste Versuch, der Geschichte als solcher Stoff für das Drama abzugewinnen."[13] (This "dramatic poem"—as Schiller himself called it—was nevertheless the most honest attempt to use history as raw material for a drama.) In other words, it was his best try.

Wagner's objection to historical drama is simple. In order to dramatize history, Wagner argues, the dramatist must falsify it. Drama demands unity, which would arise from the condensation of the historical material, and thus the dramatic form necessitates a reworking of history, which gives us only events, in order that the motives behind the events be made clear. Once it is changed, however, it is no longer strictly historical. The playwright who attempts to write a historical drama is, then, caught in an inner contradiction, a paradox. Historical drama is neither historical nor really a drama.[14] Because he felt that only myth offered the condensed world-view appropriate to drama, Wagner is, in essence, saying that history must be mythicized to be made into drama.

To illustrate his point, Wagner compares the historical dramas of Shakespeare with those of Schiller. The stage of Shakespeare's time allowed him to portray history unfalsified, for it appealed to the imagination. The medieval stage, however, yielded to the modern stage. While Schiller's historical research, according to Wagner, was superior to that of Shakespeare, Schiller's *Wallenstein* shows, Wagner argues, that he was not able to condense the historical material to dramatic unity. Wagner even uses the trilogy form of Schiller's *Wallenstein* against him. This is surprising, considering the similarity in this regard with the *Ring* cycle. Wagner argues that besides not being able to reconcile history and drama, Schiller used the multiple form for material that did not really demand it. Wagner says that Schiller portrayed the historical milieu in a separate play, that is, in a piece separate from the real drama, which he had to break into two dramas, which, after all, use only one mass of material (which Wagner did not consider especially rich anyway).

The flaw, for Wagner, was inherent in Schiller's choice of subject matter. Wagner writes that Schiller also had to use the dual form for the drama because the web of dramatic motivation was too complicated due to the muddled nature of history. (Myth, he felt, was condensed and thus easy to comprehend, lending itself to an immediate affective response.) According to Wagner, Shakespeare, in contrast, uses the multiple, cyclical form for complex plots that portray the entire lives of persons embedded in a historical center. Wagner states that Shakespeare would have portrayed the entire Thirty Years' War in three plays (which Wagner evidently wanted to top with portraying all of world-history in four mythological music-dramas).

MUSIC AND LANGUAGE, AESTHETICS AND POLITICS

A comparison of the *Ring* with *Wallenstein* will probably seem daring, especially after recounting Wagner's criticisms of Schiller. Wagner's own polemic against *Wallenstein* seems as though it ought to prevent such thoughts. Everything I wrote in the previous section of this chapter seems to make the comparison mere folly, a futile attempt to parallel two very dissimilar works that (as the composer of one of them led us to believe) defy close comparison. Before this investigation is undertaken, though, it would not be at all superfluous to consider some of the obvious differences between the two works. These include the mediums in which the two dramatists worked and the purposes that they intended their dramas to fulfill.

One can account for some fundamental differences in viewpoint by looking not only at the different ages in which these two men lived, but also at the different mediums with which they worked. Schiller was a poet and a dramatist; Wagner was first and foremost a composer. It seems trite to even assert that one would expect, therefore, major differences between the two thinkers. The parallels between the two dramatic works that I am discussing, accordingly, do not need to be direct or the resemblances literal. Rather, I would suggest that the two works relate to each other more in an indirect, complementary way, as a negative to a positive or a nut to a bolt. Wagner's passages about Schiller, which I have discussed earlier, do suggest a supersession of *Wallenstein* by the *Ring*.

The most obvious difference between the works is, of course, the fact that *Wallenstein* is spoken drama, whereas the *Ring* is music-drama. Accordingly, Wagner criticizes Schiller for having an overconcern with form and language. It was obviously not a strong enough criticism for Wagner to say that Schiller dealt exclusively with language. Schiller was too much a rhetorician as far as Wagner was concerned. Wagner's aesthetic system was more affective than Schiller's, for Wagner was a musician. He stressed that music appealed to the feeling, and language, in contrast, only to the understanding, now that it had "fallen" into the modern world, as Wagner explained in *Oper und Drama*. Thus Schiller's dramas were not yet the art-work of the future. They lacked music.[15] Therefore, Wagner revises Schiller, and music "corrects" language. The *Ring*, I will argue, rewrites *Wallenstein*.

For instance, Wagner laments (19 November 1878) the dramatic characters who, ever since Goethe and Schiller lived, continually talk, commenting that Shakespeare manages to make speech also into action (CT III, 235; D II, 205). On 1 June 1878, Wagner commented that the language of *Maria Stuart* was, though elegant, courtly and conventional (CT III, 104; D II, 81-82). This is, however, either redundant or a metalevel of criticism. Wagner felt that spoken drama, language alone, was in itself conventional, and thus artificial. In conversation Wagner was even fond of casually drafting Schiller into his theoretical schema of musical-dramatic history, and in doing so, Wagner forced Schiller to exemplify the theory that drama demands music.

According to Wagner, Schiller's dramas tend toward music. He referred, in this respect, to *Jungfrau von Orleans* (entry of 29 May 1870; CT I, 236; D I, 225). About Schiller's poetry, too, he remarked that it has the same effect as music (CT II, 661; D I, 615; entry of 27 March 1873). On another day (17 January 1870), Cosima quoted Richard as saying that the works of Goethe and Schiller all tend toward music. He also commented that one senses, when reading these German poets, the basic element of music-drama (CT I, 189; D I, 181). Some statements are (naturally enough) duplications of ideas from *Oper und Drama.* Cosima writes that Schiller constitutes the transition to music-drama, and comments on how, after Schiller's dramas, there could be only music-drama, to which Schiller, as it were, forms the bridge, an idea that seems a variation on Wagner's theoretical schema of dramatic and musical history (CT I, 178; D I, 172; entry of 14 December 1869).

Furthermore, Wagner also criticizes Schiller for a lack of political concern. In this respect, too, the *Ring* improves upon *Wallenstein.* Although both men saw the theater as some kind of moral institution that would, to some end, effect an aesthetic education, and both had a common wish to reform society, the ends they envisaged were as different as the means that they used to achieve them. In this way, Wagner's work shows a revolutionary intent in a way that Schiller's does not. Music and politics are not as unrelated as they might seem. In Wagner's system, music was essential to achieve his revolutionary purposes. Schiller was averse to the idea of revolution, whereas Wagner greeted the revolutions of the mid-nineteenth century with enthusiasm.[16] For Schiller, the aim of art was not so much political change but, rather, moral freedom. One might say that his theory and dramas are more regeneratory than revolutionary. Schiller probably would have felt that Wagner's political views were much too radical.

Andrea Mork argues that the concept of nature is central to Wagner's philosophy of art and his world-view.[17] Wagner lamented the dissociation of nature and spirit. Schiller, too, in his work on naive and sentimental poetry, stressed the poet's relationship with nature. However, Wagner put nature above morals; for Schiller, it was the other way around. Wagner's regressive tendencies are evident here. He felt that conventional morality was based on custom and thus decadent, alienated, dissociated from the living and spontaneous human being. For Wagner, art should bring one back to the material, physical world. In philosophical terms, one could say that whereas Wagner was Feuerbachian, Schiller was Kantian. In this respect, Wagner's goals are almost the direct opposite of those of Schiller. The experience of tragedy, the aesthetic condition ("ästhetischer Zustand") in general, Schiller felt, should free one from the physical world. Accordingly, because Wagner was influenced, in his revolutionary years, by the nihilism of the anarchist Mikhail Bakunin, his works written at that time show a tendency toward the radical destruction of existing institutions and social structures that Schiller would have definitely been abhorred by.

It is just this lack of political engagement that Wagner criticized Goethe and Schiller for. For instance, on 31 August 1870, Cosima notes that Richard was reading Byron, and that he commented that Byron was the only real poet of the century who followed and depicted political events, whereas

Goethe and Schiller turned their attention away from contemporary events (CT I, 279; D I, 265). On another day (3 July 1873), Cosima quotes Richard as saying that Goethe and Schiller were not very concerned with the German idea (CT II, 703; D I, 653). On 21 September 1875, Cosima reports that Goethe and Schiller were not bothered by the political mess and did not want to know what was going on (CT II, 936; D I, 864).

The main difference between the works under discussion in this chapter, though, is, I would propose, one of subject matter. For Wagner, as he outlines in *Oper und Drama*, myth implies the use of music and enables drama to be revolutionary. Thus, I will show how the differences of music versus language, and regeneration versus revolution, are expressed in a deeper, more fundamental distinction, that of myth versus history as subject matter. My thesis is that Wagner's mythological music-drama is supposed to have political, revolutionary reverberations. In this manner, the *Ring* and *Wallenstein* can be seen as complementary. Only the combination of myth and music in drama (and mythology and music, according to Wagner, imply each other reciprocally) can bring the audience to revolutionary consciousness and in this way cause a societal overthrow.

Wagner unworks (mythological) tragedy to revolutionize (historical) society. He destroys, in the finale of *Götterdämmerung*, the mythological-aesthetic cosmos that he creates from a single chord in the prelude to *Rheingold*, and with the "wisdom through feeling" that the audience has gained from experiencing the dramas, he felt that modern society would automatically be revolutionized. *Wallenstein* does not show the demise of an order that the work depicts as corrupt, nor was it written with an intent and purpose that one could describe as radical or revolutionary. Paradoxically, Wagner's mythological music-drama, though it only indirectly has to do with the "real world," has a political purpose and is more radically, dramatically, one could say societally and revolutionarily oriented than Schiller's historical drama, which uses seemingly political raw material.

HISTORY VERSUS MYTH

I argue that the difference in subject matter between the *Ring* and *Wallenstein* does not in any way preclude the analysis I am about to present. The fact that *Wallenstein* was a historical drama was, as I have shown, its distinguishing feature and main fault within the aesthetic system that Wagner presents in *Oper und Drama*. Wagner makes it clear that he totally dismisses historical drama as an illegitimate art form. These two kinds of material, historical and mythical subject matter, though, can be seen as complementary. Myth and history do not form a strict dichotomy. Myth stands in some relation to history, and history, in turn, is not always totally inseparable from myth.

Though the *Ring* is a mythological work of art, both Wagner's tetralogy and *Wallenstein* deal with history, though in different ways. Furthermore, it follows from this point that the works under discussion would show the views of Wagner and Schiller on history. Schiller's *Wallenstein* deals, of course, with history directly. Benno von Wiese remarks that Schiller does not envision some romanticized primal state of mankind. Rather, he orients himself on the constellation of the present age and tries to show, working backwards from this, how it has arisen. His philosophy of history, von Wiese explains, is not a mythical or idealistic vision ("Verklärung") of history.[18] A comparison of the *Ring* and *Wallenstein* illustrates this. Schiller refers back to the order that arose in the time of the Thirty Years' War. Past history helps explain present history.

Wagner, in contrast, tells a mythical story to explain world-history. Furthermore, he portrays an idealized or a romanticized vision of the origins of mankind. His thought demonstrates a regressive tendency with revolutionary implications. Wagner destroys the "state" in the work of art (figuratively), and this will happen literally, he hopes, in reality. For Wagner, there is a sense of (real) history, which is demonstrated by mythological drama. The *Ring* uses myth to tell the story behind history. According to Benno von Wiese, history, in Schiller's play, has assumed the role of fate or the gods. He calls the restitution that history effects "nemesis."[19] For Wagner, the notion of fate and the gods, in the *Ring*, helps him to depict the course of past and future history.

Korff explains that Schiller regarded history as, to use a term of Friedrich Nietzsche, "monumental history," as a hall of extraordinary "fates" in which the meaning of human life reveals itself. Korff writes that Schiller used history as a kind of modern mythology; that is, he used it as the ancient poets used myth and legend, as an abbreviated or condensed image of significant destinies. In a metaphysical sense, world-history ("Weltgeschichte") was, for Schiller, a judgment of the world ("Weltgericht"). It contained symbols of human existence that the poet was called upon to interpret. Herein lies, Korff points out, the difference between a poetic use of history and a scientific way of dealing with history.[20]

Thus it is ironic that Wagner, who otherwise, especially in *Oper und Drama*, drew the distinction between art and science so sharply, fails to take it into account when judging Schiller. He chastises Schiller for changing and falsifying history much as medievalists and other philologists criticize Wagner himself for tampering with and distorting his source materials, disregarding the purposes to which the material was put and the intentions behind the alterations. Korff points out that for Schiller, the poet must change history so as not to impede the clarity of the symbol.

Whereas for Schiller world-history is a judgment of the world, Wagner shows the mythological-symbolic judgment of the world, his musical-dramatic evaluation of the ills of modern society, as an image of world-history.

Schiller uses history as a kind of mythology; for Wagner, myth becomes an image of history. Wagner is concerned with depicting the mythological "truth" that Schiller abstracts from (real) history for his poetic portrayal of it. According to Korff, for Schiller, history shows the meaning of life. For Wagner, myth should show the sense of history.

Benno von Wiese writes that Schiller was intent on idealizing (i.e., showing ideas in) the real[21]; Wagner, one could say, wanted to realize (i.e., portray concretely and sensually, on the stage) the ideal (the general, typical, "das Reinmenschliche"). Furthermore, through the experience of Wagnerian music-drama, history was, he thought, to be mythicized, and thus the ideal would actually be realized in the real world, too. In writing his *Ring* tetralogy, Wagner used and refabricated myth as a metaphor for history. Whereas Wagner abstracts ideas from history, Schiller shows ideas in history. Schiller uses history as a mythology; Wagner uses myth to explain and change history. Thus I would suggest that the *Ring* is, in many ways, a myth about, or an X-ray version of, *Wallenstein*. One could even say that *Wallenstein* is Schiller's version of, or a historical counterpart to, the *Ring*.

WALLENSTEIN: A SOURCE FOR THE *RING*?

Scholars are well aware that Wagner's views on some important issues did not retain full consistency throughout his life. Every individual, of course, is permitted to change his or her mind at times, and contradict himself or herself on certain points. However, in the case of what Wagner thought about Schiller, as evidenced by his views on the *Wallenstein* trilogy, one must look for deeper reasons for these discrepancies than the basic eccentricities and character flaws of human beings in general. In particular, one must, I feel, distinguish what Wagner wrote in the treatise *Oper und Drama* from what he said and wrote elsewhere. Outside his official, theoretical persona he was freed from any obligation to fit Schiller into a preconceived musical-dramatic teleological system.

Earlier I made a distinction between Wagner the person and Wagner the theoretician. A comparison of what Cosima recorded in her diaries about *Wallenstein* with the passages in *Oper und Drama* that I have just discussed illustrates this distinction drastically and beautifully. These comments from Cosima's diaries, which were candid and thus obviously sincere, are full of praise for the work. In fact, some of them even hint at an affinity of Wagner's own dramas with those of Schiller, or indicate that Wagner might have been inspired by *Wallenstein* in creating his own dramas, as much as the theoretician who wrote *Oper und Drama* would have vehemently denied any such influence. (Both Richard Wagners are, paradoxically, speaking with total veracity. For Wagner, praise of a work does not necessarily preclude criticism of it on ideological grounds. Nothing but Wagner's work is, after all, the art-work of the future.)

On 11 November 1869 he was pleased to have Schiller's picture near him while he was working (CT I, 168; D I, 163). This seems to imply that he saw his own work within the tradition of Schiller's. On 19 May 1870, Wagner said that *Wallenstein* reminded him of what he wrote in *Oper und Drama* about spoken drama having severe limitations, as it needs to include too many details to make something clear to the audience (CT I, 231; D I, 220). That he agreed with himself is nothing remarkable. But on 17 January 1869 (CT I, 35; D I, 40–41), Wagner wants to rewrite *Wallensteins Lager* and *Die Piccolomini* in three long acts—like his own dramas, I would add. These comments are, of course, ambiguous, but some of them can definitely be interpreted as praising Schiller and his works.

Furthermore, Cosima also recorded obvious praise of *Wallenstein*, and this admiration must have been genuine. For example, on 13 May 1870 (CT I, 230), she writes, "Ich lese ihm Scenen aus 'Wallenstein' vor, und wir kommen darin überein, dass das Stück—zumal das Verhältnis von Thekla und Max—lange nicht hoch genug gewürdigt sei" (I read him scenes from *Wallenstein* and we come to the conclusion that the play—particularly the relationship between Thekla and Max—is far too little appreciated) (D I, 219). Here they even speak of having the trilogy performed in Bayreuth. This surely would never have even occurred to Wagner as a possibility if he did not hold the plays in high regard. It is, furthermore, useful to note just what Wagner praised about *Wallenstein*, and which details appealed to him. The quote I just cited shows that he liked the relationship of Max and Thekla. One can discern a similar structure, as I will show, in the *Ring*, too. Furthermore, on 18 September 1870, Cosima recorded that Hans Richter conversed with them at lunch about *Wallenstein*, and that he commented that it would be a wonderful play, except for the boring subplot of Thekla and Max. According to Cosima's report, Richard reproached him vehemently for his statement (CT I, 286; D I, 271).

Though he seems to criticize Schiller mercilessly in *Oper und Drama*, on 3 March 1879 (CT III, 312), in Haus Wahnfried, Wagner just as vehemently defends Schiller against attacks, and here he goes into greater detail than in the incident I previously referred to. Wagner explains the purpose of the Max-Thekla subplot in *Wallenstein* as follows:

Wir kommen auf "Wallenstein" von Schiller zu sprechen, und R. sagt, dass, wenn man Shak. abrechnete, was man ja immer tun müsse, so sei Schiller der grösste Dramatiker, und wie Herr Rub. meint, es sei die Episode von Thekla und Max eine von der Hauptaktion losgelöste, so stellt ihm R. dar, wie sie damit zusammenhänge, wie sie die Katastrophe herbeiführe dadurch, dass Max, von Thekla unterstützt, von Wallenstein sich trennt. R. sagt, es sei jetzt Stil geworden, Schiller, bei sonstiger grosser Achtung vor ihm, lauter Schwächen nachzuweisen.

We come to the subject of Schiller's *Wallenstein*, and R. says that if one excepts Shak., as one of course always must, Schiller is the greatest dramatist; when Herr Rub.

expresses the view that the episode of Thekla and Max stands outside the main action, R. explains to him in what way they are a part of it, how the catastrophe comes about when Max, supported by Thekla, abandons Wallenstein. R. says it has now become the fashion to point out weaknesses in Schiller, though still professing great respect for him. (D II, 273)

Wagner obviously saw the Max-Thekla episodes as basic to the dramatic conflict, and here he accords them a very important function in the work. According to Wagner, the subplot about Max and Thekla brings about the catastrophe through Max's separation from Wallenstein. This assertion is even more significant when one considers that it is a questionable interpretation; one can debate whether the separation itself really brings about the catastrophe. One suspects, as I suggest here, that Wagner was thus seeing ideas of his own. In this manner, Wagner, as I will argue, somehow projects his own composition of the *Ring* into Schiller's work.

On 26 October 1879 (CT III, 431; D II, 385) Wagner rationalizes Schiller's basically sound idea of giving a dramatic portrayal of the Thirty Years' War (which he criticized as basically fallacious in *Oper und Drama*) as failing due to Goethe's bad influence. This repeats a criticism I discussed earlier, that of an overconcern with formal considerations and language. Surprisingly enough, though, considering how he denigrated historical drama in *Oper und Drama*, here Wagner even praises the idea of giving a depiction of the Thirty Years' War, and the way the quote is phrased, it seems he is talking about a dramatic depiction of it. This, as it violates his fundamental aesthetic principles, must indicate his overwhelming fondness for Schiller.

And Cosima quotes Wagner as saying, in a discussion of Schiller's plays, on 1 December 1879 (CT III, 456), "Doch das eigentliche Stück, das, worin das meiste Leben sei, sei 'Wallenstein'." (But the play which contains the most life is in fact *Wallenstein*) (D II, 407). Even if it doesn't mean that Wagner thought it was Schiller's best play, it is still far from the faint praise in *Oper und Drama* that it was his best try, the best (albeit a totally misguided and thus failed) effort to use historical material for drama. In fact the statement that *Wallenstein* was the liveliest of Schiller's works can even be interpreted as meaning that Wagner thought it was Schiller's best. His discussion of *Wallenstein* in *Oper und Drama*, in the light of these comments, does seem to indicate an interest or even a fascination based on deep admiration.

What does *Wallenstein* have to do with the *Ring*? The length to which Wagner goes, in *Oper und Drama*, to destroy *Wallenstein* may very well indicate, paradoxically, how closely related the two works really are. A comparative analysis of the two works under discussion can penetrate the surface dissimilarities and show the divergence of subject matter to be deceptive. The resemblances, as I will show, are actually more fundamental than the differences. These affinities concern the structures and themes of the works, and thus they relate these two sets of dramas more closely than a mere coincidental agreement of type of subject matter ever could. I would even propose that the *Ring* is, in some ways, actually Schillerian. Conversely, Schiller's plays are very operatic. Other plays of his, such as *Don Carlos* and *Kabale und Liebe*, have lent themselves to operatic treatment (most notably by Verdi). I imagine Countess Terzky as a Verdi mezzo, like Eboli, Amneris, or Azucena. But can one find Wagnerian elements in *Wallenstein*?

Some elements of the *Ring* do bring Schiller's aesthetic theories or even *Wallenstein* in particular to mind. For example, Octavio, like Fricka, shows a dogmatic insistence on law.[22] In contrast, Wallenstein fatally transgresses the law. He is, in a way, a later variation on the noble criminal of Schiller's "Storm and Stress" dramas, who is immoral and unconventional. Similarly, Wagner's *Ring* is based on the conflict of law and freedom, the old and the new, or, in Wagner's terms from *Oper und Drama*, custom versus free self-determination. The world described in *Wallensteins Lager* resembles the world of the *Ring*, where theft, deception, lust, and treachery rule.

In the following comparison, I discuss how this basic difference in choice of subject matter, that is, mythology or history, affects the theories of tragedy embodied in, or represented by, the *Ring* and *Wallenstein* respectively. These works, I propose, have some of the same themes and basic dichotomies, such as the opposition of fate and freedom, and the contrast of love and power. Furthermore, both deal in some way with politics. My argument is that each work treats these topics differently, due to the historical point of time at which each of the dramatists was writing, and the dictates or constraints that the choice of material, that is, whether mythological or historical, imposed on the dramatist. These are the the points that I want to illustrate with my analysis of *Wallenstein*.

First, there are many surface affinities between the works under discussion. Despite the difference in the type of subject matter used, *Wallenstein* does bear some outward similarities to the *Ring*. The most obvious of these is, of course, the trilogy form. Thomas Mann, in his essay on *Wallenstein*, has also discussed the similarities between Schiller's trilogy and Wagner's *Ring*, noting that one work is historical, and the other is mythical. Mann points out that in each instance a single work was expanded into one consisting of several parts. If one counts the Prologue, then the *Wallenstein* trilogy really has four parts, just like the *Ring*.

The Prologue, in several details, brings Wagner to mind. It states that it was written for the reopening of the theater in Weimar; the *Ring* was, similarly, written for the Festspielhaus in Bayreuth, though before it was built. The Prologue, furthermore, calls this theater a "Tempel," and states that the work will be performed before a select circle ("vor einem auserlesnen Kreis").[23] One could say that the Bayreuth circle was also a small, select group that assumed religious significance, and the Festspielhaus in

Bayreuth was often referred to as a temple. The Prologue to *Wallenstein* proclaims "die neue Ära, die der Kunst Thaliens / Auf dieser Bühne heut beginnt" (W 4) (the new era of dramatic art that begins today on this stage). The *Ring* was, similarly, a new kind of art form. Its theoretical counterpart, *Oper und Drama*, clearly tells us that.

Moreover, the two works under discussion were written, though in different ages, under similar historical circumstances. Schiller's mention of the strifes and battles of mankind for rule and for freedom ("um Herrschaft und um Freiheit," W 4) recalls the revolutionary circumstances that gave birth to the *Ring* and even sounds like a short synopsis of the tetralogy. Similarly, the statement, "Zerfallen sehen wir in diesen Tagen / Die alte feste Form" (W 5) (Today we see the established forms falling to pieces), also sounds like a summary of the *Ring*. Schiller is talking about his contemporary age, and he says that this form was established after the Thirty Years' War, thereby also subtly introducing his subject matter. He seems to be comparing the present age of strife to the time of the Thirty Years' War. In that respect, the play that follows has some relevance to the present age, as does the *Ring* (in other ways) to the era in which Wagner was writing it. The *Ring* is a mythological image of world-history from the perspective of a nineteenth-century artist.

Furthermore, the characters of both works fall into comparable groups. *Wallenstein* has, like the *Ring*, a dual, two-tiered structure. I would even speculate that in this respect *Wallenstein* was a major influence upon the composition of the *Ring*. It is easy to understand Wagner's explanation and defense of the Max-Thekla subplot when one recalls how Wagner embeds the story of Siegfried and Brünnhilde into that of Wotan. Both Wagner and Schiller depict young couples with idyllic strivings and utopian implications who have become pawns in the larger plot, the one about a quest for power.[24] Wagner even has several young pairs in his extensive plot—the Volsungs fulfill this qualification, as do Siegfried and Brünnhilde also.

The relationship of Wallenstein and Max does resemble that of Wotan and Brünnhilde. In each instance, the two that constitute a closely bonded pair are painfully separated by irreconcilable differences. Both Wallenstein and Max are, as John Neubauer points out, on a metaphysical quest,[25] and the same can be said of Wotan and Brünnhilde. Wallenstein and Wotan play "Realpolitik"; Max and Brünnhilde begin idealistically, but they later capitulate to the system when their ideals are shattered by a corrupt reality.[26] One can call it nothing else when Brünnhilde, in the second act of *Götterdämmerung*, plots Siegfried's death with Hagen and Gunther. In the beginning, Max follows his heart, like Brünnhilde, but later he chooses the side of the Emperor. Wotan shares the "crooked paths" of Wallenstein.

Moreover, Wallenstein is eventually separated from Max, just as Wotan loses Brünnhilde. Wallenstein's sudden weakness when he pleads, "Max! Bleibe bei mir.—Geh nicht von mir, Max!" (W 271) (Max! Stay with me.—

Don't leave me, Max!), and reminds Max, at the latter's decisive moment, how much he cared for him, resembles Wotan's when he bids farewell to Brünnhilde, that is, when the god becomes a father and shows an unexpected tenderness and humanity, a moment I would designate as the destruction of the figurative mythological internalized "state" that Wagner illustrates with the myth of Oedipus. According to Wagner's revolutionary nineteenth-century retelling and reinterpretation of the mythical story of Oedipus and Antigone, when Creon becomes a father, the "state" is destroyed.

Furthermore, Wallenstein is totally dejected without Max, just as losing Brünnhilde virtually destroys Wotan. In the last scenes of Schiller's trilogy, Wallenstein remembers Max, and similarly Wotan, as Waltraute reports to her banished sister upon urgently sneaking away to visit her in *Götterdämmerung*, thinks of Brünnhilde as he awaits the end. Earlier I cited Wagner as saying that the separation of Max from Wallenstein causes the catastrophe in the work. Nobody could deny that Wotan's separation from Brünnhilde is, in some important way, connected with the doom of the gods.

The *Ring* even contains some verbal reminiscences of *Wallenstein*. These verbal similarities, I would argue, hint at deep connections between the two works. For example, Wallenstein's rationalization of his imminent treason seems to distinctly foreshadow Wotan's double-dealings in *Rheingold*. Wallenstein says to Max, "Den Edelstein, das allgeschätzte Gold / Muss man den falschen Mächten abgewinnen, / Die unterm Tage schlimmgeartet hausen" (W 208) (The jewel, the precious gold, must be obtained from the evil powers that lurk under the earth). What in Wallenstein's case is figural becomes, for Wotan, due to the mythological nature of the drama in which he finds himself, literal. In *Rheingold*, Wotan steals the golden ring from Alberich in subterranean Nibelheim.

In *Wallensteins Tod*, the protagonist's wife explains his faults to him with, "O mein Gemahl! Sie bauen immer, bauen / Bis in die Wolken, bauen fort und fort / Und denken nicht dran, dass der schmale Grund / Das schwindelnd schwanke Werk nicht tragen kann" (W 243) (O my husband! You always build, up to the clouds, constantly, and it doesn't occur to you that the narrow ground can't hold the swaying edifice). These lines, taken literally, might as well belong to the *Rheingold* Fricka, for the building of Valhalla expedites and dramatizes Wotan's inevitable moral demise, a process of deterioration that brings the whole fictional cosmos down with it. Wotan steals the ring from Alberich to pay the giants for building Valhalla for him. Wagner seems to have abstracted, for his mythological music-drama, a metaphorical layer from Schiller's plays. It seems no coincidence, taking the difference in subject matter, that what is figural in the one work is literal in the other. Mythological music-drama can portray what words alone can, in a historical work, only figuratively convey.

The most significant similarities between the two works under discussion are, though, their main characters. Many of Wagner's figures do seem to resemble the Schillerian type of "the noble criminal." They are rebels and outsiders. Wotan can be considered one of these criminals. Not only is Wotan a somewhat Schillerian type of character, but at times it is almost as though Wotan were enacting Schiller's aesthetics. Sublimity in the narrow, moralistic sense consists in a decision for duty over inclination, that is, the spiritual or the higher purpose over material pleasure, the moral over the natural. In his essay "Über den Grund des Vergnügens an tragischen Gegenständen," for instance, Schiller uses the example of a man who sacrifices his son for the welfare of the state.

Surprisingly enough, Wotan seems to be acting out Schiller's definition of sublimity. Wotan, in the second act of *Walküre*, is caught in a conflict between his godly duty ("Pflicht") and his natural inclination ("Neigung"). In decreeing Siegmund's death, Wotan resembles the fictitious man Schiller describes who sacrifices his son for the good of the state. The differences are, of course, obvious: the "state" as such does not exist in the *Ring*, and the order that dictated the decision is a corrupt one. Fricka is an unsympathetic character. Wagner exalted the natural over the moral. However, it is not going too far to say that, according to Schiller's definition, Wotan is a noble criminal, his decision is a sublime one, and the *Ring* is a Schillerian kind of tragedy. Or is it?

WOTAN AND WALLENSTEIN

Exploring the parallels between these two protagonists further reveals the veiled correspondences between the two works. Each has, after all, caused the main conflict of the set of dramas in which he exists. Neither is a simple figure. Both are unusually contradictory and paradoxical. Both Wallenstein and Wotan are rulers whose power is great but, at the same time, limited. In the second act of *Walküre*, when he forbids Brünnhilde to shield Siegmund in battle, Wotan threatens to hurl the universe into ruins if Brünnhilde does not obey him. However, the fact that he rescinds his previous command that she shield Siegmund in battle with Hunding proves, ironically, how powerless he really is. Fricka makes it painfully clear to him that law and order must triumph if he is to keep his power. Paradoxically, though, in obeying her, he loses his power. Wallenstein, to listen to the people speaking of him in *Wallensteins Lager*, seems almost invincible, like Siegfried. He is, in a way, superhuman. In a complementary way, Wotan is a god, but very human and flawed.

Though the situation in which each finds himself is a complex one, it is an obvious fact that neither Wotan nor Wallenstein is above reproach. Wotan is a corrupt ruler indeed. *Rheingold* shows him in action, participating in theft and deception in an attempt to keep his power when it is significantly threatened (or when it even looks as though it is). However, his status as lord over the rest of the gods, strangely enough, does not exempt him from the law. In fact, as Fricka makes painfully clear to him, his position actually makes his responsibility to uphold the law an even more crucial one, and his transgressions are therefore more dire. They certainly have more severe consequences than they normally would, due to his divine status. In giving up, moreover, he pulls the whole fictional universe to ruin with him.

In this respect, too, the two protagonists seem to simultaneously resemble and complement each other. In *Wallensteins Lager* the characters depicted raise the question of who is more powerful, the Emperor or the subversive general Wallenstein, outlining a precarious balance of power that seems to be a dangerous role reversal between the two. The Emperor, though, wins out. The alternation of public and private scenes in *Wallenstein* shows these two sides of the main character, as ruler and general, on one hand, and as father, on the other. Wotan is, similarly, a highly complex character. He is a god, but very human, too. Wotan and Wallenstein seem almost mirror-images of each other. They are reversed reflections of each other. It therefore seems no coincidence that one exists in a historical work, and the other in a cycle of mythological music-dramas.

The parallels of Wotan and Wallenstein can be established, as I will demonstrate, in two ways. They can be drawn either directly between the two dramatic works and protagonists, or indirectly, that is, via the theory of tragedy in *Oper und Drama*, which each of them, in some extended way, exemplifies. I may need to beg the reader's indulgence for my method, which might seem to be a detour, of discussing the similarities between *Wallenstein* and the *Ring* via the theory of *Oper und Drama*. However, I feel that the *Ring* somehow demonstrates the main ideas of this theoretical treatise, and the basic outline of Wagner's theory can also be seen as an underlying pattern in *Wallenstein*. In turn, the differences between the *Ring* and *Wallenstein*, in particular, the differences between the characters of Wotan and Wallenstein, can be seen by considering how and why the schema that I abstract from *Oper und Drama* is illustrated by each of the works under discussion in an altered form.

I will eventually make the comparison more specific by centering it on two passages in particular, for each is a pivotal one in its respective set of dramas. Both are formally comparable, too, and they can be effectively paralleled. They even have, moreover, some verbal similarities. In each, the protagonist expresses his deepest concerns. The monologues of Wotan and Wallenstein both outline the major conflicts and the ensuing course of action of each respective work in microcosm, and thus each contains the entire drama in miniature form. The similarities or other correspondences between these two sets of dramas then come to light and illuminate the relationship of these two works to each other. The central conflict of each drama is, after all, caused by the psyche and wrongdoings of the main character, Wotan or Wallenstein.

Wotan's monologue in the second act of *Walküre* is a pivotal point in the *Ring*. The necessity of pronouncing Siegmund's death sentence has wide and dire ramifications for the mythological cosmos over which Wotan rules. In his monologue, he explicates the deeper dilemma that his painful personal problems and his difficult family situation represent. This monologue shows how the conflict between convention and freedom, which Wagner explained in *Oper und Drama* as the central dramatic one in the art-work of the future as a modern rebirth of Greek tragedy, is internalized in the main character of Wagnerian drama; it takes place here within Wotan himself. At the end of this monologue, Wotan renounces his power, for he has internalized what is now a dematerialized tragic curse, that is, the curse that Alberich has placed on the ring. He feels the ring is cursed; he therefore renounces his power. His declaration of the end of the gods is an act of free self-determination and thereby self-destruction.

There is also (perhaps not coincidentally, either) a very important monologue in *Wallenstein*. I propose that some of the differences between the *Ring* and *Wallenstein*, which point toward the differences in viewpoints of Wagner and Schiller, can be illustrated by comparing the monologues of Wotan and Wallenstein. A comparative study of Goethe and Wagner would point out, for example, that Torquato Tasso is a predecessor of Tannhäuser. Each is a maladjusted artist figure caught between two women, and each has a best friend, Antonio and Wolfram respectively, who represents a more "normal" societal existence. Similarly, Wotan, I would suggest, is a mythical reincarnation of Wallenstein.

Wagner's theory of tragedy is based, structurally speaking, on the conflict between custom and freedom, tradition and self-determination. Wagner's theory of Greek tragedy and of music-drama as its nineteenth-century German counterpart actually comes in two parts. First Wagner gives a revolutionary, that is, nineteenth-century interpretation of the traditional structure of Greek tragedy, arguing that Greek tragedy was actually the repressive tool of a conservative society. Wagner defines the form of tragedy by its mythological subject matter. In *Oper und Drama*, Wagner therefore discusses the formation of myth, showing its perspectival nature and historical relativism. Myth is, according to Wagner, how one perceives things, not how they in reality are. Therefore he reinterprets the mythology of ancient drama in a demythologized way.

Wagner accordingly theorizes that "fate" was, for the Greeks, really a projection of a conservative society, which was then internalized by the tragic hero. Society, he reasoned, draws up a scenario (i.e., it tells a story or a "myth" in two senses, a literal and an extended sense) in which the protagonist of tragedy is depicted as being influenced by powers that he cannot control. The victim internalizes this story and self-image, and then he denounces himself according to the laws of the established order. According to Wagner, "fate" is a figment or a "myth" of a conservative society, intended to coerce or brainwash a freethinker and independent doer into conformity. Wagner is, in essence, saying that one makes one's fate oneself. Thus Wagner demythologizes the ancient notion of "fate." He unmasks what he thinks is an instrument of a repressive social structure. What appears as a tragedy of fate ("Schicksalstragödie") is actually, Wagner argues, a tragedy of character ("Charaktertragödie").

This makes one believe that when Wagner writes that "fate" is, in the modern world, the state, it is so because we give it power over us. Wagner's theory is a cross between a political and a psychological one. He writes that whereas Greek tragedy was conservative, modern drama should be revolutionary. Wagner's mythological revision of Greek tragedy embodies his own revolutionary interpretation of it. Accordingly, the art-work of the future is a revolutionary unworking or deconstruction of Greek tragedy. The drama he sketches in *Oper und Drama* does not deal directly with the state; rather, it portrays the conflict of custom and freedom, tradition and self-determination, via abstract concepts. The tragic conflict, according to Wagner, should be internalized in the protagonist of the art-work of the future. The destruction of the state consists in a process of coming to consciousness. The state, Wagner felt, needs to be destroyed from the inside out. It is oppressive only when we internalize its dictates, and thus it is ultimately a purely psychological force. Therefore it need not be oppressive. The choice really belongs to the individual.

The *Ring*, accordingly, demonstrates that fate is nothing metaphysical, and that one, on the contrary, makes one's fate oneself. The tragic conflict is internalized in the main character (in this case, Wotan), just as *Oper und Drama* said it should be. Wotan feels he is doomed because he touched the ring; thus he wills his own destruction, and thereby paradoxically negates any metaphysical notion of the curse. By taking his guilt upon himself, he is essentially saying that really he, not Alberich, has cursed the ring. The end of the gods must come, he realizes, because of his own inner faults, not because of any magical curses. Wotan demonstrates Wagner's theory of revolutionary drama when he takes the curse (which he thinks is literal but which is really, because of his willing of his own destruction, merely imaginary) upon himself, wills his own destruction, and thus psychologizes and transcends the curse, causing both directly and indirectly, via Brünnhilde, the cataclysm that renews the world.

In this manner Wotan demonstrates the revolutionary potential of Wagner's aesthetics of mythological-historical reflective self-consciousness. The *Ring* is a myth on the level of reflection. In the course of the tetralogy, both Wotan and Brünnhilde come to self-consciousness. Thus Wotan exemplifies the destruction of the "state" in the third act of *Walküre*. In this final scene the god, like the tyrant Creon, becomes a father. Self-consciousness is revolutionary here, for it destroys the entire mythological cosmos, and, furthermore, the *Ring* thereby self-reflectively both demonstrates its aesthetic program and prefigures the revolution of modern society that the work itself should cause. In this manner the *Ring* is built upon an affective aesthetics. The tetralogy depicts its own reception. The experience of the work was to bring the audience to some kind of revolutionary consciousness. Thus the *Ring* was to not only prefigure but also cause the revolution of modern society. Furthermore, the *Ring* is a tragedy of fate ("Schicksalstragödie") insofar as it is really a tragedy of character ("Charaktertragödie").

A cursory examination of Wallenstein's monologue shows many affinities with Wotan's monologue, even without driving the critic to *Oper und Drama* in a search for some way to link these two passages via the theoretical underpinning of the later one. Critics have noted that Wallenstein is no strict realist. Walter Müller-Seidel, for instance, notes that Wallenstein is both an idealist and a realist at the same time,[27] just as, I would add, Wotan wants both the old and the new. He wants to break the laws while keeping his power as guardian of the laws. Wotan wants both love and power, the dichotomy the terms of which in the work are established, by the curse on the ring, as mutually exclusive. Furthermore, Wallenstein's monologue, like Wotan's, deals with the theme of the opposition of the old and the new, deeds and one's reflection on them, fate and freedom, history and myth, if you will.

Wallenstein also resembles Wotan in opposing custom. In the last part of his monologue Wallenstein asks about his real motives for his deeds, and he speaks pejoratively of traditional beliefs. This, Müller-Seidel argues, shows that he is no strict realist. He has an idealistic vision. Both protagonists are also caught in contradictory situations. As Wotan's word is, according to Brünnhilde, "zwiespältig" (split), Wallenstein despairs of the "Doppelsinn des Lebens" (W 184) (duality of life), which he feels is accusing him. Müller-Seidel argues that Wallenstein is not without conscience, and Wotan's monologue, I would add, proves the same about him.

Müller-Seidel discusses the centrality of Wallenstein's monologue to the work in which it exists, pointing out that one can consider the work a "decision drama" ("Entscheidungsdrama") in which the decision is a necessary one, and thus not really a decision. In much the same way, Wotan gives in to Fricka and in his monologue rues over the fact. Wotan's decision has been made for him—his monologue is interesting, rather, in how it retells and analyzes past events. Wallenstein feels his decision has been made for him. He then makes it himself upon these premises.

Thus these monologues show how, in certain ways, the two characters under discussion can be considered reversals of each other. Whereas Wotan is dwelling on deeds that were committed long ago, Wallenstein, in contrast, is coming to terms with a deed in the future, the realization of which has not even (objectively speaking) been decided yet. While Wotan's dilemma is that he once acted but now may not act, Wallenstein's is that he must act. Wallenstein's monologue is a true soliloquy. While Wotan is speaking to himself, he is, however, not alone onstage. Brünnhilde listens in and explicitly identifies herself as his will. In order that she fully understand his present state of despair, Wotan must inform his favorite Valkyrie daughter of what went on well before her birth. Wallenstein's monologue does not recount the external events the way Wotan's does. He's alone; unlike Wotan, he doesn't have to retell the story.

Interpreters like to discuss the extent of Wallenstein's guilt for his fall, and debate about his motives for his deeds (or rather his procrastination, his lack of action).[28] Treating this topic is like asking why the gods of the *Ring* have to end. It's a difficult and complex issue, and an answer to the question will also explain what kind of concept of "fate" is at work in *Wallenstein*. Before answering the question of why Wallenstein falls, though, one must ask the not-unrelated question of why he does the deed. Why does he have to act? This is the crucial bit of (significantly enough, nonfactual) information that the monologue contains. An answer to this question will reveal the similarities between *Wallenstein* and the *Ring*. Strangely enough, Wagner's theory of the mythology underlying Greek tragedy in *Oper und Drama* can help explicate a historical drama of Schiller.

Wallenstein, like Wotan, is caught in a subtle and complicated interaction between external and internal factors. The subjective aspect is even more important than the objective. *Wallenstein* proceeds through innertextual interpretation via the title character, just as Wotan's reflection upon the previous events of the *Ring* brings the mythical cosmos to doom. Both Wotan and Wallenstein, strangely enough, will what they see as inevitable. Analyzing these monologues, for this reason, entails delving into the figures' subjective perceptions of their situations. Thus, I will not go into the real (historical) events in detail but, rather, Wallenstein's reflection on them, just as one can understand Wotan's monologue only by analyzing his subjectivity. How one perceives a situation can be much more consequential and carry far more importance than what the conditions objectively really are.

Wallenstein, subjectively at least, actually has no choice. He begins his monologue by asking himself the (rhetorical) questions:

Wärs möglich? Könnt ich nicht mehr, wie ich wollte?
Nicht mehr zurück, wie mirs beliebt? Ich müsste
Die Tat *vollbringen*, weil ich sie *gedacht*,
Nicht die Versuchung von mir wies—das Herz
Genährt mit diesem Traum, auf ungewisse

Erfüllung hin die Mittel mir gespart,
Die Wege bloss mir offen hab gehalten? (W 183)

Could it be possible? That I can no longer do as I wish? I cannot turn back, as I would like to? That I must do the deed, because I thought about it, and toyed with the temptation—I dreamed about it, but it was never certain, I merely kept the option open.

The questions are rhetorical, for he feels that they have been answered for him already. The implicit answer to these questions is that the possibility must be realized. Are the determining factors, though, internal or external? Wallenstein is in a curious position, indeed. He is no longer free, trapped as he is between past and future, guilty and innocent. He is both innocent (objectively, for he has not yet committed the actual treason) and guilty (subjectively, for in the perceptions of others, he is a traitor). But how does he see himself? In modern psychological jargon, does he have a healthy self-image?

Strangely enough, the past is somehow determining the future. Furthermore, how something that has already happened is perceived by others somehow has a decisive effect upon how Wallenstein himself perceives his own situation and why he finally determines to do a future action. Therefore, one can say that at least the circumstances in which he finds himself are the results of his previous deeds, and these past acts are certainly questionable. Objectively, he is not totally blameless; he has done much more than think about this ultimate deed. However, he even emphasizes his own innocence, as though he had done nothing wrong. He stresses that he did not intend the future treason seriously, even though he has definitely been involved in wrongdoings.

He then, like Wotan, laments about these past deeds, despairing that he (also like Wotan) has made himself unfree. Wotan's statement, "In eig'ner Fessel / fing ich mich"[29] (I have caught myself in my own fetter), which he mutters shortly before his monologue, seems to echo the line from Wallenstein's monologue, "So hab ich / Mit eignem Netz verderblich mich umstrickt, / Und nur Gewalttat kann es reissend lösen" (W 184) (Thus I have caught myself in my own net, and only violence can loosen it). Wallenstein actually, though, gives these past subversive deeds the power to ensnare him. Benno von Wiese points out that at the time he holds this monologue, Wallenstein really does have a free choice, but he sees himself caught in powers he cannot control.[30] He feels he must do the deed.

Using building imagery, Wallenstein remarks, "Bahnlos liegts hinter mir, und eine Mauer / Aus meinen eignen Werken baut sich auf, / Die mir die Umkehr türmend hemmt!" (W 184) (There is no path behind me, and a wall of my own deeds rises up, which prevents me from turning back!). This foreshadows how Wotan is caught in and by his castle, because of the pact he has made with the giants. Wallenstein feels he cannot turn back, which

Wotan, of course, has been trying to do in a very different and indirect way (regaining the ring or having someone throw it back into the Rhine for him would, he has evidently surmised, be some kind of restitution), but he can't do it directly, and now he must give up even the indirect way, too. The thought of Brünnhilde throwing the ring into the Rhine for him becomes a mere fantasy, as reported by Waltraute to Brünnhilde in *Götterdämmerung*. Wotan, after his monologue and his renunciation of his power and divine status, must become a mere spectator of the stage action, in the persona of the Wanderer in *Siegfried*.

Wallenstein's monologue, though, raises as many questions as it answers. Why have these past acts made Wallenstein unfree? Both protagonists are, one could say, in some way forced to ruin by others. Müller-Seidel links this external determinism in *Wallenstein* to the idea of fate in Greek tragedy. There is no doubt that, to a large extent, the motivating force of Wallenstein's future deed is outside of himself. Wallenstein is caught up in a complex process of reacting to counterattacks and other stimuli from outside (which he himself has, of course, provoked). Circumstances doubtlessly play a large part in prompting his actions. Korff points out that it is not Wallenstein but the Emperor who (like Loge, I would add) sets the fatal events into motion.[31] Thus the deed of treason becomes a necessity.

Furthermore, both works under discussion are tragedies of language. Wallenstein is done in by words—in his monologue, he comments that having spoken of the deed forces him to do it. In Wotan's case, the words of others force him to relinquish his power. The pronouncements of Alberich and Erda that concern the curse on the ring and the doom of the gods become reality—first in Wotan's psyche and, after Wotan mentally connects them, in external reality. Wallenstein, in his monologue, complains that having spoken about the (still tentative) event is leading to the necessity of realizing the act of treason. It is as though language had somehow assumed some objective power over him. Wallenstein is also goaded into action by his ambitious relatives. These external motivations, though, still do not explain why he acts or, rather, why he feels he must act.

To indicate a coincidental similarity between Wagner and Schiller would prove little, indeed. That they share the common goal of revising the notion of "fate" can be considered a trite observation. But, surprisingly enough, as anachronistic as it may seem, Wallenstein's dilemma can be greatly clarified and explained by analyzing it with reference to Wagner's mythological aesthetics of music-drama. The two seem to fit together almost perfectly. Wallenstein's monologue brings to mind Wagner's theory of tragedy from the second part of *Oper und Drama*. Wagner's theory of Greek tragedy describes a process of labeling and the resultant internalization of this projected image. Wagner discusses in this treatise how society perceives the tragic hero and how the protagonist, to what is intended by society as a conservative end, internalizes these projections or these perceptions.

Wagner's theory seems, in these plays of Schiller, strangely distorted, to be sure. One must make some qualifications when drawing the analogy I have just suggested. Wallenstein is, of course, a rebel, like the typical tragic hero. In Wagner's hypothetical Greek society, the conservatives use the fictional notion of the tragic curse to subtly and psychologically compel a nonconformist into conformity with the rest of society. In contrast, the people who influence Wallenstein encourage him to rebel rather than conform. But Wallenstein still fulfills the prophecy of others, thus internalizing the others' perception of him and conforming to their notions of what or who he is.

The differences between the two protagonists under discussion are also telling to the utmost. Both Wotan and Wallenstein are suffering from neither purely personal failings nor the crushing weight of external circumstances and events but, rather, a complex web, a tangled dialectic, of the inner and the outer. The subjective interacts with the objective. In the world of *Wallenstein*, the latter wins. Ironically enough, these tragic heroes, despite their strengths and eminent positions, capitulate to something that does not even exist objectively. Their psychological surrenders are the decisive moments of the dramas. The ensuing objective events that carry out what the protagonists have so painfully resolved are, in both of the dramatic works, somehow comparatively anticlimactic.

Wallenstein comments, in his monologue, on how he appears to others. If one can think anachronistically about the matter, one could say that Wallenstein seems to be strangely aware that he is, in some figurative way, "cursed," as though he had somehow read *Oper und Drama* and then applied Wagner's theory to his own situation. In his monologue, he is actually indulging in self-reflection, as he views his own drama from the outside. Thus, he rises above his own situation. At the same time, however, he elevates mere figments of the mind to real motivating forces and puts himself at the mercy of others' ideas of who he is. In doing so, he lets the subjective decide the objective. Fictions can become deadly, no doubt. In this way Wallenstein, one could say, propounds a kind of tragic subjective fatalism. He assumes the traitorous identity that the others perceive as rightly his (and that is, oddly enough, as yet unproven and also in fact, until it has been done, unprovable, as the deed has not yet even been committed), thus taking his fictitious guilt upon himself in a Wagnerian-Schillerian gesture of psychological martyrdom.

Wallenstein says, "Strafbar erschein ich, und ich kann die Schuld, / Wie ichs versuchen mag! nicht von mir wälzen" (W 184) (I appear guilty, and as much as I may try, I cannot shake off the guilt). To discuss Wallenstein's fall entails the issue of perception and perspectivism. He appears as a traitor, and therefore, to save his name, he must become one. Like the typical tragic hero, he is motivated by pride. In this respect, it is true, he falls of his own accord. But the issue is much more complex than this. It has an aspect of societal critique and it also shows subtle objective-subjective, societal-psychological interactions. Wallenstein is demonstrating a historical variation on Wagner's mythological tragedy theory.

Wallenstein anticipates that his story will be unjustly rewritten by those wanting to prove his guilt. In this way, as he explains, he has indirectly caused his own downfall by providing scattered bits of evidence that can be interpreted in a way that will apparently undeniably indict him. His deeds speak decisively against him (or so he feels). In outlining this scenario, he seems to somehow self-consciously explicate his own historical-dramatic demonstration of Wagner's theory of Greek tragedy. He laments the determinants of his inevitable "fate" by explaining,

Jetzt werden sie, was planlos ist geschehn,
Weitsehend, planvoll mir zusammen knüpfen,
Und was der Zorn, und was der frohe Mut
Mich sprechen liess im Überfluss des Herzens,
Zu künstlichem Gewebe mir vereinen,
Und eine Klage furchtbar draus bereiten,
Dagegen ich verstummen muss. So hab ich
Mit eignem Netz verderblich mich umstrickt,
Und nur Gewalttat kann es reissend lösen. (W 184)

Now they will connect what I unintentionally did by attributing crafty intentions to me, and what I angrily or courageously said, and form an artistic web from these elements, and thereby fabricate an awful accusation that will silence me. Thus I have caught myself in my own net, and only violence can loosen it.

In other words, they take the same details, his words and deeds, and put them together in a different way. That is, they misinterpret these facts and rewrite his story accordingly.

Both *Oper und Drama* and Wallenstein's monologue describe or demonstrate a process of rewriting stories, a phenomenon of mythological fabrication and refabrication, one could say. In different ways this treatise and this monologue both deal with how one forms "myths" or writes stories to explain things from one's own particular perspective. One could say that Wallenstein internalizes the "myth," story, or perception of others. He puts it into practice, and thus he historicizes it in a deadly way. In his persisting defense of his hero, Max says to his father, "Ja, ihr könntet ihn, / Weil ihr ihn schuldig *wollt*, noch schuldig *machen*" (W 171) (Yes, if you *want* him to be guilty, you can *make* him guilty). This is exactly what happens. Wallenstein himself is, in a suicidal way, the tragically fatal catalyst in the dramas so appropriately named after him.

The process that Wagner sees at work in Greek tragedy, that of society coercing the tragic hero into conformity by causing him to internalize society's views, brings Wallenstein to disaster. That the others are prompting him to rebel, rather than conform, does not change the fact that (according to Wagner's definitions) the Wallenstein plays, at least with the example of the protagonist, demonstrate a conservative world-view such as Wagner saw in Greek tragedy. The society that brings Wallenstein to ruin is, of course, portrayed with a critical eye. Furthermore, Schiller does intend to bring the audience to some kind of moral betterment through the plays. But one could not assert that the *Wallenstein* trilogy is radical or revolutionary in the same way that the *Ring* is.

What Schiller wrote about the historical Wallenstein is true, in a qualified way, for the fictional one as well. It is not that he fell because he rebelled but, rather, that he rebelled because he fell. In other words, he "falls" in the esteem of others. In assuming the others' perception of him, Wallenstein places himself in the role that others have cast him into. Then he really plays the role. In the scene before his monologue, Wallenstein says, "in Nachsinnen verloren" (lost in thought), that is, more to himself than to Illo and Terzky, "Nicht herzustellen mehr ist das Vertraun. / Und mag ich handeln, wie ich will, ich werde / Ein Landsverräter ihnen sein und bleiben" (W 181) (I cannot build trust anymore, and whatever I do, I will remain a traitor in their eyes). His deeds are at this point irrelevant, so he does as he feels he should do, or as he is at least expected to do. Which means, ironically enough, that he does what he should *not* do.

The interaction between history and character in the works under discussion is therefore a complex one. These two factors are never, after all, mutually exclusive. The decisive force of one does not exclude that of the other. To the question of whether "fate" comes from outside or from inside a person, one must reply that somehow, both possibilities are simultaneously and reciprocally true. Wallenstein is a perfect example of this. Thus von Wiese does not really contradict himself when he says that Wallenstein's character is his fate,[32] and that history takes the place of fate from Greek tragedy, for both are, in a way, true. Wallenstein attributes to history the power of fate, and how others perceive him is an impression he himself has made. Furthermore, whatever force of restitution that history has (if one, with Benno von Wiese, believes this is a "tragedy of nemesis") is provoked by Wallenstein himself.

Wallenstein, like Wotan, follows the script that others have written. Wallenstein, as Müller-Seidel notes, seeks the enemy everywhere except in himself, and this is one of his similarities with Wotan. They are, however, also alike in finding themselves in predicaments that seem to allow them no freedom and no escape, and then acting accordingly. Müller-Seidel argues that *Wallenstein* gradually reveals a tragic analysis; Wallenstein recognizes he lacks freedom. He ceases to be a subject of action and realizes that he is really an object that is being acted upon.[33] I would revise this view and emphasize the element of subjectivity in his perception of his own situation. Wallenstein, like Wotan, sees a wheel rolling downhill. Because he feels he can't stop it, he gives it a push.

Not only does Wallenstein internalize the "myth" or perception of others, thus demonstrating how a Wagnerian "mythological" pattern has somehow been transposed into his own historical dramas, but he has his own private myth, his own idiosyncratic world-view. Wallenstein's astrological beliefs contribute greatly to his ruin. Wallenstein, like Wotan, projects what is his own responsibility into metaphysical factors. Wallenstein fatally believes what he reads in the stars. Thus, interpretation is a theme of both works under discussion. Wallenstein thinks the stars decide his fate; Wotan looks under the earth, to Erda and Alberich, for his fate. Furthermore, both dramatists have, in what one could call a psychological kind of internal hermeneutic way, demythologized the ancient force of "fate."

I propose that the theme of astrology in *Wallenstein* provides the crucial link between the two works under discussion. *Wallenstein* is a critique of myth within a historical drama. It also thematizes the notion of fate. Furthermore, just as Wagner's *Ring* is not totally unrelated to history, Schiller's *Wallenstein* really, in a profound way, has something to do with myth. Moreover, both works under discussion actually thematize the topics of history and myth. To put it simplistically, ignoring for the moment the self-referentiality of these works and stressing, rather, their complementary nature, one could say the following: the *Ring* is a cycle of mythological dramas about history; *Wallenstein* comprises historical dramas that deal with myth.

ASTROLOGY AS MYTHOLOGY IN *WALLENSTEIN*

It would be a commonplace to assert that the force of "fate" in Greek tragedy was a metaphysical one. The world of Greek tragedy was, as Wagner stressed, a mythological one. Furthermore, an essential element of Greek tragedy is the tragic curse, which Wagner, in building upon Greek tragedy theory and thereby unworking it, demythologizes to a revolutionary end. This unworking and transcendence of Greek tragedy form a unifying feature of the works of Wagner and Schiller that are under discussion. The *Ring* and *Wallenstein* exemplify this. German Classical drama was, Müller-Seidel explains, oriented upon the theory of Greek tragedy. The goal of German Classicism, according to Müller-Seidel, was to transcend tragedy. In this way, Müller-Seidel finds in Schiller's trilogy untragic or "metatragic" structural elements that he sees as basically epic in nature.

With *Wallenstein*, mythology has crept into historical drama in an insidious and very destructive way. One of the epic structures that Walter Müller-Seidel finds in *Wallenstein* is the theme of Wallenstein's belief in the stars. The trilogy demythologizes this belief and shows it to be a superstition. Wallenstein himself, Müller-Seidel explains, initially sees this belief as a science, thus asserting a unity of science and religion from ancient, prescientific, or "mythical" times. Furthermore, Wallenstein understands "fate" in the sense of ancient mythology. Müller-Seidel points out that the concepts he uses indicate this; he uses "Stern" (star) and "Schicksal" (fate) synonymously. When he speaks of "fate," he is speaking of something numinous. The audience is not supposed to take his word uncritically. Wallenstein's superstition is, according to Müller-Seidel, treated in this trilogy with the device of irony.

By arguing that in the *Wallenstein* trilogy history takes the place of fate from ancient tragedy, Benno von Wiese makes it sound as though "fate" comes solely from the outside. But Wallenstein makes his own fate in several ways. The interaction between the inner and the outer is, I have shown, complex. First, Wallenstein's character is his fate.[34] Korff, for instance, explains that his external "fall" is the result of inner corruption.[35] Within the play Illo propounds this psychological interpretation of fate. He says to Wallenstein, "In deiner Brust sind deines Schicksals Sterne" (W 98) (The stars that decide your fate are in your heart). But Illo's very statement of this, just the fact that he says this in the work, opens up a whole new perspective. Not only is one shown as making one's own fate, but both *Wallenstein* and *Oper und Drama* present explicit innertextual interpretations of the notion of "fate." They thematize the essential elements of Greek tragedy. In doing so, they undo and demythologize traditionally mythological forces.

Not only does *Wallenstein* present explicit interpretations of fate, and thus reflect upon Greek tragic notions and forces, but, furthermore, in *Wallenstein*, as in the *Ring*, fate is subjective. Ironically, the subjective becomes therefore objective, just as Wallenstein's perceived necessity of doing the deed of treason pushes him into it much more so than the Emperor and his aggressive relatives do. In other words, how one sees one's fate determines how it is or what it will be in reality. In this manner, *Wallenstein* unworks the Greek notion of fate and thus the traditional structure of tragedy, as Wagner does in *Oper und Drama* and the *Ring*. What was once a metaphysical force becomes in all of these works a purely psychological one.

The gods of the *Ring*, the prime example of them being their leader and representative Wotan, in particular, have a kind of "historical" existence. They are mortal and human. As the central conflict of the *Ring* is internalized in Wotan, the supposedly accursed ring is an occasion for an inner adventure. The *Ring* portrays two stories, the one that deals with the mythical props, and the one that reveals the inner lives of the characters. It thus relates myth and psychology, the outer and the inner. The progression in the *Ring* consists of Wotan coming to terms with his own mortality, of which Erda has informed him at the conclusion of *Rheingold* in her warning. This begins the decisive inner drama of the cycle, Wotan's journey toward acceptance of his incipient and inevitable inner and therefore subsequent outer demise.

Wotan likes to believe that the universe (or the work of art) in which he exists is mythical in the sense in which traditional mythology is. The *Ring* is apparently mythological. Similarly, Wotan thinks that, as a god, he should be above all moral and ethical laws. He thinks, furthermore, that the curse that Alberich has placed upon the ring is magical. He does not know that the curse establishes the symbolic significance of the ring and is therefore merely metaphorical. He exists, simply enough, in a synthetic nineteenth-century musical-dramatic reworking of Germanic mythology. His renunciation of his power at the end of his monologue is ironic indeed. In assuming the curse, he paradoxically negates it. In other words, Wotan's belief that the ring is cursed causes him to renounce all claim to it and his desire for it, along with his power, thus ironically disproving any notion that a magical and thus traditionally mythological curse on the ring causes the loss of his power and the end of the fictional mythological world.

The curse on the ring, the one that works the doom of the gods, is therefore all in Wotan's mind insofar as the real dramatic action (or lack of action, as the conflict is to a large extent internalized, and the treaties that Wotan has made prevent him from acting) consists in Wotan, as Wagner explained in a letter to August Röckel, learning to die, to will, that is, the inevitable, of which Erda has informed him at the end of *Rheingold*. In willing the end of the gods, Wotan is tacitly accepting that his fate and his future are of his own making and that they result from his own decision. Thus he takes the inevitable upon himself and, as Wagner wrote, he rises to the tragic dignity of willing his own destruction, in what one could consider a Schillerian and sublime acceptance and affirmation of his destiny. One could even say that the decisive moment of the *Ring*, Wotan's acceptance of the end, is the realization, in his innertextual reflection upon the ring and with it the *Ring*, that what he once thought was a tragedy of fate ("Schicksalstragödie") is really a tragedy of character ("Charaktertragödie").

Like Wotan, Wallenstein feels he's in a "mythical" work or world. One could say that he thinks he's in a Greek tragedy, just as Wotan thinks he's in a work that operates according to the dictates of genuine mythology. Wotan has typically modern psychological depth and moral concerns. He seems impulsive, nondivine, and confused. He wills the end to prevent the end. Each protagonist, one could say, suffers a different end from that upon which he muses in his monologue. In other words, the end in which he goes under has different causes from that which he fears. Wallenstein is caught in the same paradox as Wotan. Because he thinks "fate" is objective, that is, external, he makes it himself. In projecting his "fate" outside, he ironically creates it. Wotan eventually overcomes myth; in taking his fate upon himself he shows that the end of the gods is not caused by a magical ring, for he wills the end himself. In contrast, Wallenstein's downfall is caused by his mythological superstitions.

Wallenstein projects the responsibility for his fate into the stars. In this manner *Wallenstein*, like the *Ring*, shows a subtle interplay between the subjective and the objective. Benno von Wiese notes that Wallenstein's belief in astrology not only is a symbol for his demise, but becomes a trap in which Wallenstein catches himself. By trying to compel earthly events into pre-ordained patterns or what he sees as a divine "fate" and thus negating his own human freedom, Wallenstein through astrology actually causes his own demise.[36]

Karl Guthke notes that the theme of astrology introduces higher powers into the *Wallenstein* plays.[37] Wallenstein feels he has some special connection to the supernatural, the metaphysical. He sees reality, then, through the lens of mythology. His belief in astrology is, one could say, his mythology, the same subjective force that fatally causes him to trust Octavio. A past event, a historical occurrence, that is, Octavio's rescue of him, has assumed "mythical" proportions for Wallenstein. It has become regulative. Thus *Wallenstein* thematizes the idea of mythology. Wallenstein has his own private mythology, his regulative fiction by which he runs his life and his career. The stars rule his life, though, merely because he thinks they do. Wallenstein, one could say, has a "mythological" world-view.

Furthermore, *Wallenstein*, like the *Ring*, shows a tension within the work between history and mythology. The stars are a mythological remnant in a historical drama. Wallenstein sees earthly reality (history) with a mythical world-view, that is, with reference to preconceived patterns. *Wallensteins Tod* opens with a scene in which Wallenstein discusses the stars with Seni, his astrologer. Wallenstein sees his fate in terms of these mythological constellations. The work in which he exists is a tragedy about tragedy, one could even say a modern tragedy about Greek tragedy, or a "Charaktertragödie" (tragedy of character) about a "Schicksalstragödie" (tragedy of fate). One can compare this scene, in its conscious and explicit deliberation on the "fate" of the drama, with the Norns' Scene that opens *Götterdämmerung*.

Previously his astrological superstition functioned in the work as retardation, like Wotan's treaties, for it caused Wallenstein's reluctance to act. Now, however, the positions of Mars, Venus, Saturn, and Jupiter determine that Wallenstein must act quickly. *Wallenstein*, like the theory of tragedy presented in *Oper und Drama*, is a strange mixture of ancient and modern elements, ancient scenarios and modern politics. Wallenstein is trying to overcome Greek tragedy on its own terms. His self-consciousness or (in Schillerian terms) sentimentality sentences him to ruin. In literary-historical terms, one could say that the contradiction between the two forms, Greek tragedy and modern historical drama, kills him. Wallenstein, like Wotan, interprets a tragedy of character ("Charaktertragödie") as a tragedy of fate

("Schicksalstragödie"). In doing so, Wallenstein does the opposite of what Wagner does in *Oper und Drama*. Wallenstein mythologizes modern historical drama; Wagner demythologizes Greek tragedy.

Wallenstein discards this "mythological" interpretation of the text in which he exists when it's actually too late, and he finds his "myth" and his mythological world-view useless to help his present predicament. Wallenstein, as Müller-Seidel points out, eventually renounces his astrological superstition, and he takes responsibility for Max's death.[38] Wallenstein, according to Müller-Seidel, does reach tragic or sublime proportions. Furthermore, Goethe wrote, in a letter to Schiller (18 March 1799), that it was the great strength of the last play of the *Wallenstein* trilogy that it ceases to deal with politics and becomes a human drama, and that here the historical is just a veil for the "fully human."[39] (Goethe, like Wagner, sees the myth behind history. According to this interpretation, Wallenstein, like Wotan, becomes fully human.) In a comparable way, Wotan, when he finds that Siegmund's death is a necessity, and he has inextricably caught himself in his own snares by trying to obtain the supposedly accursed ring from Alberich, turns inward and begins to ponder the symbolic nature of the curse that Alberich has placed upon this ring, and thus he acknowledges his own moral failings, which the plot around the ring has only served to dramatize.

The major difference between these two works under discussion is the ultimate value implicitly attributed to myth within each of them. For Wagner, according to the revolutionary-aesthetic program that he outlines in *Oper und Drama*, myth is hopefully realized in history; myth ultimately should change history. In Schiller's *Wallenstein*, however, history destroys myth. Wallenstein tries to put into practice (historicize) a preconceived pattern, that is, what he reads in the stars. Wallenstein's mythicization of history, though, fails. The planets are not regulative, and astrology is not prescriptive. Forcing historical drama into the metaphysics of Greek tragedy is deadly. The planets have mythological names, but Wallenstein cannot give them control over earthly reality by implementing their dictates and still survive. In the world of historical drama, their "mythological" value lies solely in their names. It is merely verbal.

Wotan unravels tragedy; Wallenstein affirms it. In this respect Wotan seems the reverse of Wallenstein, just as Schiller deals with history, and Wagner, myth. Wotan unworks myth and triumphs; Wallenstein mythologizes history and falls. Wallenstein's acts lead to his destruction; Wotan's past misdeeds lead to his redemption (via Brünnhilde). Wotan's renunciation of his power and subsequent loss of Brünnhilde indirectly redeem him (via her). Wagner wants to historicize myth (in reality). Wagner wanted to transcend history with myth. He felt that external (real) history should be, through the experience of art, mythified; it is to follow a mythical pattern. The redemption that Wagner sees in (or after) his "mythicized" history shows his hopes for the (real) historical future. Wallenstein's mythicization of history fails.

Wagner portrays the (figural) destruction of the "state." Schiller's trilogy ends with the continuation of a corrupt order. *Wallenstein* does not portray the destruction of the state. Perhaps this is another reason it receives no praise in *Oper und Drama*. The world-view represented by these plays does not correspond to Wagner's world-view as exemplified by the *Ring*. Wagner's tetralogy shows the demise of an order that, for obvious reasons, cannot survive. Furthermore, the work demonstrates the Romantic transcendence of tragedy. In the finale of the *Ring*, Valhalla ends. It is, of course, unclear what the new order will be like. Nothing is shown of it except men and women watching the final cataclysm. Just a musical theme points the way. But it is clear that some utopian condition, some transcendent state, has been reached. *Wallenstein* shows, as John Neubauer points out, no higher or transcendent principle in history (i.e., as shown in the work).

The transcendence of tragedy in *Wallenstein* is implicit. Müller-Seidel explains that Schiller shows the lack of a moral world-order to convey to the audience the possibility or even necessity of one in reality. Aesthetic freedom, Müller-Seidel argues, cannot be achieved within the tragedy itself, but, rather, it can be gained only in distanced reflection upon the tragedy. In other words, Schiller may be asserting at least the possibility of a moral world-order by portraying the absence of one onstage. He felt that the purpose of the experience of tragedy in the theater should be to inspire moral action in the audience.

Wagner wants to revise history via myth. His ultimate goal in reality is to mythicize modern life. Schiller shows that myth cannot dictate to history; rather, history conquers a (false) myth, as history defeats Wallenstein. Wagner saw a dialectic between history and myth. For Wallenstein, though, myth is his downfall. *Wallenstein* is a historical tragedy. For Schiller, history and myth, though they could somehow be present together in the same dramatic work, obviously constituted a strict dichotomy. *Wallenstein* shows an Enlightenment destruction of myth that Wagner and the other Romantics criticized.

This mutually exclusive dichotomy of history and myth for Schiller determines the tragic ending of the work in which they coexist. *Wallenstein*, like the *Ring*, is, in many ways, an unworking of tragedy. Wagner unworks tragedy by deconstructing myth; he places transcendence in history at the end. The future society would be the redemption of history through myth. Schiller undoes tragedy by taking transcendence out of history as portrayed in the plays themselves. Wagner historicizes myth; Schiller demythologizes history. He undermines the sense of history to create a moral awareness in the audience. Ironically, while Wotan's capitulation to custom causes him to take Alberich's curse upon himself, conquer it, and indirectly create a new world by banning Brünnhilde, Wallenstein's pursuit of his idealistic vision causes him to end tragically in the historical world of the stage reality. Wagner adds redemption to transcend tragedy; Schiller subtracts transcendence from history to undermine tragedy. The transcendence is implicit, that is, it takes place in the audience reception of the work.

Max does give an apocalyptic hint. He prophetically says at the end of *Die Piccolomini* that Wallenstein's fall will drag the whole world down with him (as Wotan's does). Wallenstein, in the same play, predicts, "Zu Trümmern / Wird alles gehn, was wir bedächtig bauten" (W 110) (What we have thoughtfully built will go to ruins). This seems a direct predecessor of Wotan's decree, in his monologue, "Zusammen breche, / was ich gebaut!" (MD 616) (May what I have built crumble!). At the end of the third act, Thekla even uses the imagery of a burning house, thus prefiguring the destruction of Valhalla:

O! wenn ein Haus im Feuer soll vergehn,
Dann treibt der Himmel sein Gewölk zusammen,
Es schiesst der Blitz herab aus heitern Höhn,
Aus unterirdschen Schlünden fahren Flammen,
Blindwütend schleudert selbst der Gott der Freude
Den Pechkranz in das brennende Gebäude! (W 135)

O! when a house perishes in fire, the clouds in the heavens gather, and the lightning courses down from the heights, from subterranean abysses, blindly raging, the god of joy slings the garland of misfortune into the burning building!

The mythological associations remain, though, on the figurative or metaphorical, one could even call it the rhetorical, level. *Wallenstein* contains an internal and implicit critique of the political system, so it is not really a conservative work, but it would certainly be mistaken to call it a revolutionary work. The state is not destroyed on any textual level. The work seems to end nowhere, with Thekla rushing amidst danger to Max's grave and Octavio displaying inner turmoil and anguish at being awarded the title that belonged to Wallenstein.

Perhaps the choice of different subject matter, that is, mythology rather than history, allows Wagner to give his work a different ending from the one that Schiller gave his. Wagner's internalization of world-history within his mythical Wotan allows him to transcend both history and myth, "redeeming" both in a higher synthesis. Perhaps Schiller's plays could not possibly show a higher purpose in history due to the constraints of the raw material with which he was working. Wagner gives a vision of destruction and renewal. Historical drama is limited, for it concentrates on the real; mythological music-drama has more options, for it has an added dimension, and extra layers of meaning. Maybe Wagner's choice of mythology allows him, in Wotan's self-destruction, to "redeem" Wallenstein.

NOTES

1. Dieter Borchmeyer, *Das Theater Richard Wagners: Idee, Dichtung, Wirkung* (Stuttgart: Reclam, 1982), p. 16.

2. Borchmeyer, *Das Theater Richard Wagners*, p. 81.

3. Helmut Schanze, *Drama im Bürgerlichen Realismus (1850–1890): Theorie und Praxis*, Studien zur Philosophie und Literatur des neunzehnten Jahrhunderts, vol. 21 (Frankfurt am Main: Vittorio Klostermann, 1973), pp. 51–55.

4. Anette Ingenhoff, *Drama oder Epos? Richard Wagners Gattungstheorie des musikalischen Dramas*, Untersuchungen zur deutschen Literaturgeschichte, vol. 41 (Tübingen: Max Niemeyer, 1987), pp. 74–79; Reinhold Brinkmann, "Szenische Epik. Marginalien zu Wagners Dramenkonzeption im *Ring des Nibelungen*" in *Richard Wagner: Werk und Wirkung*, ed. Carl Dahlhaus, Studien zur Musikgeschichte des 19. Jahrhunderts, vol. 26 (Regensburg: Gustav Bosse, 1971), pp. 85–96.

5. See: Borchmeyer, *Das Theater Richard Wagners*, pp. 63–74, 24–28. See also: Rainer Franke, *Richard Wagners Zürcher Kunstschriften: Politische und ästhetische Entwürfe auf seinem Weg zum "Ring des Nibelungen"*, Hamburger Beiträge zur Musikwissenschaft, vol. 26 (Hamburg: Verlag der Musikalienhandlung Karl Dieter Wagner, 1983), pp. 255–65.

6. See: Borchmeyer, *Das Theater Richard Wagners*, pp. 76–85.

7. Borchmeyer, *Das Theater Richard Wagners*, p. 314.

8. See: Ingenhoff, pp. 67–72.

9. On the chorus, see: Borchmeyer, *Das Theater Richard Wagners*, pp. 151–75 (the section "Chortragödie und symphonisches Drama—Wagners Anteil an Nietzsches 'Geburt der Tragödie' "); Franke, pp. 265–71 ("Die Orchestersprache als Wiederbelebung des Chores der antiken Tragödie").

10. Cosima Wagner, *Die Tagebücher*, 4 vols., 2d ed., ed. Martin Gregor-Dellin and Dietrich Mack (Munich: Piper, 1976, 1982), vol. 1, pp. 568–69 (entry of 29 August 1872); English translation by Geoffrey Skelton, *Diaries*, 2 vols. (New York and London: Harcourt Brace Jovanovich, 1978/80), vol. 1 , p. 530. References to these diaries are hereafter given in my text by volume and page numbers, with the German reference preceded by the abbreviation "CT" and that of the translation by the abbreviation "D."

11. For discussions of Wagner's views on the novel, see: Borchmeyer, *Das Theater Richard Wagners*, pp. 125–51 (section "Die 'Erlösung' des Romans im musikalischen Drama"); Ingenhoff, pp. 80–100. Ingenhoff takes issue with Borchmeyer's thesis of Wagnerian music-drama as the "redemption" of the novel form.

12. On Wagner and Shakespeare, see: Ingenhoff, pp. 44–56; Borchmeyer (see note 11, above).

13. Richard Wagner, *Oper und Drama*, ed. Klaus Kropfinger (Stuttgart: Reclam, 1984), p. 154.

14. Benno von Wiese comments on the distinction between poetic and historical truth. See Benno von Wiese, "Geschichte und Drama," DVjs 20, no. 4 (1942): pp. 412–34.

15. Wagner's ambivalence toward Schiller's works is mirrored by Schiller's ambivalence toward opera. For a discussion of Schiller's views on music, see: Hermann Fähnrich, *Schillers Musikalität und Musikanschauung* (Hildesheim: Gerstenberg , 1977).

16. For a discussion of politics and aesthetics in Schiller's thought, including his views on the French Revolution, see: Benno von Wiese, *Friedrich Schiller*, 3d ed. (Stuttgart: Metzler, 1963), pp. 446–506.

17. Andrea Mork, *Richard Wagner als politischer Schriftsteller: Weltanschauung und Wirkungsgeschichte* (Frankfurt and New York: Campus, 1990), pp. 27–35.

18. Benno von Wiese, "Schiller als Geschichtsphilosoph und Geschichtsschreiber," in *Von Lessing bis Grabbe. Studien zur deutschen Klassik und Romantik* (Düsseldorf: August Bagel, 1968), pp. 41–57.

19. See: von Wiese, *Die Deutsche Tragödie*, p. 217. Von Wiese repeats this idea in his essay "Wallenstein," in *Das deutsche Drama vom Barock zur Gegenwart*, vol. 1 (Düsseldorf: August Bagel, 1964), p. 286. In his biography of Schiller, von Wiese interprets *Wallenstein* as a "tragedy of nemesis." See: von Wiese, *Schiller*, pp. 625–77.

20. In this and the following two paragraphs I am referring to: H. A. Korff, *Geist der Goethezeit. Versuch einer ideellen Entwicklung der klassisch-romantischen Literatur-geschichte*, vol. 2: *Klassik* (Leipzig: Verlagsbuchhandlung von J. J. Weber, 1930), pp. 263–67.

21. See: von Wiese, *Die Deutsche Tragödie*, pp. 214–16.

22. Max Kommerell, for instance, interprets Octavio as a representative of law, "Vertreter des Gesetzlichen ohne Grösse." See Max Kommerell, "Schiller als Gestalter des handelnden Menschen," in *Geist und Buchstabe der Dichtung: Goethe, Schiller, Kleist, Hölderlin*, 3d ed. (Frankfurt am Main: Vittorio Klostermann, 1944), pp. 132–74 (here I am referring to p. 146).

23. Friedrich von Schiller, *Wallenstein*, vol. 8 of *Schillers Werke*, Nationalausgabe, ed. Hermann Schneider and Lieselotte Blumenthal (Weimar: Hermann Böhlaus Nachfolger, 1949), p. 3. References to this edition of *Wallenstein* will hereafter be given within my text by page numbers, preceded by the abbreviation "W." I have replaced "Sperrung" with italics.

24. Gert Sautermeister, *Idyllik und Dramatik im Werk Friedrich Schillers: Zum geschichtlichen Ort seiner klassischen Dramen*, Studien zur Poetik und Geschichte der Literatur, vol. 17 (Stuttgart: W. Kohlhammer, 1971).

25. John Neubauer, "The Idea of History in Schiller's *Wallenstein*," *Neophilologus* 56, no. 4 (1972): pp. 451–63 (here cited from pp. 455–56).

26. Karl Guthke takes issue with the interpretation of the Wallenstein-Max contrast as one of simply Realism-Idealism. See Karl Guthke, "Struktur und Charakter in Schillers *Wallenstein*," in *Wege zur Literatur. Studien zur deutschen Dichtungs- und Geistesgeschichte* (Bern and Munich: Francke, 1967), pp. 72–91.

27. Walter Müller-Seidel, "Die Idee des neuen Lebens in Schillers *Wallenstein*," in *Die Geschichtlichkeit der deutschen Klassik. Literatur und Denkformen um 1800* (Stuttgart: Metzler, 1983), pp. 127–39. Until otherwise noted, this is the article I cite in subsequent references to Müller-Seidel. See also note 26 above.

28. See, for instance: Eugene Moutoux, "Wallenstein: Guilty and Innocent," *Germanic Review* 57, no. 1 (1982): pp. 23–27.

29. Richard Wagner, *Die Musikdramen*, ed. Joachim Kaiser (Hamburg: Hoffmann und Campe, 1971; Munich: Deutscher Taschenbuch Verlag, 1978, 1981), p. 611. Subsequent references to this edition of the *Ring* text will be given in my text by page numbers, preceded by the abbreviation "MD."

30. von Wiese, *Die Deutsche Tragödie*, pp. 228–29. See also Korff, II, pp. 249–50.

31. Korff, II, p. 247.

32. von Wiese, *Die Deutsche Tragödie*, p. 227; Korff (vol. II, p. 246) says this also. Korff notes that Wallenstein's character interacts with the outside world.

33. Walter Müller-Seidel, "Episches im Theater der deutschen Klassik. Eine Betrachtung über Schillers *Wallenstein*," in *Die Geschichtlichkeit der deutschen Klassik*, pp. 140–72 (here I am referring to pp. 162–63). Unless otherwise noted, subsequent references to Müller-Seidel will be citing this article, the ideas of which I am following and building upon throughout this discussion.

34. von Wiese, *Die Deutsche Tragödie*, p. 227; Korff, II, p. 246.

35. Korff, II, 259.

36. von Wiese, *Die Deutsche Tragödie*, pp. 232–33.

37. See Guthke, pp. 89–91.

38. Müller-Seidel, "Die Idee des neuen Lebens," p. 136; "Episches im Theater der deutschen Klassik," p. 156.

39. Müller-Seidel, "Die Idee des neuen Lebens," pp. 136–37; "Episches im Theater der deutschen Klassik," p. 166.

Chapter 2

The Nibelung Legend in the Nineteenth Century: Wagner and Hebbel

*W*agner and Hebbel were contemporaries. In fact, they were even born in the same year (1813). However, the nineteenth century was rich with conflicting currents of ideas, and a comparison of Wagner's and Hebbel's views certainly proves this statement. In the nineteenth century, Idealism lived alongside Realism, which evolved out of it; the materialism of Feuerbach and Marx contrasted with the metaphysics of late Romanticism; Schopenhauerian pessimism revised Romantic utopian notions; one practiced either revolution or resignation; one strove outward, or one turned inward. External reality is manifold, as are one's options in dealing with it.

The usual procedure is to divide the nineteenth century into two parts, distinguishing between the revolutionary trends of the first half and the pessimistic resignation that was evident in the second. In literary-historical terms, one would speak of the movements "Young Germany" and "Realism." The century vacillated between these two extremes, in more general and universal terms, the objective and the subjective, the outer and the inner, politics and aesthetics, activity and inwardness, and, philosophically speaking, the currents of Realism and Idealism. When one looks at nineteenth-century drama theory, these tendencies were represented by the drama theory of Marx and Engels, on one hand, who outlined a theory of revolutionary drama, and that of Gustav Freytag, who felt that art should deal with eternal human problems.

One is strongly inclined to simply say that Wagner and Hebbel, when considered against this background, represent two entirely opposed trends of the century. Wagner seems to belong more to the trends of Romanticism and Young Germany than to that of Realism. His use of mythology as subject matter for drama, his basic three-stage social philosophy and aesthetics of a primal unity, a fall from this state, and a future utopia, and his aim to transcend tragedy in some kind of universal reconciliation in which the basic dualities of existence would be overcome are all important distinguishing features of Wagner's work that place him within the Romantic tradition. The use of mythology as subject matter and the nontragic worldview both serve to oppose his work to Hebbel's.

Furthermore, Wagner's revolutionary intentions can serve as his ties to the writers of Young Germany. The members of the rebel movement Young Germany, who wrote roughly from around 1820 to 1850, saw the theater as a vehicle for social change. They felt that the theater should demonstrate the social process and arouse the consciousness of the new age. During this period, drama in general became political drama. Heinrich Laube and Karl Gutzkow, for example, two main proponents of the movement Young Germany, thought that drama should serve the cause of spiritual and political emancipation. Wagner's thought was profoundly influenced by the tenets of Young Germany in his early years. Heinrich Laube was, after all, a friend of his. The *Ring* was formed by other currents of thought besides those usually associated with Romanticism.

Therefore, although it seems the unquestionable epitome of Romanticism in music-drama and totally opposed to the historical drama of the writers of the movement of Young Germany, Wagner's *Ring* actually represents an amalgam of the world-views of Romanticism and Young Germany. It uses the Romantic three-stage model of fall and redemption and in doing so forms a "new mythology" to a revolutionary end. Although one can debate how consistently one can interpret the *Ring* as a political allegory or parable, there is no doubt that the *Ring* is a revolutionary work. It shows this in both its mythologically subversive content and its form (its unity of various mediums and its opposition to traditional opera). The two are, after all, interdependent. Music is the only proper expression for myth, just as the return to the synthesis of the arts is somehow mirrored in the cyclical plot structure of the tetralogy.

The *Ring* not only is revolutionary in a social or political way, but in order to reform society, reforms art as well. According to the Zurich writings, one is dependent on the other. *Oper und Drama* makes it clear that Wagner needs a completely new form of music-drama in order to accomplish his ends. In the early to middle part of the nineteenth century, there was not only a prevalent desire to change reality for the sake of art, an idea that one can clearly discern in Wagner's theoretical writings. The critics had the opposite wish, too. They felt that art should be changed so as to better influence reality. Since 1830 at the latest, all seem to agree that political conditions as well as the genre of drama desperately needed to be reformed.

Wagner's writings on theater reform clearly show his desire to change artistic conditions, an intention that has political and social motives as well. The *Ring* epitomizes these trends in a complex way. It revolutionizes both art and society, both within the work and with regard to its reception. The Zurich writings embed the theory of *Oper und Drama* within a framework that treats larger concerns, such as the function of art in society, the dependence of art on political and social conditions, and the revolutionary purposes that drama can fulfill. Thus the differences between Wagner and Hebbel seem mutually exclusive, for Hebbel obviously lacked all revolutionary intent. His world-view and resultant drama theory are based on pessimistic resignation.

It seems that while Wagner's *Ring* represents, in its aesthetic program of revolutionizing society through Romantic mythological music-drama, an amalgam of Romanticism and Young Germany, and thus embodies drama theories of only the early part of the century, Hebbel, though he died twenty years earlier than Wagner and was a representative of Realism, belongs intellectually to the second half of the century. The issue, however, is not that simple, the contrasts not quite as clear-cut and clean as literary histories might make them seem. The investigation of such generalizations using specific textual examples is, after all, the task of literary criticism.

Tidy systems are often deceptive and suspicious in their simplicity. Literary currents usually do not exist in complete and total isolation from each other, much as literary histories, for the purpose of simplicity and cataloging, make it seem that way. Rather, literature or drama is usually influenced by history and philosophy in a nonsystematic, subjective way. Furthermore, in the minds of great artists, influences and trends become merged in a complicated way, and opposing terms of dualities somehow strangely interpenetrate. Wagner and Hebbel might very well represent two combinations of similar trends, though in different ways.

Of course, one does not often think of Wagner's works in relation to Realism. This seems as though it would be totally incongruous. When Wagner's dramas are discussed in a critical work about "realistic" literature, one is often looking for Wagner allusions in Keller or Fontane novels, thus foreshadowing the prominent role of Wagner's works in the narrative fiction of Thomas Mann (who, after all, represents late Realism gradually and subtly turning into Symbolism). For instance, Dieter Borchmeyer explores the pairing of Wagner and Fontane.[1] Borchmeyer has also discussed Wagner with reference to Stifter, who had a negative opinion of Wagner's works.[2] However, Wagner's dramas themselves, one would say, are anything but "realistic." When one scrutinizes the basic characteristics of "realistic" literature, though, one must acknowledge under the superficial differences some deep affinities between Wagner and this literary current, thus justifying the comparison that I am about to undertake.

For instance, the entire century had a deep interest in history, and this was reflected in the drama of the age. Dramatists were interested in portraying historical progressions. The dominant dramatic form in the age of Young Germany was, accordingly, the historical drama. Portrayal of the past was anything but escapism for the writers of Young Germany. In historical dramas written during the age of Young Germany, unlike giving a Romanticized image of, say, Nuremberg, important crises of history were portrayed in a manner that made them transparent for contemporary conditions. Grabbe, for instance, was interested primarily in the use of history in drama.[3]

This is certainly one factor that serves as a link between Wagner and Hebbel. Wagner's historicism is clear, though he links it with an interest in myth. The *Ring* is, underneath its mythological exterior, a profoundly historical work, and this, too, is a link with the dramatists of both Young Germany and Realism. Nobody could deny that Wagner intended his *Ring* as a model of the world-historical process. Hebbel is primarily known as a historical dramatist. Furthermore, the trend to change reality can be discussed with relation to its converse, the negative to the positive, the resignation that occurred in the age of Realism. History in the nineteenth century had two aspects, as it usually does, and reality often paradoxically causes a retreat from the real world.

After all, history does not necessarily entail revolution or optimism, as it did during the earlier part of the century. The revolutionaries wanted not only to portray but also to change history. They intended the experience of drama in the theater to arouse some kind of revolutionary consciousness and inspire productive activity to change the social and political environment. On the other hand, though, in the nineteenth century history became overpowering and senseless.[4] Not all writers of the nineteenth century felt that drama could change reality. Often reality was portrayed in drama as triumphing over the individual. Georg Büchner's dramas, for instance, reflect the pessimism and melancholy prevalent during the age. They show the utter senselessness of existence, with the title characters victims of historical and social circumstances, powers that they are helpless to control.

One can also discuss the converse, myth, the opposite pole, most would agree, from history. Wagner's work is complex indeed. The inwardness of Romanticism does contrast with the direct political awareness of Young Germany, both of which the *Ring* (in some way or other) expresses. Similarly, I will discuss a historical, dramatic work of Hebbel that has many mythological elements. The uses to which Wagner and Hebbel put myth in drama are, though, vastly different. It is also characteristic of these two men, given their respective world-views, that one would choose history, and the other myth as his primary type of raw material. Moreover, history and myth are not always mutually exclusive. For each of these dramatists, history contrasts with myth in his work. Furthermore, the stance of each toward myth is, reasonably enough, in some way related to his stance toward the historical reality of his time.

Myth and history are not only related but, for Wagner, even imply each other. The one actually determines the other. For Wagner, myth is historically conditioned and determined. Furthermore, he felt that myth could affect history. Thus, in this chapter I will discuss an interrelationship between myth and history in the works of Wagner and Hebbel, and use this mythical/historical axis as a point of comparison between the two dramatists. How one sees and uses myth determines the portrayal of history in his work, and vice versa. In writing the *Ring*, Wagner has veiled his image of world-history under a mythical exterior. This has instrumental social value. He uses myth to change and mythicize history. As the *Ring* seems a mythical work but is, under the surface, profoundly historical, Hebbel's historical drama is indirectly and intricately tied to the topic of myth. Absences can be as significant as presences.

Literary critics also explain that the drama, in the age of Realism, was seen as portraying some sort of totality, and that it was intended to show the individual as standing under universal laws. Even the historical drama strove to achieve some kind of timelessness, with history, one could say, being raised to "mythical" status. Idealism lived on, albeit not in an "unbroken" form, through the latter part of the nineteenth century. In these respects, then, the *Ring* is typical of the late as well as the early nineteenth century. The *Ring* gives what can be considered a total cosmology, for it portrays, according to its composer, the beginning and end of the world. Moreover, it views history through a veil of mythical timelessness. When considered from these angles, the *Ring* is, surprisingly enough, in many ways a "realistic" work. A comparison of the *Ring* with a work of realistic literature (and a mythical-historical set of Nibelung dramas at that) therefore does not seem at all out of place.

When discussing Wagner in relation to the drama of the latter half of the nineteenth century, one must also take into account the fact that the drama, in this period, was almost all but nonexistent, despite the wealth of theoretical works that dealt with the form. Although the nineteenth century had an unprecedented interest in, and enthusiasm for, the theater, most critics agree that the dramatic form was in a state of decline in the second half of the nineteenth century, when judged by what was being written at that time. In the age of Realism, roughly from 1850 to 1890, the theater was still a popular form of entertainment and a major cultural institution of bourgeois society. There was also an increase in the number of performances and new stagings. In fact, the drama was theoretically considered the highest form of art, one that pointed beyond concrete reality to embody some metaphysical truth. However, the age of Realism was not noted for drama.

The primacy that he accorded the dramatic form is clear from Wagner's theoretical writings. Furthermore, the sorry state of drama in the latter half of the nineteenth century, that is, a wish to reform or resuscitate the form in Germany, may also have been an impetus for Wagner to stress that his works were drama, not opera. Thus, one could say that Hebbel and Wagner were both reacting, albeit in different ways, to this state of drama and the crisis that the form was suffering. Though their reworkings of the Nibelung legend are worlds apart, they are both answers to the same state of affairs, the solutions, or (in the case of Hebbel) lacks thereof, to the same problems. Therefore this chapter presents not only the comparative analysis of two works and two dramatists, but also an exploration of the various currents and problems of nineteenth-century German drama in general.

A comparison of the works of Wagner and Hebbel must also, of course, take into account the various political, literary, and philosophical trends that found expression in the dramas and world-views of either or both of them. I outline and contrast these briefly in this chapter. Then in the latter part of this chapter, I demonstrate the parallels and divergences between the views of the two men on life in general and drama by undertaking a comparison that just seems made to order. In this analysis I will use two sets of texts that, being based on the same subject matter, lend themselves easily to showing these affinities and differences in especially stark relief.

When the topic is Wagner and Hebbel, the comparison that comes most readily to mind is, of course, Wagner's Ring and Hebbel's Die Nibelungen.[5] Both projects were series of dramas, and the composition of both spanned a number of years. Wagner took over twenty-five years to write the Ring. Hebbel's project took more than four years. He began Die Nibelungen the end of September 1855, and ended it in March 1860. In fact, these two dramatists were, in part, writing their dramatizations of the Nibelung legend at the same time. The two works are, though, very different. They are anything but two slightly altered versions of the same basic source material. This chapter investigates and theoretically grounds, within the aesthetic and philosophical system of each dramatist, the radical differences between their dramatic versions of the Nibelung legend.

Hebbel, like Wagner, was very concerned with the political situation of his day. As Wagner intended to reveal and in doing so resolve the ills of modern society, Hebbel, too, felt that his dramas should address contemporary social and political issues. Hebbel, like many other historical dramatists of the nineteenth century, considered the drama as somehow symbolic of the laws of existence. It was supposed to portray universal progressions and eternally valid events. Thus the drama symbolized historical progressions. One could even say that this raises history to the status of myth. Herbert Kraft discusses the interrelationship of the standard three phases of time for Hebbel. The past was, by Hebbel, considered relevant to the present and future.[6]

One can also assume that the Nibelung legend was given special significance by Wagner and Hebbel because of its Germanic national character.

The *Nibelungenlied* was considered the German national epic, and the nineteenth century was certainly a time when historical consciousness and an awareness of the nation (or, rather, of the lack thereof) were particularly strong. It thereby acquired almost mythical significance that anybody using it as the basis of a literary and/or musical work would have surely been aware of. It seems likely that with the use of this raw material, each of the dramatists under discussion was saying something about the past, present, and future of Germany.

Thus I take each of the Nibelung drama cycles under discussion as not only expressing its author's views on life, or demonstrating the aesthetics of its creator, but also symbolically conveying a certain message about political issues of the day. If we raise Hebbel's *Nibelungen* to eschatological or national significance, what is it saying? In other words, what kind of future do these plays envision for mankind and, in particular, for Germany? How does that differ from Wagner's message and intent in writing the *Ring* cycle?

After a general discussion of Wagner and Hebbel and a preliminary consideration of Hebbel's drama theory in relation to Wagner's, this chapter ends with a comparison of Hebbel's *Nibelungen* and Wagner's *Ring*, in which I show how these works are characteristic of the viewpoints of, and therefore exemplify the differences between, the two dramatists. In particular, I discuss the interrelationship of history and myth in the work of each of these dramatists, as demonstrated by their differing dramatic versions of the Nibelung legend. This point of comparison is present in both the plot of these dramas and the choice of raw material. Nobody could deny that the *Ring* is meant to portray some kind of mythologically veiled historical progression. Furthermore, it is a revolutionary work. It was intended not only to portray but also to change history. Hebbel, however, in his realistic and pessimistic resignation, destroys any kind of dialectical interrelationship between myth and history in the plot of his dramas and in the aesthetic program upon which they are based.

I will discuss how the differences between the world-views of Wagner and Hebbel, as reflected by the mediums in which they were working, that is, spoken drama for the one, and music-drama for the other, are expressed in a more profound way by the use of myth by each of the works under discussion. Wagner's *Ring* uses mythical raw material and forms a myth about history. Its aim is to mythicize history, that is, bring about a future regeneration of modern society and a new "mythical" Golden Age. Hebbel degrades myth in his *Nibelungen* trilogy and denies the possibility of any such interchange between history and myth, thus, within the same subject matter or raw material from which Wagner (partially, of course) worked in writing the *Ring*, defeating the aesthetic program upon which Wagner's tetralogy is based.

WAGNER AND HEBBEL

Wagner and Hebbel had, it seems, nothing good to say about each other. Their differences, which were much more than personal enmity, can be seen as deriving from their different world-views and, not totally unrelated to that, the different mediums within which they were working. Wagner theoretically deplored spoken drama. *Oper und Drama* makes this clear. Wagner felt that spoken drama appealed only to the intellect and was therefore deficient. Real drama, according to Wagner, would address all faculties, the total person, including the senses. It therefore needed music. Furthermore, for Wagner, only myth was the appropriate subject matter of music-drama. Myth and music implied each other reciprocally, as far as Wagner was concerned.

Hebbel, in turn, was skeptical of Wagner's theory of music-drama. He did concede that music was, of course, an appropriate medium for mythological subject matter. In a diary entry of 5 March 1863, he wrote:

So viel ist an Richard Wagners lächerlicher Theorie richtig, dass die Oper ihre Stoffe immer aus der Mythe entlehnen sollte; wenn ein Schwanen-Ritter singt, wird sich Niemand wundern, denn ein Mensch, der den Ozean auf dem Rücken eines Vogels durchschneidet, kommt aus einer Welt, worin es anders her geht, wie in der uns'rigen; aber wenn ein Notar sich in Rouladen erschöpft, während er einen Heiraths-Contract zu Papier bringt, klafft uns ein Widerspruch entgegen, den wir uns nur dadurch erträglich machen, dass wir uns bemühen, das Ganze über das Einzelne zu vergessen und also auf die höchste Wirkung der Kunst, die umgekehrt alles Einzelne in's Ganze auflösen will, Verzicht leisten.[7]

This much is right about Wagner's ridiculous theory, that opera should take its subject matter from myth. Nobody would marvel at a swan-knight who sings, for a human being who traverses the ocean on the back of a bird comes from a world that is different from ours; but when a notary expresses himself in trills while he draws up a marriage contract, there is a huge contradiction facing us, which we make tolerable by trying to forget the whole to the advantage of a single detail and thus do without the supreme effect of art, which consists in the opposite, integrating the details to the advantage of the whole.

According to Hebbel it is, of course, fitting for mythological subject matter that it be sung. But the way Hebbel phrases it, this is no compliment. Hebbel completely discounted Wagner's theory as ridiculous. In this respect, as I will show, it makes sense that the (spoken) plays of Hebbel that are under discussion destroy myth by history.

In a letter to Robert Schumann of 21 June 1853, Hebbel also declared his inability to accept without qualifications the ideas in Wagner's *Oper und Drama:*

Ohne Richard Wagners Buch im Ganzen oder im Einzelnen irgend acceptiren zu können, schwebt doch auch mir, und zwar von meinem ersten Auftreten an, die Möglichkeit einer Verschmelzung von Oper und Drama in ganz speciellen Fällen vor, und meinen Moloch, an dem ich seit zehn Jahren arbeite, habe ich mir immer in Bezug auf die Musik gedacht.[8]

Though I am unable to accept Wagner's book in its entirety, a synthesis of opera and drama has always seemed to me in very special cases possible, and I have always thought of my *Moloch*, on which I have been working for the past ten years, in connection with music.

He does not sound truly convinced of the feasibility of Wagner's theory. One can argue that Hebbel misunderstood Wagner's intent, and that Wagner never advocated a fusion of opera and drama. However, that the two men had radical differences is obvious from these quotations. Neither dramatist considered the works of the other true "drama." One therefore has a right to expect their reworkings of the Nibelung legend to differ drastically, as though the different mediums in which they were working were lenses that construed (or, each would say of the version of the other, distorted) the legend in a manner appropriate to each of them.

Wagner's comments on Hebbel's works were about as bad as, or worse than, Hebbel's views on Wagner's drama theory. For instance, on 17 November 1878 Cosima reported in her diary that they discussed "die korrupte Phantasie der Modernen (Tieck, Hebbel, Schumann)" (CT III, 232) (the corrupt imagination of the modern writers [Tieck, Hebbel, Schumann]) (D II, 203). On 7 February 1881 they read the last two acts of *Herodes und Mariamne*. They did find this reading interesting, though their response was anything but fully positive. Cosima mentions in her diary that they also found it disturbing; it seems that they were fascinated by it because they felt it was strange, being at the same time, as she put it, both passionate and arid, profoundly perceptive and operatic (CT IV, 685; D II, 617).

One can sort out Wagner's statements concerning various dramas of Schiller with reference to the subject matter and style of these dramas and, in turn, their resultant place within Wagner's aesthetic system, which determined how he evaluated them in *Oper und Drama*. Wagner's opinions of Hebbel's plays, however, are much more uniform. Wagner obviously disliked them. From the evidence at hand, he didn't appear to have praise for any of them. Whereas Wagner's opinions of some of Schiller's works vacillated, as I have shown with the example of *Wallenstein*, depending on whether he was speaking as a private person or on his public platform, none of Hebbel's dramas, it seems, appealed to Wagner. He was a voracious reader, and his interests were indeed wide. It seems, though, that he did not enjoy reading Hebbel's plays, nor did they really interest him.

Most of Wagner's remarks about Hebbel's work, all of which are negative and deprecatory, are directed against, specifically, Hebbel's *Nibelungen*.

On 5 August 1872 Cosima wrote, "Abends liest er mir zum Spass den ersten Akt von den Hebbel'schen 'Nibelungen'; unglaublich schlechtes Machwerk" (CT I, 558) (In the evening he reads me the first act of Hebbel's *Nibelungen* for fun—an incredibly bad piece of work) (D I, 520). The comment "zum Spass" (for fun) indicates that, just as Hebbel thought Wagner's theory was ridiculous, Cosima and Richard, in turn, couldn't take the Hebbel plays seriously. Similarly, on 8 August 1872, Cosima recorded in her diary:

Wie wir schon uns zu Bett begeben haben, müssen wir sehr über die Hebbel'schen "Nibelungen" lachen (Siegfried—Münchhausen; die Helden, die in den Kulissen Heldentaten ausüben und dann erscheinen und höhnisch darüber sprechen; Hagen, der den todverwundeten Siegfried verhöhnt). (CT I, 559)

After we have gone to bed we still cannot help laughing over Hebbel's *Nibelungen* (Siegfried-Münchhausen; the heroes performing heroic deeds offstage and then appearing to relate them scornfully; Hagen mocking Siegfried as he lies wounded to death). (D I, 521)

That they laughed at these plays is clearly a derogatory comment of the most severe kind. The description of these figures as scornful and mocking seems to indicate that Cosima and Richard found them unsympathetic because they seemed to lack human sensitivity. Obviously these Nibelung plays of Hebbel were simply, to Wagner, intolerable.

On 9 August 1872, Cosima explains even more about what was wrong with the Hebbel trilogy. In conversing about Hebbel's *Nibelungen*, her husband commented, "In den grässlichsten Situationen sagten die Leute sich noch Pointen; und wie trocken alles Grauenhafte hier geschieht" (even in the most horrible situations people still indulge in polished speech. And how dull are all the gruesome happenings!). The composer compared Hebbel's plays unfavorably to the plays of Shakespeare. Hebbel's plays, according to Wagner, depict things "platt" (flat) and "nackt" (naked) (CT I, 559; D I, 522). Wagner seems to have found Hebbel's plays boring and dry. These plays evidently lacked a certain sincerity and depth of feeling as far as he was concerned.

The comments that I have quoted concerning how the characters speak in the most horrible situations echo Wagner's criticism of what he considered an overemphasis on language and rhetoric in Schiller's plays. To explain Wagner's contempt for Hebbel's plays by the fact that Hebbel wrote spoken dramas does not go deep enough. There were other reasons, which were further ramifications of this fact, concerning the basic subject matter and plot. Music-drama, for Wagner, needed to be mythological. He obviously considered Hebbel's plays callous and his figures cold. Wagner's music-drama appealed primarily to the capacity of feeling. Wagner obviously knew that the polished speech of Hebbel's plays contrasted, of course, with the music of his own dramas (which, along with the mythological subject matter, was the means by which to appeal directly to the capacity of feeling).

In fact, in many of Cosima's diary entries concerning Hebbel's Nibelung plays, Hebbel is paired with others who also reworked the Nibelung legend in the nineteenth century. Hebbel did not incur Wagner's scorn alone. The other culprits were Geibel and Jordan. In her diary entry of 24 July 1872 (CT I, 553; D I, 515-16), for instance, Cosima reported that when the reworkings of the Nibelung legend by Hebbel and Jordan that her husband had ordered had arrived, they were horrified by how these writers had ruined the subject. The composer commented that these writers had ruined the legend in the same way that Meyerbeer had ruined "Eine feste Burg" (CT I, 553; D I, 515-16). Wagner obviously objected to Hebbel's and Geibel's treatment (or, rather, mistreatment) of the Nibelung legend. The comparison with Meyerbeer is clearly the utmost negative comment he could make.

On 25 August 1872, also, Cosima reports that she and her husband laughed over Geibel's version of the Nibelung legend, and they conversed about the relative strengths (or, rather, weaknesses) of Hebbel's and Geibel's Nibelung works. Hebbel and Geibel were, for Richard and Cosima, different though comparable in quality. Cosima reports that Geibel is the classicist or the academic, for he took the heroine by herself and neglected all subplots, and that Hebbel is the Romantic, and then she adds, "beide so platt und erbärmlich, dass man staunt, nicht über sie, sondern über die Leute, die das ertragen oder gar loben" (CT I, 567; entry of 25 August 1872) (but both so flat and pitiful that one is amazed, not about them, but about the people who tolerate and even praise their work) (D I, 528-29). Wagner evidently considered the Nibelung legend a complex structure, and he obviously did not avoid subplots or use a small cast of characters in his own Nibelung work. To isolate, as Geibel had done, one figure from it, in Wagner's opinion, did it an injustice. Wagner certainly modified, but nobody could accuse him of oversimplifying, the Nibelung legend.

The term "erbärmlich" ("pitiful") recurs in the entry of 2 July 1873, in which Cosima exclaims, "Erbärmlichkeit Hebbel's und Geibel's!" (CT II, 702) (The pitifulness of Hebbel and Geibel!) (D I, 652). On 10 October 1877, too, they laughed over Hebbel and Geibel. Cosima writes,

Das Gespräch führt uns auf die Nibelungen von Geibel und Hebbel, R. liest einiges daraus vor, und unter grosser Hilarität können wir uns kaum darüber beruhigen, dass derlei Produkte nicht mit Hohn und Schmach von der deutschen Literatur zurückgewiesen werden. (CT II, 1076)

Our talk leads us to the *Nibelungen* of Geibel and of Hebbel, R. reads some passages from them amid great hilarity, and we find it hard to overcome our amazement that such products are not banished with scorn and contumely from the realms of German literature. (D I, 987)

Again, they found the work hilarious. They felt that it deserved only scorn and contumely. The negative comments show that the humor was a clear denigration of these plays. As these plays were not comedies, he must have felt they were outrageously failed dramatic attempts, a judgment that, I propose, was consistent with Wagner's basic aesthetic theories.

It seems only natural, of course, that Wagner would consider his own *Ring* to be the only true version of the Nibelung legend. The matter, however, is not that simple. His mockery of Hebbel's treatment of the Nibelung legend is firmly rooted in a fundamental difference in their world-views, which are reflected by their respective drama theories and thus by extension also the dramas under discussion. A comparison of Wagner's and Hebbel's drama theories and the world-views that form their foundations shows that Wagner's negative comments on Hebbel's *Nibelungen* signified vast differences in their outlooks on life and drama. In the next section, I show how Wagner's laughter, like Kundry's, has a much deeper source.

DRAMA THEORY AS WORLD-VIEW

Wagner's theory of mythological drama is firmly rooted in the tradition of German Idealism. According to the philosophy of German Idealism, art was the sensual revelation of the Absolute. Despite his Young Germany revolutionary political sympathies and his interest in Feuerbachian materialism, Wagner's philosophy of art is, in this respect, typically Romantic. It seems only natural, therefore, that Wagner would feel that mythology was the only proper subject matter for music-drama. Mythology provided Wagner with raw material that was Absolute, general, symbolic, or, as Wagner termed it, "purely human" ("reinmenschlich").

Hebbel's drama theory, like the rest of Realism, is also rooted in the philosophy of German Idealism.[9] In contrast to Wagner's aesthetics, though, Hebbel's drama theory clearly signifies the breakdown of this Idealistic world-view. The Idea can be considered the Absolute in Hebbel's theory. For Hebbel, though, the Idea itself is dualistic or split, and for this reason the Absolute is no longer absolute. Conflict can therefore never be reconciled in a utopian fashion. Not only was the relation of mankind to the Idea debated, but also the validity of the Idea itself. One could consider Hebbel's pessimism another version of post-Romantic solipsism or nihilism. Hebbel presents no values that are clearly transcendent or "redemptive" in a metaphysical sense.

According to Fritz Martini, Hebbel's plays represent the last examples of German tragedy within the Classical tradition.[10] Hebbel's theory, he points out, arose from his awareness of the crisis that the form of drama was suffering in the nineteenth century. Martini, seeming to echo Wagner's interpretation of Greek tragedy, as Wagner saw individualism as being represented as fate, writes that Hebbel's dramas demonstrate the meta-physical, psychological, and artistic problematics of individualism as fate in the nineteenth century.[11] Whereas Wagner's world-view is not essentially tragic but, rather, utopian, most agree that Hebbel's world-view and his dramas are tragic.

The Idea must realize or embody itself in the individual, and this, according to Hebbel, creates the tragic conflict. By virtue of his or her independent will, the individual violates the Idea. Conflict is thus a char-acteristic of life. In Hebbel's system, there is a clear rift between the indi-vidual and the universe. Even though Wagner was influenced by Feuerbachian materialism during his revolutionary years, his resultant world-view was, in comparison with Hebbel's, still very much in the German Romantic tradition. Wagner seems to have felt that dualism could be overcome in a utopian redemption that would lead history to a mythical Golden Age.

For Hebbel, though, an irreparable discrepancy exists in the world between the individual and the World-Spirit, the Idea and appearances, the norm and the specific case. Human life has, by definition, guilt, which lies in will itself, not even in a specific use of the will. Hebbel felt that the individual is at odds with the world-order. The individual has freedom, which makes demands that conflict with those of the Idea. The personal will runs into the general "world will" regardless of how the individual acts. One's deeds are irrelevant; one's downfall is inevitable. The individual must necessarily perish and is always doomed to failure. Action is identical with suffering.

This world-view has important implications for Hebbel's drama theory. For Hebbel, drama illustrates the basic tragedy of existence. Drama, accord-ing to Hebbel, should demonstrate, as he put it, the very process of life itself. One can argue that Hebbel's world-view is inherently dramatic. Since for Hebbel life itself necessarily, by definition, consists of conflict, there seems no problem in putting this world-view into the form of a play. Drama consists of a conflict, within oneself, between different value systems, or between the individual and the higher order, that cannot be fully resolved. For Hebbel, though, drama, which reflects and symbolizes the basic condi-tions of earthly existence, is always necessarily a tragedy.[12] According to Wagner's drama theory as set out in his Zurich writings, a modern rework-ing of tragedy, without transcendence (even an immanent kind) or revolu-tionary value, is just not the proper kind of tragedy.

Commentators call Hebbel's world-view "tragic idealism." In contrast, one could call Wagner's outlook, at the time he wrote the *Ring*, "metaphysi-cal materialism," for it is a revolutionary sort of Feuerbachian Romanticism. Wagner's *Ring* shows the transcendence of tragedy in a utopian reconcili-ation and massive universal redemption. For Hebbel, though, tragedy is not a condition that shows the dualism of existence that is to be overcome, as it was for the Romantics. Rather, for Hebbel, tragedy is a basic and inevitable condition of life. There is no redemption. Hebbel deals with only the middle phase of the three-stage model of the Romantics. For Hebbel, human existence is irrevocably "fallen." It cannot be saved in any viable way. Hebbel's world-view is bleak indeed. His basic philosophy of life holds out little hope of social improvement.

There is some room for a possible reconciliation in Hebbel's system, but this happens in the interest of the general, the larger picture, not the individual. It is definitely not the all-encompassing, universal redemption that occurs at the end of Wagner's *Ring*. Hebbel writes in a diary entry (Paris, 11 November 1843, Entry Number 2845), with a metaphor that makes one think of *Parsifal*, "Versöhnung im Drama: Heilung der Wunde durch den Nachweis, dass sie für die erhöhte Gesundheit nothwendig war"[13] (Reconciliation in drama: Healing the wound by proving that it was necessary to achieve a higher state of health). The individual must perish. The Idea, the general, destroys the individual, the particular. Only the downfall of the individual can repair or remove the dualism, though Hebbel's statements on whether or not dualism can really ever be fully repaired are, Hans-Joachim Anders notes, contradictory.[14] It does seem unlikely, given the basic outline of Hebbel's ideas, that it could ever be totally done away with; rather, it seems a perpetual state of affairs.

It seems no wonder, then, that the two dramatists I am discussing in this chapter could not appreciate each other's works, and that they did not think highly of each other. There is a basic disagreement in their world-views. Although it is not a directly political work, the aesthetic program of Wagner's *Ring* clearly aims at the revolution of modern society. The end of the *Ring* is a new beginning that signifies the Romantic transcendence of tragedy. The fictional cosmos is redeemed through Brünnhilde's sacrifice. Wagner exalts the free individual who opposes society and convention. In contrast, the world-view that underlies Hebbel's drama theory completely obviates the possibility of revolution or reform. According to Hebbel's world-view, existence is hopelessly tragic. For Hebbel, despair is metaphysically grounded. Human life will always be doomed to failure, and activity is permanently condemned to constant futility. His *Nibelungen* trilogy, accordingly, lacks any such ray of hope at the end.

Thus the plots of these works reflect the world-views of their respective dramatists. Wagner portrays, in an abstract, extended sense, the conflict of the free individual and society. In Hebbel's dramas, the individual is destroyed to restore the societal order. Hebbel sees individuals as products and victims of society. Wagner extolled autonomy; through the cosmic cataclysm at the end of the *Ring*, Siegfried and Brünnhilde overcome fate, as does Wotan also. Wagner's *Ring* revises and overcomes tragedy in a utopian reconciliation. Hebbel's *Nibelungen*, I will show, demonstrates his basic conservatism. It depicts the tragedy of existence. In doing so, it offers, unlike the *Ring*, no hope of societal betterment, whether in the plays themselves or by the audience experience of the plays.

In this manner, an analysis that compares and contrasts the dramas of Wagner and Hebbel demonstrates how their world-views clash. The dramas themselves differ vastly, as do the aesthetic programs of audience reception upon which these dramas are, in turn, based. Wagner's *Ring* shows that a corrupt order must be destroyed by a cataclysmic glorification of the humanistic values that it has violated. Wagner's *Ring* does, of course, portray tragic conflicts in the world, irreconcilable clashes of wills, but these problems are ultimately transcended. In the *Ring*, Wagner totally eradicates, through a vision of destruction and renewal, the order portrayed onstage. Hebbel did not see the drama as a social, revolutionary instrument in the way that Wagner did. Hebbel's dramas, as Herbert Kaiser notes, show the tragedy of existence, but they do not eradicate it.[15]

Wagner, in contrast, wants to repair it, that is, to do away with the contemporary problematic societal order and replace it with a utopia. The *Ring* depicts the destruction of the state only in an extended fashion, as I have argued, but it is no doubt a revolutionary work. Furthermore, Wagner felt that, through the performance of the cycle, the state would (or could) actually be destroyed. According to Wagner, the real destruction of the state would necessarily follow upon the psychological one that the dramatic experience would induce. Hebbel, however, did not share with Wagner the hopes for the destruction of the state. Hebbel, it seems, considered the problem a more basic one of human existence, one that could never be overcome because of its fundamental nature.

Whereas Wagner's *Ring* shows love triumphing over power, Hebbel's *Nibelungen* trilogy portrays a grim and brutal struggle for power that, despite Dietrich's Christianity, which ostensibly assumes the lead at the end of the work, seems somehow unalleviated and unredeemed by higher humanistic principles. For Kriemhild, whose progression, according to Herbert Kraft, shows the destruction of humanism most vividly,[16] power overcomes love. She sinks to the slaughter of her own relatives as revenge overcomes grief. Neither Kriemhild's nor Brunhild's feelings of love for Siegfried portray a romantic ideal, and their love dimly fades away, yielding in both cases to some form of inhumanity, a brutal or a gruesome one, respectively.

The differences that Wagner and Hebbel had with the works of each other were obviously much more than personal enmity. The friction between Wagner and Hebbel, though, just might have been intensified by rivalry that resulted from their concurrence for the same legendary material that was popular in the nineteenth century.[17] In the next section, I show how the world-views of Wagner and Hebbel are illustrated not only by the course of the action of each of their Nibelung works, and the presence or absence of some kind of redemption at the end of each, but also by the very choice of setting, whether mythical or historical, that each of them gives to his version of the Nibelung legend.

THE NIBELUNG LEGEND: MYTHICAL OR HISTORICAL?

Since the time of the Romantics, the Nibelung legend had a national significance in Germany. After the disappointments of the failed revolutions and the resultant shattering of the German consciousness of 1848, the Nibelung legend offered a symbol of national unity that led into the distant historical depths of the "Volk." Hebbel's *Nibelungen*, like Wagner's *Ring*, was therefore an attempt to attain some national significance for the Nibelung legend.[18] Wagner had both Idealistic and materialistic revolutionary hopes; the *Ring* makes this clear. If given some kind of deeper eschatological significance and interpretatively taken to be somehow representative of the age in which he lived, Hebbel's *Nibelungen* envisions, for Germany, a bleak future indeed.

The difference in the world-views of Hebbel and Wagner is also reflected by a deeper distinction in the type of subject matter that each chose to make the basis of his version of the Nibelung legend. The choice of history or myth was, it seems, not accidental for either of them. The general nature of each work is obvious. Wagner uses myth, and Hebbel, primarily history. Their different ways of using their common source, the Middle High German *Nibelungenlied*, reflect their differing concerns. I propose that the contents of the dramas under discussion, that is, the plots that are depicted in these drama cycles, are determined by the world-views of their respective dramatists. Furthermore, not only is there some correlation between the plot-line (whether tragic or nontragic) and the choice of subject matter (historical or mythical), but, in addition, within these works, myth is used differently. The plot of each cycle, by reflecting the world-view of its dramatist, actually determines how myth is treated in each of these works under discussion.

Like Wagner's *Ring*, Hebbel's trilogy deals in various ways with the interrelationship between history and myth. Furthermore, Hebbel's *Nibelungen* trilogy, like the *Ring*, implicitly demonstrates its own aesthetic program. These reworkings of the Nibelung legend both depict their own receptions. A comparison of their Nibelung works, though, shows that Wagner and Hebbel had fundamental differences concerning the use of myth in drama and the proper (or existent) relationship between history and myth. The two issues, drama and life, were not separate spheres for these men but, rather, in some way interconnected. Moreover, just how Hebbel's *Nibelungen* trilogy uses mythical elements, that is, what it does to myth in the plot, demonstrates its derogatory stance toward myth, an attitude that Wagner would, understandably enough, not only object to but also abhor.

Wagner's *Ring* is an artificial myth to explain and change history. The aesthetic program of Wagner's *Ring* outlines the reform of history through mythical music-drama. Wagner's *Ring* was conceived in his revolutionary years, the late 1840s. Peter Wapnewski has called it the artistic realization of a political utopia.[19] Wagner immersed himself in works of the Germanic past to construct images of a future utopia. Wapnewski points out that the *Nibelungenlied* uses elements of legends and places them in a historical context to teach the people of the present age a lesson. It is basically a conservative work. Wagner was anything but a conservative. Rather than trying to save the world of the past, Wagner wanted to establish a new one. The *Ring* was written using ancient sources, Germanic and Nordic folklore, but to revolutionary purposes.

Thus the *Ring* is Janus-faced, both retrospective and future-oriented. Wagner used one as a means to the end of the other. He looked backward to project forward. Art, drama in particular, as the highest form of art, he felt, could be instrumental to life. It could not only foreshadow but also bring about the future utopia. He extracted from the *Nibelungenlied* a mythical "core," as he termed it, "das Reinmenschliche" (the "purely human" essence) and expanded the story of Siegfried's death to a pair of dramas, later extending the work still further forward to dramatize the more and more remote beginnings of the story and shifting the tragic interest from Siegfried to Wotan and Brünnhilde. In the final version of the *Ring*, it is actually the "love story" of the god and his favorite daughter that unifies the massive work.

Wagner embedded the plot that he took from the *Nibelungenlied*, which is basically a historical work and which furnished the rough outlines of the character constellation and the central plot structure of *Götterdämmerung*, in a mythological Scandinavian context, pieced together from the *Edda*s and the *Volsunga Saga*. In the composition of the *Ring*, then, the story of Siegfried and Brünnhilde was embedded into the broader context and larger story of Wotan and the stolen ring. The *Ring* as we know it today is the result of an elaborate, nonsystematic method of mythological syncretism. Wagner used Jacob Grimm's *Deutsche Mythologie* and many other Nordic mythological sources, too, in addition to those works I previously mentioned. I do not intend a survey of the composition or sources of the *Ring*. This has been done elsewhere. My point here is that the *Ring* is basically a mythological work. It is the story of Wotan and his godly dilemma.

Wagner wanted to issue in a mythical Golden Age and thus mythicize history, and he hoped to accomplish this with the audience experience of his music-drama. Not only does Wagner portray a cosmic cataclysm in the *Ring* itself, but he also intended to accomplish an analogous reform of modern society and a mythicization of history with the experience of his work. In this respect, his *Ring* is a Romantic drama, for both in it and with it he hopes to mend the dualism of earthly existence that the Romantics lamented. Accordingly, in the *Ring*, Wagner uses the dichotomy of love and power, glorifying the former. The inner repairs the outer. The end signifies redemption and a new beginning. Wagner also exemplifies the social and revolutionary trends of the Young Germany movement of the nineteenth century.

Wagner's Zurich writings use the standard Romantic three-stage model, expressed in, among other works, Kleist's "Marionettentheater" essay, of a primal state, a "fall" from this unity, and a re-establishment of unity. Kleist writes that by eating from the Tree of Knowledge a second time, mankind can re-enter Paradise through the back door. Wagner states this three-stage model, which usually implies the "fall" from primal unity and a reattainment of some new kind of conscious unconsciousness, in terms of history and myth. He says that myth is the beginning and end of history. Wagner wants to replace nineteenth-century society with a mythical utopia. As paradoxical as it sounds, to reform corrupt modern historical society, that is, because of his political involvement, Wagner uses myth as subject matter for his music-drama. According to Wagner, history was some kind of "fallen" state that was to be overcome in some kind of "mythical" synthesis.

Furthermore, Wagner's aesthetic program states that myth is the only proper kind of subject matter for music-drama. Wagner felt that true drama needs to be mythical, for myth was readily comprehensible. According to Wagner, only mythical raw material could portray the free individual; history, the subject matter of the modern novel, on the other hand, depicts mankind as a product of societal restrictions and custom. Thus, for Wagner, mythological music-drama was the only kind of art-work that could revolutionize modern society. It is well known how Wagner's *Ring* resulted from a decision for myth over history when Wagner was faced with the possibility of writing a work about either Friedrich Barbarossa or Siegfried. History and myth were, of course, not mutually exclusive as far as Wagner was concerned. In his essay "Die Wibelungen: Weltgeschichte aus der Sage," he derives, as the title indicates, world-history from myth, and he makes Friedrich Barbarossa, accordingly, a historical reincarnation of Siegfried.

But in deciding to write a drama cycle about Siegfried rather than using Friedrich Barbarossa as his protagonist, Wagner was therefore giving myth some kind of priority over history. The *Nibelungenlied* seems to have left Wagner cold. The Siegfried that was portrayed therein was, he felt, distorted by historical features. He therefore sought to unmask the purely human version of this figure and free him from all of the historical trappings that obscured him from view. For this reason the composer delved further back, to the more archaic versions of the Siegfried story, the source materials of the Nordic mythology.

Wagner's *Ring* is, accordingly, first and foremost a mythological work. This statement does need to be qualified, due to the fact that it was written in the mid-nineteenth century. It has all the outward trappings of a mythological world, such as gods, goddesses, a dragon and the bright-eyed lad who slays him, a ring that supposedly accords its owner world-dominion, potions, a Tarnhelm, an important spear, and a sword that is broken and then reforged. The cosmos that the *Ring* depicts is inhabited by gods, goddesses, dwarfs, Valkyries, Rhinemaidens, Norns, all of whom are, from all appearances, beings who belong in primal works of northern folklore.

Nevertheless, the world of the *Ring* is, due to its essence as a nineteenth-century synthetic reconstitution of mythological source materials, marked by qualities that betray its historicity. For example, in the *Ring*, the gods think like modern human beings. Wotan, the prime example of this, has a nonmythological psychological depth, blatant character weaknesses, and a growing guilt and paranoia somehow inappropriate to a genuine Germanic god. The allegedly magic requisites are apparently mere props. Their magic per se is, it seems, oddly nonmagical. One of the progressions of the *Ring* is Wotan's coming to terms with his own mortality. In this manner an incongruity arises between the mythological trappings of the work and the modern psyches of the characters depicted therein.

In Wagner's *Ring*, one could say, the gods are very human, and they must end. They are thus not almighty and immortal, as gods should be. Erda makes this clear to Wotan and the others onstage in her warning at the end of *Rheingold*. Wotan wills his self-destruction with a Wagnerian kind of mythological grandeur. However, one could say that the gods of the *Ring* actually have a kind of "historical" existence. Despite the mythological costumes and props of these music-dramas, these gods onstage are apparently individuals with feelings and problems just like normal people. Thus the *Ring* betrays its own historicity. Although the viewer/listener is usually swept away by the music in performance, the *Ring* is, indeed, upon close analysis an extremely paradoxical work. Its main character, a Germanic god from all appearances, must come to terms with his humanity. A strange plot-line, to be sure.

One could say that history occupies the same place in Hebbel's world-view and drama theory that mythology does for Wagner. Hebbel's *Nibelungen* seems to be some kind of blueprint or negative/positive version of Wagner's *Ring* cycle, with regard to the relative merits of history and myth in each set of dramas. Hebbel's *Nibelungen* is basically historical. It is thus clear from these dramas where the priorities of each dramatist were. There is a controversy in Hebbel research concerning the function of history in his dramas. Scholars discuss Hebbel and history as they do Wagner and myth. The positions have changed with time. Oskar Walzel's position was, for a long time, the dominant one, stating that Hebbel's dramas portray the historical process. This view was revised by Klaus Ziegler, who argued that Hebbel's dramas illustrate more general problems. At any rate, it seems fair to say that Hebbel is primarily known as a historical dramatist.

Hebbel, unlike Wagner, worked from a single source, and this was the basically historical *Nibelungenlied*. Hebbel saw his plays as a dramatization of the *Nibelungenlied*. He sought to rework the dramatic elements that were latent in the epic. He felt that the *Nibelungenlied* itself was actually, in a way, a tragedy, and thus he was actually formulating a thesis similar to Wagner's theory of the evolution of modern drama from medieval romance. In his preface to his Nibelung dramas, Hebbel asks, "Der geneigte Leser aber wird gebeten, auch in dem Trauerspiel hinter der 'Nibelungen Noth' Nichts zu suchen, als eben 'der Nibelungen Noth' selbst"[20] (The gracious reader is asked to look for nothing behind the tragedy of the Nibelungs as the tragedy of the Nibelungs itself). But it would be fallacious to think that the dramas did not, of necessity, show in some way Hebbel's basic concerns.

In Hebbel's theoretical writings, one can find a theoretical justification of historical drama, just as Wagner's theoretical treatises deal with the necessity of mythological music-drama. In "Mein Wort über das Drama!" Hebbel even writes that history is a vehicle through which the poet can convey his views. Hebbel's theory about the intrinsically tragic nature of life is embodied in, and demonstrated by, the course of history. The essential tragedy of existence is intensified to critical proportions in periods of historical transition, or the Hegelian "Zwischenzeit." It was a common view in the age of Realism that tragedy took place at the turning-points of historical crises.

One could build a theory (as Wagner might have) that the weaknesses of Hebbel's *Nibelungen* come from the author's trying to use epic materials unchanged and fit epic content as is into the drama form. According to Wagner's aesthetic system, by making spoken, historical dramas out of the *Nibelungenlied*, Hebbel had thus created some kind of nonentity. Wagner, one can surmise, must have felt that placing the Nibelung legend into a cycle of Realistic, historical dramas that embody Hebbel's world-view just meant creating a positive atrocity. Therefore, one can clearly see how Wagner thought Hebbel's *Nibelungen* trilogy was not true drama but, rather, a ridiculous debasement of a Germanic legend.

Furthermore, Hebbel's *Nibelungen* trilogy expresses his basic pessimistic resignation. The historical progression seems to lead nowhere; it is oddly unproductive. The dramatic development is a kind of pointless one. One could say that this work shows the Idealistic world-view at its absolute worst, portraying the capitulation of Idealism to a harsh reality that it finally feels it is helpless to alter from the inside out. Another tragic transition illustrated by Hebbel's *Nibelungen* plays is that of Idealism yielding to reality, the inner surrendering to the outer, the transcendental to the concrete and actual, the imaginary to the tangible. Wagner deconstructs myth; Hebbel deconstructs history.

Hebbel's world-view ruthlessly destroys any possibility of progress ever being achieved within the compass of earthly existence. Thus he demolishes all possible revolutionary hopes and reduces history to senseless clashes that will never be resolved. Wagner's *Ring* is a cycle that symbolically depicts and is supposed to cause the redemption of modern society. Hebbel's world-view, from the evidence of his *Nibelungen* trilogy, remains stuck in the Hegelian "Zwischenzeit." Furthermore, in the plays under discussion, Hebbel also demonstrates an aggressively negative stance toward mythological drama. A comparative analysis of Wagner's and Hebbel's versions of the Nibelung legend with regard to the themes of history and myth does seem to indicate what sound like sardonic comments on each other.

Whereas, for Wagner's *Ring*, history is a phase to be overcome, as the *Ring* is a mythical account of history to the end of mythicizing real-life, that is, bringing about the future utopia, the dissolution of history into myth, Hebbel, in the course of his Nibelungen plays, destroys myth and replaces it with history. This happens in his *Nibelungen* trilogy, both in the choice of raw material, and in how the various kinds of raw material, mythical or historical, that the work contains are treated and portrayed therein. Hebbel's *Nibelungen*, I would argue, defeats the Romantic idea of history that Wagner expressed in his *Ring*, via, by use (or abuse) of, myth.

The nineteenth century, as Fritz Martini points out, was the century in which mythology was superseded and replaced by history and bourgeois society.[21] Martini explains that the world of the nineteenth century was endangered by individuation, the dissolution of metaphysical systems, and the loss of binding societal forms—that is, in all, by the loss of myth. One could well argue that when myth (i.e., a transcendent, metaphysical system) is debased, and history becomes such an overpowering force that it negates free will, what is usually defined as tragedy no longer exists as such. This is the basic literary-dramatic dilemma that Wagner and Hebbel were dealing with, each in his own way.

Wagner, among others, observed that such a shift in orientation results in a preference for different literary genres, as he explained in *Oper und Drama*. In the age of Realism, drama was not what writers were intent on producing; rather, artists (seemingly demonstrating Wagner's theory that drama needs mythology) turned to narrative literature. Realism was the age of the novel as the dominant form. This turn from myth to history in the age of Realism was evidently what Wagner was rebelling against. Thus, he was at odds with both his literary and his dramatic contemporaries. Wagner said history was not the proper subject matter for the drama. Rather, he felt that the novel typically portrayed history and bourgeois society. It seems, in this respect, that Hebbel's *Nibelungen* is mocking Wagner in a premature response to how Wagner was to later mock him.

Building on Martini's statement that tragedy in the Classical tradition ends in Germany with Hebbel, I suggest that the two works I contrast demonstrate different ways of ending tragedy. Myth is, in some way, essential to each. In these works, though, tragedy is ended in different ways, to vastly different purposes. Wagner's *Ring* represents the Romantic transcendence of tragedy with and through myth. In his *Nibelungen*, Hebbel, through the use of myth, implicitly asserts the impossibility of the traditional form of tragedy, which presupposes the existence of a mythical world-order, the power of a metaphysical fate, and the ruling force of transcendental gods, in the nineteenth century. Accordingly, in Hebbel's *Nibelungen*, which I thus take to be representative of his work, myth is degraded and conquered by history.

HISTORY AND MYTH IN HEBBEL'S *NIBELUNGEN*

One could argue that Hebbel's *Nibelungen* is, in a sense, a "mythical" work. Any story that explains something can be considered a myth, regardless of the subject matter that it uses and the features that it has (though myths usually do have some particular distinguishing elements). In this manner, people have interpreted Hebbel's *Nibelungen* as a myth, that is, a fiction (that happens to use conventionally mythical elements), to explain history. I discuss one such interpretation in more depth in the next section of this chapter. For now, I will just mention that this slant exists, and postpone closer consideration of it until then.

Thus, for one thing, Hebbel, like Wagner, has formulated a myth, in other words, a story, that explains history; that is, it portrays in some veiled way modern society and shows through the plot-line how it got to be the way it is. Suffice it to say that in this regard, calling the trilogy a "myth" means pointing out that it is an explanatory story. Like Wagner's *Ring*, Hebbel's *Nibelungen* is an image of world-history. Herbert Kraft, for instance, feels that Hebbel, with his *Nibelungen*, wanted to help the age in which he was living understand the forces at work in it.[22] Helmut deBoor, too, writes that Hebbel's Nibelung plays represent world-history.[23] According to this mode of interpretation, history assumes some kind of mythical, that is, symbolic significance. Fritz Martini explains how Hebbel, in his *Nibelungen* plays, formed the Nibelung legend into a cycle of dramas that portrayed a historical progression. Hebbel's trilogy shows the mythical heathenism of Brunhild being succeeded by the Germanic heroism of the Burgundians, which, in turn, yields to a more humane ethic of Christianity.[24]

However, it is unclear just what the entire "myth" means. This is open to interpretation. One is tempted to interpret the trilogy as representing, due to the influence of Hegel on Hebbel, some teleological historical progression.[25] However, deBoor notes that it is no accident that in Hebbel research, the Nibelung plays stand in the shadow. The historical progression demonstrated in these plays does not fall comfortably into the familiar three-stage model of thesis, antithesis, and synthesis. Neither the opposition of Siegfried and Hagen, the antagonists of the first part, nor that of Kriemhild and Hagen, those of the second part, represents the clash of two stages of world-history from the conflict of which a new world arises.

Furthermore, that the work uses traditionally mythological elements makes the situation even more complicated. One could therefore say that these plays have a "dual" mythical nature. They can be interpreted as basically explanatory, but they also use traditionally mythical elements. They have specific features that resemble real myths in the usual, conventional sense of the term. The elements that resemble conventional mythology are placed against the backdrop of history, and this doubtlessly affects the way one interprets them. Meaning is often dependent on context. Myths usually do not have historical settings or use historical subject matter.

Moreover, the dichotomy of history and myth, as represented by these plays, is also not a simple one. One cannot say that either the conventionally mythical elements or the potentially veiled, explanatory nature of the work qualifies it as truly mythical in the traditional sense. Nor can one define this trilogy as historical in the way that, say, *Wallenstein* is. Historical plays usually do not contain familiar superhuman figures such as Siegfried and Brunhild. The basically historical setting prompts one to seriously question the purpose and function of the mythical elements. What is the status of myth in this work? Are the mythological elements just projections of the dramatic figures? Hebbel's Brunhild has visions that betray her "mythological" origin. Myth is, after all, madness in the realm of a historical work. A discussion of how myth functions in this trilogy must account for the historical elements in it, too.

Alois Bönig proposes several ways of viewing the relationship of history and myth in these dramas. First, he explains that history functions in Hebbel's dramas the same way that myth does in ancient drama.[26] Both history and myth give order and sense to life. In other words, Bönig is arguing that the plays are actually historical to the end of being mythical in the extended sense of this term. He mentions, however, that this may not be necessarily advantageous to the tragic depiction of the world of the plays. To say that Hebbel's *Nibelungen* represents a change from historical to mythical subject matter would, however, be an oversimplification. The issue of history and myth in these plays is a complex one.

Bönig also suggests that Hebbel's use of myth in these plays represented an attempt to place these dramas within the tradition of tragedy, which arose from a religious source. The potential success of this motive, Bönig mentions, is however questionable, as the modern public was alienated from its mythology. Hebbel's *Nibelungen* trilogy is neither strictly historical nor traditionally mythical. When applied to his *Nibelungen*, the classification of Hebbel as a historical dramatist must be qualified. History and myth do not constitute a simple dichotomy for Hebbel, as they do not for Wagner also.

Whereas Wagner's *Ring* is basically a mythological world with historical features, Hebbel's dramatic version of the Nibelung legend is just the opposite. Hebbel's drama cycle presents a world that is clearly situated in historical time and in a real location. This historical world has, though, mythological interpolations. Siegfried and Brunhild are clearly superhuman creatures who are, for some reason, placed (or misplaced, rather) in history. Hebbel has thus done the opposite of what Wagner did. In this respect, his *Nibelungen* trilogy seems the converse of the *Ring*. Hebbel's plays are basically set in historical times, in real places. But Hebbel's characters have "mythical" qualities. Siegfried and Brunhild are somehow more than human. They are superhuman creatures who have been misplaced into history.

Hebbel's *Nibelungen* trilogy functions, to a large extent, on the opposition of Christianity and heathenism. In this way Hebbel presents a "mythicized" account of history, as does Wagner's *Ring*, only differently. Heathenism and Christianity, two different kinds of belief systems or myths, collide in Hebbel's *Nibelungen*. Like Wagner, Hebbel also seems to deal with history via myth. One could say that Hebbel has "mythicized" his historical plays by depicting the collision of mythologies, and also by giving these mythologies of Christianity and heathenism some traditionally mythical qualities that serve to undermine the differences between them (and thus somehow make the clash seem less a progression than a stasis or a repetition, an aspect I will discuss shortly).

Hebbel's Nibelung plays seem to be an application of *Oper und Drama* to the *Ring*, like a rewriting of the tetralogy with reference to the tension, if not strict dichotomy or linear historical progression, of Christianity after Germanic myth in the schema that Wagner sketches in the second part of his treatise. Wagner argues that the world-view of the modern world was characterized by these two strands of myth, which clashed. The collision of Christianity and the indigenous heroic myths of the Germanic peoples formed, according to Wagner, the medieval knightly romance. Wagner laments the demythologization of the modern world. These plays by Hebbel thus seem to demonstrate Wagner's history of mythology from the second part of *Oper und Drama*. Furthermore, in showing the succession of Christianity after Germanic heathenism, Hebbel destroys myth in the plot of the trilogy.

Brunhild, however, along with several other figures, is a "mythical" figure in the literal sense. Iceland, though a real geographical location on this earth, is a "mythical," that is, timeless world. Brunhild says, "Wohl steht die Zeit hier still, wir kennen nicht / Den Frühling, nicht den Sommer noch den Herbst, / Das Jahr verändert niemals sein Gesicht, / Und wir sind unveränderlich mit ihm"[27] (Here time stands still, we don't know spring, summer, or autumn. The seasons don't change, and we don't either). Brunhild is a complex figure, indeed. In Hebbel's trilogy, Brunhild is one of the figures who spans both levels, those of history and myth. She has a paradoxical existence. She represents the simultaneity of history and myth. One could say she opens the mythological "window" in Hebbel's work.

In Wotan's monologue in *Walküre*, he tells his favorite daughter of her origin—who her mother was, and the circumstances of and reasons for, even the events preceding, her birth and that of her eight Valkyrie half-sisters. In Hebbel's work, Frigga fulfills the same function with regard to the analogous character. She tells Brunhild how an old man from the mountain, clearly a legendary character, presented the baby (Brunhild) to them, and how the attempted baptism was repeatedly foiled by other powers. Therefore it is clear to both Brunhild and the reader or viewer, from the story that Frigga tells, that Brunhild, like Siegfried, is a supernatural, that is, mythological creature, a being who is extraordinary in the literal sense of the word. Brunhild fights with men and usually wins. DeBoor notes that the opposition of Christianity and heathenism is present in this story of Brunhild's baptism.

Within mythological material, in the course of the tetralogy, even before our eyes, Wagner demythologizes Brünnhilde. The story of her banishment from Valhalla is one of the main unifying themes of the tetralogy. She is thrown out of Valhalla, stripped of her immortality and her Eternal Wisdom, and she becomes mortal. Hebbel, within a realistic (historical) work, mythologizes the corresponding figure. The works of the two dramatists thus seem mirror-images of each other. What in Wagner's *Ring* is a temporal progression is in Hebbel's trilogy a strange simultaneity of myth and history. Hebbel's Brunhild, in fact, seems to personify the conflicts of these plays in which she exists. She represents the dichotomies of history and myth and of heathenism and Christianity. One could consider her an embodiment of the work as a whole.

DeBoor writes that heathenism and Christianity are signs or symbols for the same mythical mode of existence, the same timeless mode of being. In doing so, I would add, Hebbel collapses the dichotomy of Christianity and heathenism. In Hebbel's trilogy, then, the "myths" of heathenism and Christianity are also invested with literal mythological attributes. Hebbel has thus "mythicized" his picture of history in another sense. He has made both these "myths" or belief systems (using the term "myth" in the extended sense) "mythical" in the sense in which genuine mythology is. Furthermore, these two senses of "myth" seem to work against each other, for they function in different ways.

Hebbel actually collapses the duality of Christianity and heathenism by giving them similar characteristics and undermining their differences.

DeBoor points out that the idea of an exemplary "noble" stance binds Christians and heathens in these plays much more than religion separates them. Even Dietrich von Bern, the representative of Christianity, has contact with nixies at the fountain, and Brunhild was (finally) baptized. Fritz Martini points out that the Christian ethic of humanity—forgiveness, humility, and renunciation—does not become a real dramatic motivating force in these plays.[28] Thus heathenism and Christianity do not constitute some kind of deep structural or ideological conflict in the Hebbel trilogy. They are, rather, mere scenery or props.

One must ask, then, why Hebbel uses myth in this curious way and puts these mythological interpolations into a fundamentally historical work. In so doing, he trivializes myth and, paradoxically, demythologizes it. In other words, myth becomes strangely nonmythical. If myth or mythical attributes link opposing trends and different modes of (historical) existence, then does myth really have any meaning anymore? The matter is one of interpretation. Hebbel thus reduces what might seem a historical progression to some kind of eerie stasis that does not quite qualify as "mythical" timelessness, but that seems to designate, rather, its complete obliteration and the futility of ever hoping or striving to achieve the final mythical Golden Age or synthesis of history and myth.

One can devise a scale that designates what one could call the "levels" of myth in the work. There are Worms, a historical place, and Iceland, also a historical place but in addition, it seems, a mythical land. Brunhild's origins, one could say, are in traditional mythology, a land that is more mythical than Iceland, a past she remembers vaguely, in visions. Myth, it seems, is, in Hebbel's trilogy, more a state of mind than a physical place or a literary-dramatic substance. There is even a still higher level of myth in Hebbel's *Nibelungen* that I will now explore, and that invites comparison most strongly with Wagner's *Ring*. Furthermore, in Hebbel's *Nibelungen*, as I show in the next section, myth is debased and destroyed in the characters of Siegfried and Brunhild.

REGENERATION DEFEATED

No discussion of the relative uses of myth and history in Hebbel's trilogy, both in the choice and in the portrayal of the raw material (i.e., what happens to the mythical elements in the plot of the dramas), would be complete without some consideration of not the content itself but, rather, what was not in the content. Hebbel's *Nibelungen*, as I have already noted, contains "mythical" elements that somehow, oddly enough, show how nonmythical the work really is. To effectively analyze this aspect of the work, one must, also paradoxically, step outside of the work for a while.

I have already outlined how one can see the dramatic representatives of the belief systems (or myths) of heathenism and Christianity being portrayed as truly mythical figures in Hebbel's trilogy, as they are invested with traditionally "mythical" qualities. Furthermore, the work as a whole can be considered as being "mythical" in an extended sense because it uses the Nibelung legend, which had representative status or "mythical" significance in the nineteenth century. However, the use of "mythical" (in two senses) heathenism and Christianity, one could even say that this "myth" or story that tells a "mythicized" version of history in several ways, is embedded within a larger, more traditional myth, that of the divine mission of Siegfried and Brunhild and the plan of the gods to renew the world.

Within Hebbel's trilogy (or, perhaps more correctly, beneath or even beside it) there is a mythical teleology that Hebbel composed and then omitted, though for external reasons. We know he attached great importance to it and considered it the core of the drama. According to these passages, the gods have destined Siegfried and Brunhild for each other (which is what Wagner's Wotan does indirectly). This match of Siegfried and Brunhild, according to Hebbel's fiction, is supposed to renew the world, but because it threatens mankind with destruction, so it (mankind) opposes this match with a second bride, Kriemhild.

Dietrich von Bern describes this renewal of the world with apocalyptic imagery. In telling the myth, he says, "Das Vergangene / Ringt aus dem Grabe, und das Künftige / Drängt zur Geburt, das Gegenwärt'ge aber / Setzt sich zur Wehre"[29] (The past struggles to rise up from the grave, the future presses to be born, but the present resists). Like the *Ring*, Hebbel's *Nibelungen* deals with the old and the new, the opposition of utopian visions and the repressive, reactionary force of custom. In doing so, it thematizes its own aesthetic program. Wagner shows one age succeeding another, which he feels the performance of the works will cause to happen in reality. Hebbel shows a chaos of what seems to be more a bunch of simultaneous world-views that will probably, it sounds as though he is saying, never stop clashing.

In a quotation recorded by Cosima in her diaries, Wagner designated Brünnhilde and Wotan as the two "tragic" figures of the *Ring*, for they both come to full consciousness. Wagner said that Siegfried was not a tragic figure, for he did not come to full consciousness of his transgression (see CT II, 703, entry of 4 July 1873). Tragedy, for Wagner, entails coming to consciousness. Paradoxically, for these reasons Wagnerian tragedy is not "tragic" in the full and usual sense of the term. The *Ring* represents, rather, the Romantic transcendence of tragedy. The drama is internalized. Consciousness was, for Wagner at the time he was working on the *Ring*, revolutionary. The art-work of the future was supposed to induce some kind of revolutionary consciousness in the audience.

Furthermore, the stories of Brünnhilde and Wotan, interlinked as they are, unify the tetralogy. Brünnhilde's defiance of Wotan and her banishment from Valhalla connect *Walküre* and *Götterdämmerung*. The associations that the ring has, Hagen as Alberich's son, and Brünnhilde's constant cries to Wotan (at crucial moments, at the climax of each act) serve to remind the viewer/listener that the story of Siegfried and Brünnhilde is embedded in the "Göttertragödie," is "framed," so to speak, by Wotan's story. The final scene of *Götterdämmerung* is Brünnhilde's reckoning with Wotan. Valhalla is, after all, finally burned at the end of the cycle, linking the rectification and cleaning up of the mess that the final drama depicts with the righting (and the burning) of the wrong that goes back several evenings to the prologue of the cycle, and that was given rise to by Wotan's treaties with the giants for the building of his castle.

Moreover, the *Ring* is a tragedy on the level of reflection. The portrayal of a process of coming to consciousness and the thematization of the conflict of custom and free self-determination establish the *Ring* as a clearly self-referential work. It portrays its own aesthetic program or performance, and it thematizes its own premises or audience reception. In the *Ring*, the dialogue of Wotan and Fricka in the second act of *Walküre* is an innertextual explication of the conflicts that are illustrated by the tetralogy. This debate involves the relation of the gods to mankind. In this manner, the *Ring* is about itself; it comments on its own themes with Romantic irony. In other words, the *Ring* thematizes what Wagner presents in *Oper und Drama* as his reworking of the traditional structure of Greek tragedy. I wish to investigate the function of the mythological "window," the passages that Hebbel omitted that "embed" the match of Siegfried and Brunhild in the plan of the gods to renew the world.

The myth of the divine predestination of Siegfried and Brunhild, that is, the plan of the gods to renew the world, serves the same function in Hebbel's *Nibelungen* as do the building of Valhalla and Wotan's double-dealings in Wagner's *Ring*. In each case the story of Siegfried and Brünnhilde-(or Brunhild, as the case may be) is embedded in this larger framework. For Hebbel, because this union failed, the world was not renewed. Wagner, however, has a three-stage view similar to that of the Romantics. Precisely because the union failed, Brünnhilde is moved to cause the cataclysm at the end and thus renew the world. She has suffered fully and gained tragic insights. She brings good from evil. Siegfried unknowingly betrayed her so that a woman might gain wisdom. Brünnhilde therefore redeems the corrupt mythological rule of her divine (but, in many ways, all too human) father.

Thus this more "traditional" myth, within the conglomeration of myth and history that Hebbel's work contains, expresses his attitude toward myth. Hebbel's *Nibelungen* represents, in various ways, a process of demythologization. Reading these plays seems like experiencing the *Ring* only backwards, beginning with *Götterdämmerung*. The story of the humans or half-mortals somehow points toward the larger cosmic drama of the gods and goddesses, in which the mortals are caught. One could even state the analogy mathematically. I would suggest that if you take *Götterdämmerung*, that is, the culmination of the *Ring*, and somehow subtract *Rheingold* from it, you get Hebbel's *Nibelungen*. Then subtract the Immolation Scene. This is what Hebbel's trilogy would sound like if set to the music of the *Ring*. Imagine that the music that represents Sieglinde's glorification of Brünnhilde is never repeated. The gods are absent, with the disastrous events of earthly reality lacking the grandeur of a metaphysical, an other-worldly foundation. Redemption remains at best an unrealized possibility.

Hebbel undoes the "cosmic," teleological, didactic implications formally (he omits the "frame," that is, the plan to renew the world), and with regard to content (Siegfried and Brunhild do not renew the world). In doing so, Hebbel undoes the three-stage model of the Romantics that Wagner was using. Wagner, like the Romantics, portrays the dualism of existence in order to show it being repaired, and thus also to repair it in reality. For Hebbel, however, the dualism of existence is not repaired and perhaps not even reparable. One could say that with his use of these themes in this manner, Hebbel presents or formulates an anti-myth that inevitably fails and that functions only to show its futility or impotence. Hebbel's *Nibelungen* thus seems a negative, or perhaps one could say a distorted, version of Wagner's *Ring*.

For these reasons, Hebbel's *Nibelungen*, like *Wallenstein*, can be considered a complement, a reversal, of the *Ring*. It seems an anti-*Ring*, almost a parody. Where the *Ring* is a positive, Hebbel's *Nibelungen* is a negative. Where the *Ring* is mythological, Hebbel's *Nibelungen* is historical, and vice versa. Whereas the *Ring* is outwardly mythological, the work by Hebbel is basically historical, not mythological. It merely has mythological interpolations. Moreover, in Hebbel's trilogy, the divine plan doesn't work as it is foretold. Whereas Wotan's schemes to regain the ring and forestall the end of the gods are foiled, his futility has positive value, for it is ultimately redeemed with the rest of the fictional universe. Thus, when one compares Hebbel's *Nibelungen* to the *Ring*, one has the opposite kind of material (history, as opposed to myth) going in the opposite direction (the world is not, and cannot be, renewed).

Hebbel's work seems the opposite of Wagner's as regards the process of composition, too. Wagner's *Ring* was the product of a massive backward expansion. Wagner originally planned a story about Siegfried, and then he embedded this into the "frame" of the gods' tragedy. He gradually reached *Rheingold*, the metaphysical foundation for the story in which Siegfried and Brünnhilde find themselves trapped. What Wagner eventually includes, Hebbel excludes from his version of the Nibelung legend. Whereas Wagner embeds the story of Siegfried and Brünnhilde (the constellation of the last drama, which was inspired by Hebbel's only source, the *Nibelungenlied*) in the story of the gods, Hebbel omits (for external reasons, of course) the teleology of the divine predestination of Siegfried and Brunhild from the trilogy.

Wagner felt that a process of coming to consciousness was essential to tragedy. For Hebbel, tragedy entails not coming to consciousness. Perhaps this is even, for Hebbel, essential to tragedy. Wagner, after all, was concerned with unworking and transcending tragedy in a Romantic reconciliation. Wilhelm Emrich argues that in Hebbel's dramas, the battle of the sexes is the struggle for the articulation of a "female consciousness."[30] He observes that in Hebbel's dramas the women live outside of time (in, I would add, some kind of "mythical" existence). Brunhild's absolute wisdom does not enter her waking consciousness. The intrigue of Siegfried and Gunther kills it. The renewal of the world, characterized by the equality of women and men, fails to materialize. While Wotan and Brünnhilde, in the *Ring*, both come to full consciousness, Hebbel's *Nibelungen* depicts the failure of the same process.

In a different article from the one cited earlier, Emrich discusses how the *Nibelungen* trilogy demonstrates Hebbel's ideas about myth and history, and what consciousness (or lack thereof) has to do with myth. Emrich's interpretation takes into account both senses of "myth" in Hebbel's trilogy as I have outlined them. As his interpretation sheds light on the differences between Wagner's and Hebbel's versions of the Nibelung legend, it is, I feel, worth recounting here. Emrich explains that Hebbel's *Nibelungen* portrays a symbolic (i.e., veiled or "mythical") progression (or lack thereof) of world-history.[31] Emrich argues essentially that for Hebbel in his *Nibelungen* trilogy, myth (within the work) represents a stage of history, and thus myth is used by Hebbel in some roundabout way to portray history. By analyzing what happens to myth in the course of the trilogy, that is, by exploring what one could call the diachronic aspect of the topic of myth in the *Nibelungen* trilogy, Hebbel's pessimism is blatantly shown.

Emrich's interpretation seems to resemble Wagner's theory of the origin of mythology that he proposes in *Oper und Drama*. Wagner, too, theorized that gods were mere Feuerbachian projections of humans. Hebbel, Emrich argues, interpreted them in a similar way. According to Emrich, the gods represent, for Hebbel, the powers that determine all earthly reality in the psychic, physical, or societal realm. Emrich explains that the belief in gods that people of previous times held was just projection due to a lack of self-consciousness. Humans, when they become autonomous, can control gods. Hebbel, though, felt that humans had not yet become fully autonomous. Thus the renewal of the world never takes place as planned. The regeneration of society fails when mankind does not overcome the gods and recognize them as its own Feuerbachian projections. Thus, mankind never achieves autonomy.

Emrich argues that Hebbel's *Nibelungen* trilogy takes place in modern society. In other words, it is a "myth" that accounts for why the world is the way it is. According to Emrich, the fight for gold is the central motivation in these plays of Hebbel, as it is, I would add, in Wagner's *Ring*. The gold ring did, after all, lend its name to the tetralogy. Emrich feels that Hebbel's Siegfried brings about modern society with its greed for gold. This interpretation shows the radical differences between Hebbel's and Wagner's Nibelung works. In Wagner's *Ring*, Siegfried's death indirectly, by helping Brünnhilde gain full wisdom, helps end the fight for material wealth that somehow stands for the evils of modern capitalistic society.

Both Wagner and Hebbel use myth to destroy it, but in different ways and to different ends. Wagner uses myth in order to portray the end of myth. In doing so, however, he extols myth. In contrast, myth is, in Hebbel's work, not overcome, and it is not a positive force. Hebbel writes a historical work that shows that myth is never overcome (i.e., humans never became fully autonomous), and thus it depicts the grim continuation and perpetuation of myth. Myth is negatively evaluated as a stage that should be overcome but can't be, due to deficiency of humans. In other ways, it debases myth. The overcoming of myth by history is also represented by Brunhild's degeneration by Siegfried's tomb. Quite unlike Wagner's erstwhile Valkyrie who redeems the mythological cosmos with fire and water, thereby having her say about her divine but corrupt father, Hebbel's Brunhild has an unheroic end as a vampire in Siegfried's tomb, clawing at her skin and his coffin.

At the end of Wagner's tetralogy, myth yields to history in several ways—the gods end, and the work opens onto reality in a programmatic way. The *Ring* is a mythological metaphor for, or explanation of, (real) history. The end represents the renewal of reality, which the work in turn should cause. Wagner mythicizes history; that is, he writes a mythicized view of world-history, so he can thereby historicize myth, that is, turn history, the external world, into myth, by leading it to a mythical Golden Age. One of the ways he states his three-stage model in *Oper und Drama* is by saying that myth is the beginning and end of history. In Hebbel's *Nibelungen*, in contrast, mythicized history fails to fulfill a mythical pattern. The pessimism of external reality triumphs over myth.

Brunhild and Siegfried, Hebbel's main mythical figures, are conquered, victimized by history. After being overcome and betrayed, Brunhild, in Siegfried's burial vault, seems to "fade away." With her, Romanticism and mythological tragedy die out in the late nineteenth century. Brunhild's end prefigures how myth will later become macabre in the age of Expressionism. The deaths of Brunhild and Siegfried in Hebbel's *Nibelungen* signify that Germanic mythology is debased and killed off by nineteenth-century political and societal reality. According to Herbert Kraft, Siegfried's "flaw" is a betrayal of historical reality through his "mythical" ability.[32]

Not only do the two main "mythical" figures die away, but in Hebbel's *Nibelungen* the future "mythical" world is never realized in history. The renewal of the world, as described in the section that Hebbel omitted, sounds like a mythical age, a new Golden Age. Wagner wants to historicize a myth in reality. Hebbel, however, undoes Wagner's dialectic of history and myth. Whereas for Wagner, myth is a metaphor for history, Hebbel shows history trapped within myth. One mythicized realm of being succeeds another. Furthermore, for Hebbel, history simply fails to follow a mythical pattern. There is no reconciliation between history and myth. The two terms do not converge as they do for Wagner. Whereas Wagner presents the renewal of the world, Hebbel's plays represent pessimism.

In Hebbel's *Nibelungen*, the failure of myth to affect reality may very well express Hebbel's resignation to a crass external reality, and his rejection of the Romantic idea that fictions, products of the mind, can regenerate the external world. Art has no revolutionary function for Hebbel. The reality of the plays can only be explained with reference to myth in a negative way. Reality does not fulfill the hoped-for "mythical" pattern. The myth within the work even foretells its own failure, that is, the use of the "second bride" (Kriemhild) to defeat the renewal of the world. For Hebbel, history fulfills myth by not fulfilling a mythical function. For Wagner, myth revises history; for Hebbel, history defeats myth.

Wagner's *Ring* is a cycle, a spiral. Hebbel's trilogy shows a linear progression. History is more an eerie "eternal recurrence" than any kind of sensible progression. Dynamics are reduced, by the common "mythical" features of Christianity and heathenism, to stasis. The *Nibelungen* plays of Hebbel show only opposite poles of a dialectic, without the synthesis that is the last phase of the usual three-stage model. For Hebbel, the doubling might very well reflect the fact that the dualism is in the Idea itself. The dichotomy (which Hebbel implicitly collapses with myth) of Christianity and heathenism can also be seen as an instance of this dualism.

Because Hebbel has collapsed the dichotomy of Christianity and heathenism, he has "deconstructed" any sense of a historical progression. Unlike the *Ring* cycle, Hebbel's *Nibelungen* dramas do not come full circle. Nothing is really changed at the end of the *Nibelungen* trilogy, and there is none of the reconciliation or redemption of society that is essential to tragedy. According to Fritz Martini, Christianity is never adequately synthesized with Germanic heathenism in these plays.[33] Wagner's *Ring* represents in both its content and its aesthetic program of audience reception some kind of utopian redemption of history in and by myth. The Hegelian "Zwischenzeit" is, in Hebbel's *Nibelungen*, a condition that will never be overcome. According to Fritz Martini, for Hebbel's *Nibelungen*, tragedy arises from the destruction of myth. Siegfried and Brunhild fail to fulfill their mythical predestination.[34]

DeBoor points out that Hebbel saw Christianity as a mythology among many. He did not think that it would bring the redemption of the world. Toward the end of the trilogy, Dietrich states, concerning the final catastrophes, "Hier hat sich Schuld in Schuld zu fest verbissen, / Als dass man noch zu einem sagen könnte: / Tritt du zurück! Sie stehen gleich im Recht"[35] (Here guilt confronts guilt, so that one cannot say to one of them, "Step back!" They are both in the right). Wagner's *Ring* is, one could say, nihilistic in that it shows a vision of total destruction. In his revolutionary years, Wagner was, after all, a friend of the Russian anarchist Mikhail Bakunin. But the *Ring* presents the renewal of society, and, despite the fact that most of the characters are neither totally good nor totally evil, such as Wotan and Alberich, the cycle clearly shows the values that Brünnhilde champions to be supreme.

Wagner might have revised Brünnhilde's final solo to make it less sententious, but he ends the cycle with the violin melody associated with Sieglinde's glorification of Brünnhilde from the third act of *Walküre*. Wagner reconciles the real and the ideal. In contrast, Hebbel's *Nibelungen* shows a lack of transcendent values, and it ends in mythological solipsism. Hebbel's work reflects the attitude of nineteenth-century writers, in the age of the novel, toward myth. In this respect the content of Hebbel's Nibelung dramas is suitable to the historical subject matter. Wagner unworks tragedy by unworking myth. Hebbel affirms tragedy by defeating myth.

NOTES

1. Dieter Borchmeyer, *Das Theater Richard Wagners: Idee, Dichtung, Wirkung* (Stuttgart: Reclam, 1982), pp. 316–24.

2. Borchmeyer, *Das Theater Richard Wagners*, pp. 305–16.

3. On German drama in the age of Young Germany, see: Horst Denkler, "Politische Dramaturgie. Zur Theorie des Dramas und des Theaters zwischen den Revolutionen von 1830 und 1848," in *Deutsche Dramentheorien. Beiträge zu einer historischen Poetik des Dramas in Deutschland*, ed. Reinhold Grimm (Frankfurt am Main: Athenäum, 1971), vol. 2, pp. 345–73.

4. On German tragedy in the nineteenth century, see: Benno von Wiese, *Die Deutsche Tragödie von Lessing bis Hebbel* (Hamburg: Hoffmann und Campe, 1948; 6th ed., 1964), pp. 535–71.

5. For other comparisons of Wagner and Hebbel, see also: Otto Kayser, "Die Nibelungensage bei Hebbel und Wagner," *Hebbel-Jahrbuch* (1962): pp. 143–59; Otto Oster, "Der Nibelungen-Stoff bei Richard Wagner und Friedrich Hebbel," *"Die Walküre": Programmhefte der Bayreuther Festspiele* (1966): pp. 37–44; Rolf Schneider, "Der fortgeschriebene Mythos," *"Die Walküre": Programmhefte der Bayreuther Festspiele* (1989): pp. 17–27; Otfrid Ehrismann, "Siegfried. Studie über Heldentum, Liebe und Tod. Mittelalterliche Nibelungen, Hebbel, Wagner," *Hebbel-Jahrbuch* (1981): pp. 11–48.

6. Herbert Kraft, *Poesie der Idee: Die tragische Dichtung Friedrich Hebbels* (Tübingen: Max Niemeyer, 1971), pp. 132–39.

7. Friedrich Hebbel, *Sämtliche Werke*, ed. Richard Maria Werner, *Tagebücher*, vol. 4 (Berlin: B. Behr's Verlag, 1905), pp. 274–75.

8. Friedrich Hebbel, *Sämtliche Werke*, ed. Richard Maria Werner, *Briefe*, vol. 5 (Berlin: B. Behr's Verlag, 1906), p. 109.

9. On Hebbel's drama theory, see: Hans-Joachim Anders, "Zum tragischen Idealismus bei Friedrich Hebbel," in *Deutsche Dramentheorien. Beiträge zu einer historischen Poetik des Dramas in Deutschland*, ed. Reinhold Grimm, vol. 2 (Frankfurt am Main: Athenäum, 1971), pp. 323–44.

10. For Martini's summary of Hebbel's drama theory, see: Fritz Martini, *Deutsche Literatur im bürgerlichen Realismus 1848–1898*, 4th ed. (Stuttgart: Metzler, 1962, 1981), pp. 130–49 (here cited from p. 130).

11. Martini, *Deutsche Literatur im bürgerlichen Realismus*, p. 133.

12. On tragedy in Hebbel's world-view and drama theory, see: Herbert Kaiser, *Friedrich Hebbel: Geschichtliche Interpretationen des dramatischen Werks* (Munich: Wilhelm Fink, 1983), pp. 139–44.

13. Friedrich Hebbel, *Sämtliche Werke*, ed. Richard Maria Werner, *Tagebücher*, vol. 2 (Berlin: B. Behr's Verlag, 1903), p. 295.

14. See: Anders, pp. 331–33.

15. Kaiser, p. 170.

16. Kraft, p. 265.

17. On the Nibelung legend in the nineteenth century, see: Elizabeth Magee, *Richard Wagner and the Nibelungs* (New York: Oxford University Press, 1990). See also: Wolfgang Frühwald, "Wandlungen eines Nationalmythos. Der Weg der Nibelungen ins 19. Jahrhundert," in *Wege des Mythos in der Moderne. Richard Wagner, "Der Ring des Nibelungen"*, ed. Dieter Borchmeyer (Munich: Deutscher Taschenbuch Verlag, 1987), pp. 17–40; Klaus von See, "Das Nibelungenlied—ein Nationalepos?", in *Die Nibelungen. Ein deutscher Wahn, ein deutscher Alptraum. Studien und Dokumente zur Rezeption des Nibelungenstoffs im 19. und 20. Jahrhundert*, ed. Joachim Heinzle and Anneliese Waldschmidt (Frankfurt am Main: Suhrkamp, 1991), pp. 43–110.

18. Martini, *Deutsche Literatur im bürgerlichen Realismus*, p. 177.

19. Peter Wapnewski, *Der traurige Gott: Richard Wagner in seinen Helden* (Munich: C.H. Beck, 1978; Deutscher Taschenbuch Verlag, 1982), pp. 120–28.

20. I am citing from: Friedrich Hebbel, *Die Nibelungen*, ed. Helmut deBoor (Frankfurt am Main and Berlin: Ullstein, 1966), p. 274.

21. The ideas of Martini that I am summarizing are taken from: Fritz Martini, "Drama und Roman im 19. Jahrhundert: Perspektiven auf ein Thema der Formgeschichte," in *Literarische Form und Geschichte: Aufsätze zu Gattungstheorie und Gattungsentwicklung vom Sturm und Drang bis zum Erzählen heute* (Stuttgart: Metzler, 1984), pp. 48–80; *Deutsche Literatur im bürgerlichen Realismus*, pp. 116–18.

22. Kraft, p. 247.

23. See deBoor's section "Der Geschichtsmythus in Hebbels 'Nibelungen,' " in his Introduction to his edition of Hebbel's *Nibelungen*, pp. 23–37. Unless otherwise noted, subsequent references to deBoor are to this discussion, upon which I have also based parts of the previous discussion.

24. Martini, *Deutsche Literatur im bürgerlichen Realismus*, p. 179.

25. On the relationship of Hebbel and Hegel, see: Birgit Fenner, *Friedrich Hebbel zwischen Hegel und Freud* (Stuttgart: Klett-Cotta, 1979).

26. Alois Bönig, "Hebbel und das Drama der Griechen—Zur Funktion des Mythos und der Geschichte in der Tragödie," *Hebbel-Jahrbuch* (1974): pp. 44–68.

27. Hebbel, *Die Nibelungen*, p. 105.

28. Martini, *Deutsche Literatur im bürgerlichen Realismus*, p. 179.

29. Hebbel, *Die Nibelungen*, p. 275.

30. Wilhelm Emrich, "Friedrich Hebbels Vorwegnahme und Überwindung des Nihilismus," in *Geist und Widergeist. Wahrheit und Lüge der Literatur. Studien* (Frankfurt am Main: Athenäum, 1965), pp. 147–62. Some of the same ideas about the "absolute consciousness" of the female figures recur in Emrich's article "Götzen und Götter der Moderne," cited in the following note.

31. Wilhelm Emrich, "Hebbels *Nibelungen*—Götzen und Götter der Moderne," in *Friedrich Hebbel*, ed. Helmut Kreuzer and Roland Koch, Wege der Forschung, vol. 642 (Darmstadt: Wissenschaftliche Buchgesellschaft, 1989), pp. 305–26.

32. Kraft, p. 254.

33. Martini, *Deutsche Literatur im bürgerlichen Realismus*, p. 179.

34. Martini, *Deutsche Literatur im bürgerlichen Realismus*, p. 180.

35. Hebbel, *Die Nibelungen*, p. 238.

Chapter 3

Brünnhilde on Naxos: A Study of the Wagnerian Influence on Hofmannsthal's Dramas and the Hofmannsthal-Strauss Dramas

*T*he collaboration of Hugo von Hofmannsthal and Richard Strauss is usually thought of as standing in the tradition of the Wagnerian music-drama.[1] The parallels between aspects of the literary output of Hofmannsthal alone, both in and aside from his collaboration with Strauss, with Wagner's works are certainly numerous. For instance, the names of Wagner and Hofmannsthal are associated with the places Bayreuth and Salzburg, which are the two major, exclusive summer music festivals in Germany and Austria respectively, and it seems likely that the latter was influenced by the former.[2] Scholars have written about the theme of music in Hofmannsthal's works,[3] and this invites the topic of words and music, one so familiar to Wagner research. Early in his career Hofmannsthal even wrote a poem entitled "Zukunftsmusik." The allusion could not be more obvious.

That Wagner influenced Hofmannsthal seems a blatant fact and a trite assertion. Borchmeyer notes that Hofmannsthal was familiar with Wagner's dramas, and he gives ample proof of this from Hofmannsthal's notebooks.[4] For instance, Borchmeyer states that Hofmannsthal repeatedly drew analogies between the figures of his own works and those of Wagner's.[5] Critics are fond of comparing the Marschallin with Hans Sachs, as both figures are older protagonists, and each renounces a young lover. The resemblances between works of Hofmannsthal and those of Wagner often extend to minute textual details. For example, Borchmeyer finds a verbal reminiscence of the announcement of death scene from *Walküre* in the title of *Der Tor und der Tod*.

The music of the Hofmannsthal-Strauss works just reinforces and at times even seems to unequivocally prove their similarity to Wagnerian dramas. Strauss' music is, after all, usually classed as "post-Wagnerian." However, to designate superficial influence does not serve as an interpretation of the function of various elements in a work of art as a whole. It is somehow tautological and thus deficient as textual analysis. Isolated elements and scattered resemblances always need to be considered in the context of each work in its entirety. How a work creates meaning is a complex, comprehensive process.

Discrete similarities, furthermore, can prove to be deceptive when a work is analyzed in its entirety. They entice one to assert that there is a complete agreement between two works that simply does not exist. Even at a cursory glance, one cannot possibly overlook the fact that the Wagnerian legacy was radically changed by Hofmannsthal and Strauss. The Viennese comedies are, in fact, often seen as an antithesis to the mythological, serious Wagnerian works. Dieter Borchmeyer sees the works that Strauss and Hofmannsthal collaborated on as representing a "productive reception" of the Wagnerian form. These works, he feels, were influenced by Wagner's dramas, but maintain a critical distance from their models. Wagner, it seems, usually inspired mixed reactions in those who bore the weight of his influence. Hofmannsthal was no exception.

Borchmeyer indicates that Hofmannsthal wanted the works that he created in collaboration with Strauss to be understood as some kind of antithesis to the Wagnerian music-drama. The prototype of these works of Hofmannsthal and Strauss was to be, rather, Mozart and the older "Spieloper."[6] Hofmannsthal, for instance, wrote to Strauss that Octavian and Sophie should be Mozartian. They were not to scream at each other in a Wagnerian way (he uses the term "Liebesbrüllerei," "love-howling").[7] It is easy to say that the use of mythological subject matter for opera is Wagnerian. Furthermore, Elektra does howl for her murdered father in a way that Hofmannsthal probably would have considered Wagnerian. However, can one describe Elektra as a Wagnerian character? Or is Ariadne more Wagnerian than Zerbinetta?

The Wagnerian influence, one could surmise, might even make the Hofmannsthal-Strauss works somehow internally contradictory, as they were jointly written by a poet and a composer who were very different individuals and did not always get along with each other. Wagner, of course, united both faculties within himself. Hofmannsthal, Borchmeyer explains, respected Wagner as a poet and a dramatist, even though he was critical of the music of Wagner's dramas. Borchmeyer points out that the negative comments of Hofmannsthal about Wagner concern his music, not his dramas or his theory.[8] An investigation into how the works that resulted from this collaboration relate to Wagner's work is no simple matter.

Furthermore, the relationship of Hofmannsthal and Strauss, which one can find well documented in their correspondence, was not without friction. Besides working in different mediums, the two men had very different temperaments and backgrounds. To say that the music of Wagner influenced that of Richard Strauss is to repeat a commonplace of musicology. Because Hofmannsthal actually had an ambivalent relationship to Wagner, and his mixed feelings concerned the various elements or the different mediums with which Wagner worked, one could therefore suspect that his ambivalence might affect how the various elements of the operas he himself helped create would work together.

Thus, undertaking an analysis of the Hofmannsthal-Strauss works in comparison with those of Wagner means tackling a very complicated, multifaceted issue. One must, to this end, discuss how words and music function with and/or against each other in each music-drama. This raises important questions concerning not only how the various elements of a work of art relate to each other (such as music to words), but also how the various mediums, such as words and music, express and thereby thematize the mythological raw material used. Hofmannsthal uses mythological raw material for *Elektra* and *Ariadne auf Naxos*, as Wagner does for almost all of his music-dramas. How does the critical stance of Hofmannsthal toward Wagner's music affect the works he created with Strauss, whose music stands very much in the Wagnerian tradition?

Hofmannsthal's works therefore could have been influenced by Wagner's in a very complicated way. What happens when a poet relates to a musical style differently from the way he relates to the theoretical notions and the literary motives inspired by the same composer? When one notes these considerations and dissects the tradition into which Hofmannsthal and Strauss were consciously placing their works, then even drawing discrete parallels with Wagner's work, and noting what seem to be simple similarities or differences, become almost impossible to do in any kind of uncomplicated fashion. The collaboration of Strauss and Hofmannsthal produced a complex phenomenon indeed.

In this chapter, I expand upon the work that has previously been done on the relation of the Hofmannsthal-Strauss collaboration to the Wagnerian music-drama by exploring one aspect of the possible Wagnerian influence on the Hofmannsthal-Strauss dramas. I inquire more specifically into how Wagner's theory of myth and his dramas as mythological music-dramas might have affected the use of myth in selected works by Hofmannsthal. A detailed investigation and analysis of the use of myth by Wagner and Hofmannsthal show Hofmannsthal's use of myth, as exemplified, I propose, by the dramas *Elektra* and *Ariadne auf Naxos*, to be an unworking of Wagner's theory of myth as presented in *Oper und Drama* and exemplified by the *Ring* tetralogy. At first glance one sees parallels, but, upon closer examination, these similarities are really polar opposites and direct inversions.

The theme of myth is closely intertwined with the mediums involved, and thus it involves the topic of words and music. I ask how Hofmannsthal's collaboration with Strauss, that is, his conscious writing of texts for music, affected his views on myth. Not only is this an investigation into how a poet writes differently depending on the medium and goal, that is, whether he is writing a spoken play or an opera libretto, but it can also point to subtle evidence in the works under discussion of Hofmannsthal's stance toward Strauss and Wagner. In addition, debating this topic involves raising the issue of interpretation and, in doing so, also performing hermeneutics. Superficial impressions can often be misleading. Elements that are apparently Wagnerian and a style that seems to be Wagnerian can be used to actually cause a work, when analyzed in its entirety, to be a critical comment upon Wagner. Strauss' music often seems Wagnerian. Just how Strauss' music relates to that of Wagner is, in the case of *Ariadne auf Naxos*, though, a complex issue.

A methodological quandary arises when one considers that *Elektra* really exists in two versions, the play and the opera. I may be criticized for discussing the play *Elektra* and contrasting it with the opera *Ariadne auf Naxos*. However, I defend my choice as sound when understood with reference to my topic, which focuses on myth, language, and music. *Elektra* was originally a spoken play and only later, on Strauss' initiative, used, with minor revisions, as the text for an opera. *Ariadne auf Naxos* was written as an opera text. There is a close interrelationship between language and myth, and between music and myth, for Hofmannsthal and Wagner, respectively. By comparing a spoken text with a text that was specifically written during a collaboration with a composer who was setting it to music, one can discuss how Hofmannsthal's use of myth in his texts differed as a result of whether or not the text would be set to music. In this chapter, I show how Hofmannsthal the poet replies to Wagner the composer on the topic of myth in drama.

HOFMANNSTHAL AND WAGNER ON MYTH

It is much more difficult to discuss Hofmannsthal's views on mythology than it is to present Wagner's. The second part of *Oper und Drama* contains an elaborate theory concerning the origin, interpretation, and synthetic reconstitution of mythology. In contrast, Hofmannsthal has no theoretical works the size of *Oper und Drama*. His views are not presented systematically in any large treatises. Rather, they are scattered throughout essays, notebooks, and letters. The critic, rather than being able to take one text and analyze it carefully, seeking internal coherence (which even then might be tenuous), must rather piece together these bits and try to form a complete picture from them. Scholars, though, have found some continuity in Hofmannsthal's thoughts about mythology. In the ensuing section I summarize some of these observations and, in doing so, discuss the ways in which Hofmannsthal's thoughts on myth are similar to Wagner's.[9] I argue that

Hofmannsthal's works, like those of Wagner, are mythical in multiple and complex ways.

Eva-Maria Lenz explains that in his early statements concerning mythology, Hofmannsthal defines myth as an expression of some kind of primal state that was once alive, but that has now become lifeless and stale. Like Wagner and the rest of the Romantics, Hofmannsthal laments the decline of mythology with time. A characteristic of the modern age, for these thinkers, is the petrification of mythology. Hofmannsthal writes, "Natur-zustand.—Mythische Lebendigkeit, wo für uns starre Allegorien"[10] (State of nature.—Mythical animation, whereas we now have only stale allegories). Furthermore, like Wagner, Hofmannsthal considers mythology an explanatory system, and in addition, both of them see an affinity between art and myth.

For instance, Hofmannsthal wrote in his notebook (1893), "Poet—Mythenbildner: er humanisiert die Phänomene der Welt" (A 361) (The poet is a creator of myths. He humanizes the phenomena of the world). Later in the same entry, Hofmannsthal states, continuing the analogy between art and myth, "Kunst die Antwort des Menschen auf die undurchdringliche Rücksichtslosigkeit der Natur. Kunst expliziert alles, schon die Mythologie Explikation des unheimlichen Naturwaltens" (A 361) (Art is the reply of mankind to the impenetrable ruthlessness of nature. Art explains everything, and mythology is the explanation of the eerie tyranny of nature). Similarly, Wagner felt that mythology arose from a natural artistic ability. For Wagner, mythology is an artistic fiction that expresses one's perception of the world and thus explains external phenomena.

According to Hofmannsthal, myth balances (and thus unites or somehow "erases") antinomies, and he consequently likened myth to the drama ensemble, a phenomenon that he termed "Konfiguration." One can even consider this line of thinking analogous to how Wagner saw the rules of tragedy in Greek mythology itself, and therefore he could define the form (tragedy) by referring to its raw material (myth). One can also understand Hofmannsthal's statement that myth balances (and thus unites or somehow "erases") antinomies and Hofmannsthal's consequent likening of myth to the drama ensemble, a phenomenon he terms "Konfiguration," as analogous to how Wagner sees the rules of tragedy in Greek mythology itself, and therefore he can define the form (tragedy) by referring to its raw material (myth). This point of Hofmannsthal is exemplified by his talk on Shakespeare. (Interestingly enough, Wagner saw Shakespeare as a historical playwright, while for Hofmannsthal, however, the plays of Shakespeare are really mythological.)

Thus Hofmannsthal, like Wagner, actually uses the term "myth" in two different senses. Thus Hofmannsthal's works, like those of Wagner, are mythical in multiple and complex ways. The concept of myth, when applied to Hofmannsthal's works, remains an ambiguous term. Not only is there an analogy between art and myth in Hofmannsthal's thought, but for Hofmannsthal, as for Wagner and the Romantics, the poet creates new myths. Any explanatory story can be a myth. Original, genuine myths, however, are different from the myths that a poet creates. A play based on traditionally mythical material is thus doubly mythical. If myth-making is an artistic activity, then mythical art, it seems, is a mythical myth. One could say that mythological art, such as Greek tragedy, is a kind of "potentiated" kind of art, a higher level of myth.

As Wagner felt that the poet should use and interpret traditional mythology to create new myths, according to Hofmannsthal, the task of the poet was to give new life to old myths. Hofmannsthal wrote, "Dichter ein umgekehrter Midas: was er Erstarrtes berührt, erweckt er zum Leben" (A 338) (The poet is a reverse Midas: when he touches stone, he makes it come to life). In a letter to Gustav Schwarzkopf (23 January 1891), Hofmannsthal wrote, "Ein gut Teil unserer poetischen Arbeit ist Auflösung erstarrter Mythen, vermenschlichter Natursymbole in ihre Bestandteile, eigentlich Analyse, also Kritikerarbeit"[11] (A large part of our poetic efforts is the dissolution of petrified myths or anthropomorphized symbols of nature into their component parts, which is actually analysis and criticism). In a notebook entry written in 1894, Hofmannsthal says, "Alle Mythen sind aufs Menschliche gebrachter Ausdruck des allgemein Natürlichen. Der Dichter schafft neue Mythen" (A 382) (All myths are expressions of the purely natural given human form. The poet creates new myths).

Like Wagner, then, Hofmannsthal presents, in his works that deal with conventionally mythological subject matter, what I would term a "duality" of myth. A synthetic reconstitution of myth, that is, an explanatory fiction, a myth in a modern, extended sense, will invariably differ from genuine myth even when it is based, as Wagner's works are, on traditional mythology and uses this as its raw material. Wagner's *Ring* is mythical in two ways. Wagner uses elements of genuine myth, or mythical raw material, to form a new myth that is, and at the same time is not, mythical. For instance, his gods are very human, and definitely not immortal. Hofmannsthal's mythological works, similarly, invariably unmask their modernity.

Thus one must distinguish between traditional myth and this myth as it appears in the works of Wagner and Hofmannsthal. The task of both Wagner and Hofmannsthal was to interpret traditional myth on the stage of modern consciousness and with regard to, in the light of, contemporary history and their present-day world. For both of them, the task of the artist was one of mythological reinterpretation and refabrication. According to Eva-Maria Lenz, myth for Hofmannsthal has a "double source," one in reality, and one that is an artistic, artificial one. Thus not only does myth refer to the past, but, rather, as an artistic product it has utopian qualities. Hofmannsthal, I suggest, has a theory of mythological refabrication that is comparable to Wagner's.

I would like to apply these different definitions of "myth," after a theoretical excursion, to Hofmannsthal's drama texts themselves. Hofmannsthal, like Wagner, uses, for one thing, mythology as raw material. One could say he also inevitably forms a "new myth" from it. But when discussing *Elektra* and *Ariadne auf Naxos*, I will outline a third and extended, one could say psychological way of understanding the term "myth" in Hofmannsthal's works by showing how he uses myth to create what could be called a second-order myth that thematizes myth and thus itself. I consider this the self-referentiality of Hofmannsthal's works as concerns their mythological nature. That is, traditionally mythological figures in conventionally mythological subject matter are shown in the process of commenting upon and creating myths. To show how in the texts under discussion myth itself is thematized within mythological material, I will outline a sense in which myth can be seen in Hofmannsthal's theory of pre-existence ("Präexistenz").

The main theoretical framework that Hofmannsthal is known for has to do not with myth or even aesthetics but, rather, with stages of existence. Wagner is concerned with aesthetics and politics in history. Wagner sees myth as a way of interpreting the external world and understanding history. Wagner felt that myth could cause an inner change and enable one to become wise through feeling, thereby reforming society and history from within the person. One could say that Hofmannsthal takes Wagner's inner/outer dichotomy and intent to renew society from within one more step inward. Hofmannsthal writes mostly about psychological processes and the course of the life of an individual.

Central to Hofmannsthal's schema is his doctrine of pre-existence. Rolf Tarot sees the pre-existence as a state of nature ("Naturzustand") characterized by paradisiacal timelessness ("paradiesische Zeitlosigkeit") and a mythical world-view ("mythisches Bewusstsein"). He also uses the terms "naive" ("naiv") and "unreflecting" ("unreflektiert") to characterize this stage. Here one has, he theorizes, a "mythical" sense of unity ("mythisches Einheitsgefühl"). Hofmannsthal, in his notebooks, wrote that in the pre-existence, one sees only totalities. This, one could conjecture, is a marked characteristic of a mythical world-view. Thus, myth is to a large extent subjective. It is a way of viewing external, objective reality.

Tarot designates the second stage as the phase in which the "mythical" consciousness enters a crisis ("Phase des in die Krise getretenen mythischen Bewusstseins"). This is the stage of "guilt" ("Verschuldung"), in which the pre-existence is half lost ("halb verlorener Zustand der Präexistenz"). Tarot also notes that really these first two phases can be termed "pre-existence" in that they are simply pre-existence in the literal sense; that is, they precede the phase of existence. This third phase is "life" ("Leben").[12] Hofmannsthal is clearly working within the German tradition of which Wagner was also a part. Hofmannsthal's three-stage model thus enables one to discuss his works with reference to subjective myths, mythical world-views, and stages of existence.

Hofmannsthal's schema is, of course, not simple or unambiguous. Benjamin Bennett addresses the issue of whether or not the state of pre-existence is truly naive and without reflection. He explains that pre-existence is characterized by intense self-awareness. He also points out that pre-existence and existence are not distinct developmental stages, and that existence is not a state that can be achieved once and for all but, rather, that the transition from pre-existence to existence occurs over and over again, in every transition, every deed, and that pre-existence is never past but always present, at least as a possibility. Bennett explains that consciousness, because it implies a separation from the self by a distance, causes a disintegration of the totality of which one is conscious. Existence, he writes, is not knowing the truth but being the truth. Pre-existence is total consciousness of what one is. Existence is a newly unconscious condition.[13]

One can reconcile Bennett's system with Tarot's system by postulating a state of nature before Bennett's brand of pre-existence or discussing the relations between reflection and consciousness. Much more has been written about these concepts than I can possibly present here; a complete survey and an analysis of the research literature are not my purpose. I do not imply that these matters of definition are simple issues, or that Hofmannsthal's dramas can all be seen as somehow exemplifying these stages of existence. Furthermore, how to interpret the dramas with regard to these concepts would certainly be open to debate, as such theories and conclusions as regards each individual work of literature would, of course, vary with different literary critics.

Thus, in the preceding paragraphs, with my summary of these stages of existence being, of course, an oversimplification, I am merely outlining certain general ways in which such an approach can be undertaken and the term "myth" applied to Hofmannsthal's works and, in doing so, presenting ideas that I render more specific when I subsequently apply them to individual works under discussion in this chapter, *Elektra* and *Ariadne auf Naxos*. What interests me in particular is Tarot's terming of the pre-existence as some kind of mythical existence and Bennett's distinction between knowing and being. There is a difference between mythic material and a mythical (i.e., unified) world-view such as characterizes pre-existence. Only some of the figures in the dramas, all of whom were created by Hofmannsthal, were created within conventional mythological material. Not all characters in mythological subject matter live in a mythical world-view.

One can use these various stages of existence to understand Hofmannsthal's texts as thematizing myth, often within mythical raw material. Even from a cursory consideration of the theoretical schema that I have outlined, one would expect Hofmannsthal's works to show that he had various and ambivalent feelings about myth, and that his valuation of myth changed with time. The pre-existence was a privileged position, but Hofmannsthal later in his life rejected a sterile aesthetic existence for a more social one. I would like to show how two texts of Hofmannsthal, the latter in conjunction with the music of Strauss, illustrate very different views of Hofmannsthal on myth. Furthermore, Hofmannsthal, like Wagner, wanted to reconstitute myth to combat and cure the modern fragmentation of society. Their works present various solutions (or lacks thereof) to the crisis of modern life. Both dramatists present what Friedrich Schlegel, with significant terminological ambiguity, called a "new mythology." Hofmannsthal's dramas, I propose, thematize myth. Thus they thematize themselves. This self-referentiality can be either tragic or comic.

I propose that *Elektra* and *Ariadne auf Naxos* deal with the use and abuse of mythology. *Elektra* is evidence of an unhealthy view of myth, or perhaps rather a healthy skepticism about the viability of myth. The play uses mythical raw material, but, at the same time, it also shows that Hofmannsthal is highly critical of mythical drama. Perhaps the aesthete who has just undergone the "Chandos crisis" is coming to terms with his earlier existence, and thus he is particularly critical of this mythical world as a sterile pre-existence. However, later in his life, Hofmannsthal seems to have accepted that myth can, when used correctly, be applicable to life, though in a figurative or a metaphorical way. *Ariadne auf Naxos* thus represents this later view of the importance but also the limited, qualified applicability of myth to life. One might even liken Hofmannsthal's new perspective on myth with how his early narcissistic interest in poetry and lyric drama later yielded to a devotion to the social form of drama and a commitment to the larger, outer world.

Hofmannsthal's notebooks attest to the importance he ascribed to myth, especially in the 1920s, the epitome of which critics take to be *Die ägyptische Helena*. For instance, a note in "Ad me ipsum" dated 1921 reads, "Der Einzelne und die Epoche als Mythos gesehen" (A 617) (The individual and the epoch seen as myth). He began to see things in mythical terms. In his notebooks, Hofmannsthal wrote (1927), "Das Wagnis, ins Mythische zu gehen: mythische Bewegtheit unseres dunklen Untergrundes heute. Okzident—Orient. Heranfluten alter Elemente heute" (A 588) (The hazardous undertaking, to venture into myth: the mythical activity of the dark undercurrent in our present-day. Occident—Orient. Ancient elements rise up today). He also asked (1927), "Das Mythische steht über der Zeit. Haben wir denn nichts Unvergängliches?" (A 589) (The mythic transcends time. Do we have nothing that is immortal?). Martin Stern discusses Hofmannsthal's concern with decadence and confidence in the regeneratory effect of "mythic" thinking.[14] This certainly resembles the program of Wagner's aesthetic writings. Wagner also wanted to reform modern society through art, and myth was an essential element of his aesthetics.

Both *Elektra* and *Ariadne auf Naxos* are implicitly, in some way, playing off of Wagner's use of myth for drama. I will show this by analyzing both in conjunction with Wagner's views, as represented by *Oper und Drama* and the *Ring*. Furthermore, in both *Elektra* and *Ariadne auf Naxos*, language is, significantly enough, the decisive factor, not music. The later work shows a tension between words and music that resulted from his tenuous relationship with Strauss. In *Elektra*, it forms myth; in *Ariadne auf Naxos*, by interacting with the music, it interprets, relativizes, and thus destroys the mythic grandeur of heroic, Wagnerian, mythological opera.

LANGUAGE, MYTH, AND TRAGEDY IN *ELEKTRA*

Wagner's *Ring* tells the story behind history and, in doing so, forms the myth of world-history. For Wagner, there was an interrelationship of the inner and the outer, the subjective and the objective, myth and history. Myth, Wagner theorized, arose through the interaction of primitive individuals with their surrounding world. According to Wagner, myth makes the outer world—that is, history—understandable. Wagner even felt that myth could change history and revolutionize society. In *Elektra*, Hofmannsthal severs the link of myth to external reality in both directions. Here myth excludes and even destroys history. There is no productive interchange between the two. In contrast to the *Ring*, *Elektra* has little or nothing to do with history. Rather, it deals exclusively with itself as a mythical and a linguistic work. It is not meant to portray or, in turn, cause some real historical progression. The work turns completely inward.

Furthermore, it does this not with a narcissistic glorification of its own mythological material but, rather, with an internal contradiction, a suicidal skepticism about itself. It portrays itself with self-doubt and displays an inherent cynicism about the usefulness and viability of mythological drama. The play is thus based on an internal contradiction. *Elektra* shows that when this link with history is severed with mythological self-doubt, the result for the dramatic characters is disastrous. Furthermore, its skeptical denigration of its own medium (language) and content or raw material (myth) seems to rob the work of any instrumental, regeneratory societal value. *Elektra* seems evidence of the distrust with which Hofmannsthal, after his Chandos crisis, regarded the sterile and asocial pre-existence of the aesthete and the writer or poet.

Karl G. Esselborn discusses Hofmannsthal's use of Greek mythology with reference to the theories of Nietzsche.[15] The resemblances can be blatant. For instance, in a Nietzschean vein, in his notebooks (1893), Hofmannsthal writes, "Der tragische Grundmythos: die in Individuen zerstückelte Welt sehnt sich nach Einheit, Dionysos Zagreus will wiedergeboren werden" (A 359) (The basic tragic myth: the world that has been mangled into pieces longs for unity, Dionysos Zagreus wants to be reborn). Similarly, in 1903, he writes, "Wir müssen uns den Schauer des Mythos *neu* schaffen. Aus dem Blut wieder Schatten aufsteigen lassen" (A 443) (We must create the horror of myth anew, and let shadows arise from the blood again). Nietzsche's emphasis on the Dionysian aspect of Greece was clearly iconoclastic within the tradition of Schiller and Winckelmann, which stressed the calm grandeur and noble simplicity of the Greeks.

The discussion of *Elektra* with reference to Nietzsche's ideas about myth is definitely not a forced comparison. The bloody, horrible, Dionysian aspect of *Elektra* as a mythical drama, with its gory talk of blood sacrifices, is clearly Nietzschean. However, it should not be overlooked that this drama is also highly critical of this Dionysian use of myth. Furthermore, the text of *Elektra* can also be understood with reference to Wagner's theory of myth. The work in which Nietzsche discusses Wagner's works and myth, a treatise that had profound influence on the young Hofmannsthal, was *Die Geburt der Tragödie*.[16] This treatise might, strangely enough, account for some of the discrepancies between the *Ring* and *Elektra*.

Wagner's works are not really tragic, as they somehow transcend tragedy in a universal reconciliation, and he did not advocate a simple return to Greek myth. However, in *Die Geburt der Tragödie* Nietzsche extolled Wagner's dramas as a rebirth of Greek tragedy through their use of music and Dionysian—that is, tragic—myth. On the most superficial level, Hofmannsthal seems to be agreeing with Wagner and Nietzsche. Simply enough, he writes a mythological drama. This interpretation, though, is far too simplistic. The play by Hofmannsthal that is under discussion is actually a bitter and destructive commentary on the use of myth in drama. In many ways *Elektra* shows the unhealthy aspects and societal unproductivity of Dionysian, Greek myth in drama. When analyzed with reference to Nietzsche and Wagner, *Elektra* thus seems an ironic work indeed. *Elektra* might have been influenced by Nietzsche's writings on Wagner, but one could say that it displays an un-Wagnerian use of myth in drama. In other words, in building on or answering Nietzsche, it takes issue with or un-works Wagner.

Wagner felt that only a drama that uses the medium of music could communicate to the capacity of feeling the shared, unified world-view expressed by the mythical content, and this seems an appropriate view for a composer. Wagner does, of course, include the notion of the "fall" and redemption of language in his three-stage aesthetics.[17] The art-work of the future was to have a reconstituted musical language that appealed to the feeling as well as the understanding. But nobody would argue with the assertion that the focus of his theory is music. The essence of reconstituted language was, after all, that it would be made more musical. Language, in the former "mythical" age, was, Wagner theorized, inseparable from music. Wagner's system is progressive as well as regressive.

For Hofmannsthal, though, there is as profound an interrelationship between language and myth as Wagner saw between music and myth. Lenz remarks that the language crisis of Lord Chandos resulted from the loss of a mythical world-view.[18] The primal unity that Chandos has lost can be described as mythical. Whereas Wagner felt that music helped the drama realize and communicate its mythical nature, for Hofmannsthal, from the evidence of *Elektra*, language forms myth. Furthermore, the play removes the redemption or reconciliation that the *Ring*, still within the Romantic world-view, had. The Romantics, as is inherent in the very nature of their standard three-stage model, were intent on overcoming the dissonance and conflicts of existence and attaining some kind of harmonious reconciliation of dualities. Wagner's unworking and transcendence of tragedy clearly place him within the Romantic tradition. There is, however, no transcendence for the characters of *Elektra*. Valhalla has become the House of Atreus.

Lothar Wittmann discusses how language becomes tragic in *Elektra*.[19] In doing so, he outlines the paradox of Hofmannsthal's use of the traditional form of Greek tragedy and his personal revision of it. For Hofmannsthal, Wittmann explains, language is the criterion of humanity, for memory is intricately related to language. The paradox of this, though, is that Elektra becomes like an animal. Language becomes her tragic fate. Furthermore, Elektra extracts revenge for the murder of Agamemnon through language, and her role as prophetess, which gives her a regal quality, is tied to language. Finally, language is the medium through which Elektra's tragic sacrifice occurs. The basis of tragedy, Wittmann points out, is the existence of a mythical order that is embodied by the gods. However, in Hofmannsthal's modern reworking of this Greek myth, the gods don't care about mankind.

Lothar Wittmann discusses the interrelationship between the thematization of language in Hofmannsthal's works and their various dramatic forms. He explains that in Hofmannsthal's output, the language crisis of the "Chandos Letter" (1901) formed the transition between two different genres, the tragedy *Elektra* (1903) and *Das Bergwerk zu Falun* (1899), which critics usually interpret as representing Hofmannsthal's early "magical language."[20] That language is tragic in *Elektra* is, he argues, a result of the Chandos crisis. Chandos realized that the individual had no language. The significance of this is that, for Hofmannsthal, the realm of individuation was that of speechlessness. Language extinguishes one's humanity. For Elektra, then, the fact that deadly language would be the proof of humanity is necessarily tragic. I wish to build upon and vary Wittmann's ideas about *Elektra*. Not only is this play self-referential as regards language, but in Wittmann's analysis, he also demonstrates how it thematizes myth as well. What he sees as the paradox of Hofmannsthal's modern reworking of Greek tragedy can also be considered the plight of modern mythological drama.

The tragic nature of this play not only has to do with Hofmannsthal's ambivalent feelings toward language, but may be inevitable in its very nature as a modern-day reworking of Greek mythology in the medium of language. Because the play portrays a modern refabrication of the Greek myth that furnished the raw material, the characters are actually somehow very human. They have modern psychological depth and what can be termed a historical existence. As they exist in a twentieth-century synthetic version of mythical subject matter, the characters of this drama seem to be suspended between myth and history. Though it uses mythological raw material, the play is actually antimythological.

What Wittmann writes of the problematic of language in *Elektra* can also be said, in an analogous way, of the stance of this work toward myth. *Elektra* is both mythological and non- or antimythological at the same time. *Elektra* thematizes myth within mythical raw material. Not only does the play contain, as Wittmann points out, a strong linguistic criticism, but just as strong is its negative commentary on its own raw material, as language forms myth. *Elektra*, I propose, really dramatizes the plight or crisis of twentieth-century mythological refabrication.

Furthermore, insofar as it is a spoken play based on the Greek myth, it actually thematizes itself. The topics of myth and language are, when discussed with relation to this play, interrelated. The idea that the reflexivity of the play as regards language necessarily demythologizes the mythical raw material used as its subject matter needs to be taken further. The paradox of *Elektra* can be thought of as necessarily residing in its essence as a modern reworking of Greek tragedy or of the Greek myth that furnished the raw material. As a modern work based on Greek tragedy, it is inevitably a deconstruction of Greek tragedy. Its tragic end is inherent in the very nature of the raw material used, as well as the medium of which the play is formed.

In unworking tragedy, the *Ring* demonstrates its own revolutionary potential, overcoming tragedy in the process of depicting its own audience reception. One can say that it transcends the distinction between history and myth. Wagner wrote, in *Oper und Drama*, that myth was the beginning and end of history. The third stage of the model, it seems, is really a synthesis of the first two. In willing his own destruction, Wotan actually leads the fictional universe to a mythical Golden Age. Brünnhilde both destroys and redeems the mythological cosmos. With the audience experience of the tetralogy, Wagner hopes to mythicize modern historical society and bring about a future utopia. *Elektra*, however, is tragic, and thus it reverses Wagner's Romantic transcendence of tragedy.

Furthermore, Wagner glorifies myth. In his theoretical works, he advocates mythological drama—by definition it is, he felt, the only true drama, for it is modeled on Greek tragedy. There can be no doubt that for him it has a useful societal purpose. In contrast, *Elektra*, I propose, is an implicit critique of mythology and, by extension, mythological drama. Because it thematizes itself, being like the *Ring* a myth on the level of reflection and self-reflection, it is necessarily a tragedy. In this drama by Hofmannsthal, the tragedy is unmitigated by hopes of societal revolution. Wagner's *Ring* was supposed not only to depict the destruction of the state, but also to cause, by making analogous events happen in reality, the mythicization of history. *Elektra*, within mythological material, portrays myth as necessarily yielding to history. The play is distrustful or critical of its mythical raw material, and it also shows a language skepticism, a linguistic critique. As a spoken play based on Greek tragedy, the work is a tragedy about tragedy. The self-referentiality of *Elektra* as a work of language that uses mythological subject matter is, as the play is critical of both myth and language, lethal.

Elektra's opening monologue both thematizes and practices the idea of ritual repetition. At the same time every day Elektra wails for her slain father. The second attendant explains, "Ist doch ihre Stunde, / die Stunde wo sie um den Vater heult, / dass alle Wände schallen"[21] (It is her hour, the hour that she howls for her father, so that all walls resound). Elektra herself is conscious of the temporal correspondence. She addresses Agamemnon with, "Es ist die Stunde, unsre Stunde ists! / Die Stunde, wo sie dich geschlachtet haben" (E 190) (It is our hour, the hour that they slaughtered you). The monologue also encompasses the past and the future tenses. Elektra repeatedly relives the murder of Agamemnon and envisions the day of revenge. She even anticipates a second coming of Agamemnon.

The description of Agamemnon's return is almost apocalyptic, as is the end of *Götterdämmerung*. This all exists, however, solely in Elektra's mind. The end of the play shows the vast and appalling difference between Elektra's anticipations and external reality. In her monologue, Elektra cries, insisting that her father will one day return, "Vater! dein Tag wird kommen! Von den Sternen / stürzt alle Zeit herab, so wird das Blut / aus hundert Kehlen stürzen auf dein Grab!" (E 191) (Father! Your day will come! Time will fall from the heavens and blood will fall upon your grave from a hundred throats!). Elektra then describes an elaborate, bloody, Dionysian feast, at which the family will slaughter dogs and horses and dance around Agamemnon's grave.

In discussing Elektra's monologue, Wittmann explains that through language, Elektra can transcend time. In her monologue, Elektra evokes the past and the future. When she communes with her dead father, she is in touch with this world-order that transcends "natural time" and that was violated by the murder of Agamemnon. In Elektra's monologue, Wittmann explains, time stands still. As opposed to Wittmann, I would expand upon the subjective facet of this monologue. Elektra has a mythical world-view. The figure of Agamemnon has clearly assumed mythical significance for Elektra. The cyclical nature of her outlook is specifically mythical. After all, one of the definitions of mythology is that in a mythical world-view prototypical events are considered mirrored in earthly reality, and all temporal existence is seen as the repetition of these primal events.

Thus myth becomes a theme of *Elektra*. The title figure, like Wagner and Hofmannsthal, creates a myth on the level of reflection. She mythicizes history. Elektra, as she herself admits, cannot forget the past. But the problem goes much deeper than that. For Elektra, a real, historical event (the slaughter of Agamemnon) has become mythological. It was an event of the relatively recent past; she remembers her father. She has lifted it out of time and made it regulatory. This supposedly mythical event rules Elektra's life. She sees history as an eternal recurrence. She has even kept the ax with which Agamemnon was killed, almost as a relic. With the second use of it, to murder the murderers, Elektra hopes to reverse time and bring back her dead father.

When she hears noise inside the palace, she even imagines that murders are being committed. Chrysothemis urges her to leave the past behind her, but to that Elektra replies, "Vorbei? Da drinnen gehts aufs neue los!" (E 196) (Past? Inside it is happening again!). It is as though the murder of Agamemnon is not, for Elektra, a single incident in the past. And Elektra wants to change history at its second occurrence. She resolves, "Diesmal will ich dabei sein! / Nicht so wie damals. Diesmal bin ich stark. / Ich werfe mich auf sie, ich reiss das Beil / aus ihrer Hand, ich schwing es über ihr!" (E 197) (This time I want to be present! Not like last time. This time I will be strong. I will throw myself upon her, grab the ax from her hand, and swing it over her). For Elektra, the murder of Agamemnon recurs in history, like a mythical event. Wagner's *Ring* is a cycle; Elektra expects a strict repetition of the past and thereby a direct 180-degree reversion and regression.

The play questions its mythological material, reducing myth to a purely imaginary product, a psychic creation. In *Elektra*, Hofmannsthal implicitly and paradoxically (given that the raw material is mythical) demythologizes myth. The characters merely make reference to the gods; there is no evidence that these powers have any ontological status. The gods are, in *Elektra*, a system of explanation, regulative fictions, necessary lies. Nothing supernatural happens in the drama. Gods do not appear in the play, which seems to hint that the gods are merely rhetorical entities and purely linguistic creations. As such, they are suspect.

When she encounters Elektra, Klytemnestra apostrophizes the gods. Thus she attributes her own bad conscience to the gods, and sees her own unruly daughter as a punishment of the gods, though the psychical and familial situation she bemoans is really her own doing, as it results from her past misdeeds. Klytemnestra has actually brought her misfortune upon herself. Klytemnestra laments, "O Götter, warum liegt ihr so auf mir? / Warum verwüstet ihr mich so?" (E 199) (O gods, why do you oppress me so? Why do you destroy me this way?). Klytemnestra describes a pathological weakness and lack of energy. One suspects that the figures of *Elektra* merely like to think that the gods exist. In *Elektra*, myth doesn't comment on history. It comments on its creator and his or her psychology. The comment is a critical one. It says that myth is pathological.

The play actually depicts a pathetically demythologized mythical world. The gods of this world are obviously Feuerbachian projections of the characters portrayed. In this manner, the work recapitulates and portrays its own performance. In *Elektra*, myth is portrayed as being subjective to the point of being meaningless and dangerous. Hofmannsthal thus gives a psychogram of myth. The gods are portrayed (or not portrayed, for they do not appear in the drama) as Feuerbachian projections, mere figments of the imaginations of humans. Myth is reduced, that is, to psychology. With the tragic ending of the play, Hofmannsthal seems to be saying that myth cannot have revolutionary value. Rather, it has little real value at all. It seems more harmful than good. From the evidence of Elektra's mythological world-view, it is obvious that myth can be quite dangerous when it causes one to lose touch with reality.

The *Ring* is essentially a revolutionary work. Mythical works, Wagner felt, could grant one human autonomy and revolutionary power. For Wagner, according to his revolutionary interpretation and modern reworking of Greek tragedy in *Oper und Drama*, "fate" is really nothing metaphysical but, rather, a very powerful, societally contrived figment of the imagination. Recognizing it as such allows one to overcome it and achieve a revolutionary kind of consciousness. From the evidence of *Elektra*, freeing the characters from metaphysical foundations produces an ontological crisis and a grim destiny indeed, not revolutionary hopes. The play depicts pathological states of mind and tragic events, all of which not only refer to, but also are determined by, its mythological subject matter or raw material, which the play thematizes. Elektra's revolutionary consciousness or second unconsciousness is, in the realm of this play, deadly. If myth is really psychology, and language forms myth, the conclusion must be that myth is pathological.

Hofmannsthal's personal revision of Greek tragedy, because he places responsibility for one's actions with the individual human being, is not the only thing that necessarily demythologizes the mythological world-view that is the essence of tragedy. That the play also self-referentially thematizes language, in doing so reducing myth to language, creates another paradox and thus further deconstructs myth and demythologizes the originally mythological raw material used as subject matter for the play. The dramatic characters may talk about the gods. Language, though, is shown to be a means of deception. Both language and myth are, in the world of *Elektra*, potentially lethal forces. The self-referentiality of *Elektra* as a work of language that uses mythological subject matter is deadly. Ultimately the content undermines the vehicle that conveys it.

Shortly before Orestes' return, practically coincidental with it, a story is reported that states he is dead. When Orestes arrives, he keeps his identity secret, thus dissimulating. In her conversation with him, before he reveals his identity to her, Elektra, similarly, lies and tells him she is a servant of the house. The characters seem to be pathetically groping around in the dark, unsure of whether they are in a modern or a genuinely mythological work. Their lines often seem to be instances of Romantic irony, that is, comments on the fictionality of the work of art in which they exist. The dramatic figures seem to comment on the possible interpretation of the linguistic work in which they find themselves. In this manner, the work thematizes itself. The dramatic action arises out of its raw material, which it deconstructively discourses upon. The end of the play is necessarily tragic. Mythology is problematic, indeed. As a modern work and a spoken drama based on Greek tragedy, *Elektra* is actually a deconstruction of Greek tragedy.

Because the characters are somehow human, with a modern psychological depth, the mythical atmosphere seems to be stifling for them. There seems to be a destructive or deconstructive interaction between the mythological raw material of this play and the verbal medium of which it is formed. It is almost as though the choice of the mythical raw material in which the dramatic characters exist had somehow made the verbal medium as it is used in this play both exalted and deadly, magic and at the same time inadequate and futile. The words of the play, though they can conjure up an entire world, are somehow out of whack and, at their worst, fatal.

Epistemological uncertainty is surely epidemic in the House of Atreus. The characters deceive each other and even themselves. Klytemnestra laments, lapsing into total solipsism, "Was die Wahrheit ist, / das bringt kein Mensch heraus. Niemand auf Erden / weiss über irgendein verborgnes Ding / die Wahrheit" (E 201) (Nobody can find out what truth is. Nobody on earth knows the truth about anything). The antimythological sentiment of this mythological drama illustrates this dictum beautifully. As *Elektra* implicitly problematizes both myth and language in a spoken play based on mythological raw material, its tragic outcome is sealed from the very beginning; indeed, it is implicit in its very nature. Not only is the play paradoxical, but insofar as it is a spoken play based on mythology, it is, one could say, mythologically and linguistically self-destructive or deconstructive. The paradox of its very nature causes it to turn tragically against itself.

Chrysothemis seems to be the only main character who speaks with total veracity. Thus it somehow seems appropriate that she has the last line of the play, crying for Orestes. She lives in the state of existence, and therefore she is trapped in the play, in the House of Atreus and in the mythological material. Chrysothemis wants to marry and have children, which signifies the epitome of "existence" in Hofmannsthal's works. When she exclaims, "Ich will hinaus!" (E 196) (I want to get out of here!), it is almost as though she were talking with Romantic irony, referring to her literary existence, speaking, that is, as a consciously fictitious character. She says to Elektra, "Wärst nicht du, / sie liessen uns hinaus" (E 193) (If it weren't for you, they would let us out of here). The destruction of the mythological material, that is, the end of the play, is the (dubious and nonviable) liberation that she is longing for.

It is almost as though the entire play were from the perspective of the title figure, or as though it showed the world she conjured up for herself. The name of the work is, after all, her name. When thus interpreted, *Elektra* portrays its own performance. Elektra somehow becomes an image of the playwright who wrote the work. Hofmannsthal makes a mythical work out of language (by writing the play). Elektra does the same thing within the play. Klytemnestra praises Elektra's verbal abilities. Klytemnestra laments that Aegisthus reproaches her, and she has nothing to answer. "Aber du hast Worte. / Du könntest vieles sagen, was mir nützt. / Wenn auch ein Wort nichts weiter ist!" (E 203) (But you have words. You could say many things that would be useful to me. Even if a word is nothing more than that!). Thus Elektra seems to stand above the work. She apparently has a privileged position with regard to the dramatic action. In this way, the drama comments bitterly and tragically upon itself as a modern reworking of tragedy. It is almost as though the fact that Elektra seems to have conjured up the mythical raw material in which the dramatic characters exist had somehow made the verbal medium as it is used in this play inadequate, futile.

The rest of the characters may think they are in a genuine Greek myth or an authentic Greek tragedy. Elektra, however, seems to somehow know that they are not. Elektra says to Klytemnestra, "Die Götter sind beim Nacht-mahl! so wie damals, / als du den Vater würgtest, sitzen sie / beim Nachtmahl und sind taub für jedes Röcheln!" (E 210) (The gods are out to dinner! Just as they were when you murdered my father, they are away and they are deaf to our pleas!). Thus Elektra seems to see through the "mythical" facade of the play. She apparently realizes that it is a theater set. Thus, as she invented it, she also eventually makes it crumble. Elektra deconstructs from the inside a mythological universe that is an imaginary, Feuerbachian projection. She sees through myth at the beginning of the play and escapes it (tragically) at the end.

The House of Atreus, one could even, by extension, say the mythical subject matter of this linguistic work, is a prison. Chrysothemis runs from one empty room to another in an anxious and futile attempt to escape from Elektra's sick trap. In contrast, myth was, for Wagner, a means of liberation, something positive, a beneficial force. Wagner intended his mythical music-drama to regenerate modern society and thus free mankind from the oppression of the (internalized) "state" and custom. Chrysothemis says to Elektra,

Wär nicht dein Hass,
dein schlafloses unbändiges Gemüt,
vor dem sie zittern, ah, so liessen sie
uns ja heraus aus diesem Kerker, Schwester!
Ich will heraus! (E 193)

If it were not for your hate, your wild sleepless character that makes them tremble,
they would let us out of this prison, sister! I want to get out of here!

The aesthetic program of Wagner's *Ring* dictates a productive exchange and
dialectical interrelationship between myth and life, art and reality. For the
characters in Hofmannsthal's *Elektra*, though, myth is a kind of sterile
pre-existence that hinders their participation in the flux of life.

Elektra needs to break out of mythical existence, which she does when
Orestes murders Klytemnestra and Aegisthus. It is no coincidence that this
is the end of the verbal art-work. At the end of the play, the events depicted
spring open the dramatic form, and it shatters. The antagonism between
the content and the raw material that carries it determines that the play
must end when it does. Elektra's veil of illusion has been lifted. Esselborn
discusses how Hofmannsthal's Greek dramas dissolve the traditional dramatic form, for instance, plot and dialogue.[22] I argue that, from the evidence
of *Elektra*, they also, in a very subtle way, dissolve myth. This happens in
the very portrayal of the mythical content, as it is dematerialized and
psychologized, and also in the plot of the drama itself. Wittmann interprets
the play as having a tragic contradiction. I see this as having to do with its
ambivalent stance toward its own mythical raw material; the content is
totally at odds with the vehicle that conveys it.

With the tragic ending, Hofmannsthal is vehemently denying any correspondence between history and myth. It is as though he were saying that
it is not viable to form myths about history, the outer world, one's world,
and one's past. This causes, he seems to say, a dangerous confusion of myth
and history. Bennett discusses Elektra's tragic situation of knowing the truth
and thus not being it. She is aware of a totality, but she does not possess it,
only at the end, when she (silently) dances.[23] According to Tarot's scheme,
she is living in some kind of pre-existence. The tragic ending is the inevitable result of the doubt that the play expresses about its own medium and
subject matter. The *Ring* shows the revolutionary potential of myth. *Elektra*
reflects sarcastically and cynically on the idea of mythical drama, blatantly
showing that it is skeptical of myth ever changing history.

The work is based on a paradox, a contradiction. It undermines its own
premises. The mythological material forms the frame for Elektra's mythical
world-view. At the end of the play, when Elektra's myth collapses (into
history), so does she. The apocalyptic anticipations of Elektra are disappointed. The murder of the murderers does not bring back her dead father.
The end of the play is paradoxical, and Elektra's death is deconstructive.

The content undercuts the raw material within which this content is portrayed. Chrysothemis cries that before she dies, she wants to live. She would rather be dead than living a life that was not life. However, entry into life is, for Elektra, death. Her only reality is myth. With the fulfillment of her vengeance, the reason for her existence (or, rather, pre-existence) is negated.

For Wagner, the mythological work of art should interact profitably with the outside world. The *Ring* was supposed to regenerate modern society. The *Ring* not only mythologically portrays history but is also supposed to change and mythicize history. Wagner's theory as set forward in *Oper und Drama* is based, broadly speaking, on an affective aesthetics of audience reception. The failure of Elektra's regressive hopes may be a comment of Hofmannsthal on what he might see as the reactionary intent to return to a mythical Golden Age by the use of mythical drama that portrays its own aesthetic program. Time progresses forward, not backward, as the Marschallin well knows. Mythical timelessness is simply not a viable alternative.

At the beginning of her opening monologue, Elektra laments being all alone. The plight of the solitary, dejected title figure of *Elektra* is symptomatic of the mythological nature of the work. The gods are absent and silent, Agamemnon is not one of them, and the humans are pitifully abandoned. The resurrection of Greek mythology following Nietzsche's recommendation in the age of Neoromanticism was, from the evidence of Hofmannsthal's *Elektra*, not totally successful. Myth in the twentieth century just becomes further broken than it was in previous modern eras. Furthermore, the theme of fathers and daughters links Wagner and Hofmannsthal here. But Brünnhilde's playful "Hojotoho" has become, in the twentieth century, Elektra's howling lament for Agamemnon.

THE HERMENEUTIC DECONSTRUCTION OF MYTH IN *ARIADNE AUF NAXOS*

I have shown how *Elektra* implicitly raises doubts about mythological drama. But it does so fully with language, being a spoken drama. In *Elektra* language formed myth for the world of the play as play, and language expressed myth for the figures within the play. Hofmannsthal was, however, obviously ambivalent toward language when he wrote *Elektra*. As the play is evidence of a problematic stance toward language, with language being portrayed as both exalted and deadly, priestly and tragic, this situation set the scene for dramatic mythological disaster.

Ariadne auf Naxos[24] shows that Hofmannsthal now sees myth as useful to life. The use of words and music in this opera, however, makes what is supposedly a heroic mythological opera laugh at Wagner himself. *Ariadne auf Naxos* dissects the *Ring* in various ways. In *Ariadne auf Naxos*, the tension between language and music subtly dismantles the Wagnerian mythological and heroic ideal. Mythical opera, the work seems to show, needs music, but insofar as myth is reduced to metaphor, it is undone and thus "redeemed" by language. In the process, the words gently and subtly ridicule the holy art of music, which supposedly unifies the various art forms and creates an aesthetic harmony, for the poet may very well, despite his words, be laughing at the composer.

Thus, myth has a correct and an incorrect use. It is applicable to life, but not in a serious, heroic, or "Wagnerian" way. It must be minimized and, surprisingly enough, trivialized. Elektra's belief in an ahistorical, mythical world-view was portrayed as dangerous. Myth cannot be taken "as is," at face value. The Wagnerian transcendence or mythological deconstruction of tragedy must be replaced by another kind of redemption that relativizes myth and makes it blatantly comical. The Wagnerian, heroic ideal needs to be qualified in order to be at all viable. Parts of Strauss' music are clearly within the Wagnerian tradition, but this tradition is relativized and thus drastically changed by the work as a whole. Hofmannsthal's scenario is definitely not Wagnerian in an unqualified way, nor is the "play within the play" really a heroic opera. In general, the entire joint collaboration is Wagnerian only in isolated elements. On the whole *Ariadne auf Naxos* is a Wagner parody.

The work is explicitly self-referential in several ways. *Ariadne auf Naxos* is complex in what I would call its reflective and hermeneutic nature. For one thing, it is outwardly split into two parts, separated by an intermission. The Prologue, as Barbara Könneker notes, explicates the opera within the opera.[25] The implicit Romantic irony of *Elektra* is in *Ariadne auf Naxos* explicit. In *Ariadne auf Naxos*, myth is again re-created, this time a stage higher, on the next level of reflection. The text is explicitly reflexive. The characters of the Prologue know they will be in, or watching, a performance. Just having a fictional Composer onstage who has supposedly written the entertainment that is to form the latter part of the work and then having this opera within the opera rewritten and improvised by another work that represents another art form are, after all, Romantically ironic to the deconstructionist utmost.

The work, when taken in its entirety, is a performance of a performance. Insofar as the work as a whole loops back on itself and thematizes its own performance, that is, the planned performance, and also the interpretation of this performance, of the story of Ariadne and Bacchus, the work within the work, the microcosm of the work as a whole, nominally connected with the entire work through the same name, the work has explicit Romantic irony. The work, in fact, conforms beautifully to Bernhard Heimrich's definition of Romantic irony. According to Heimrich, the fiction as a whole consists of two levels, appearance and reality, the fictional level (what happens within the fiction) and the objective level (e.g., a play is being performed onstage). Romantic irony consists of a reduction, which occurs when an element of the fictional reality refers to the objective reality, and an improvisation (because the reduction is a break in the fictionality, an uncalculated moment).[26] Accordingly, *Ariadne auf Naxos* is explicitly a performance, and it is no coincidence that the performance within the performance—in other words, the opera that is staged within the opera—is improvised.

Furthermore, the work contains clearly different frames of reference, which complicate things more by not corresponding strictly to the two parts of the "frame" and the work that is later performed. The Prologue shows what is going on "behind the scenes" of a performance. It takes place in the home of the richest man in Vienna, a Straussian or aesthetically self-referential version of Valhalla and a far cry indeed from the House of Atreus. The opera that is finally performed takes place on a Naxos that is located within this Viennese home. The settings relativize each other. The myth of Ariadne and Bacchus is blatantly juxtaposed with both the quasi-reality of the affluent Viennese society (the artistic depiction of the audience, that is) and the banality of the troupe of comedians led by Zerbinetta. Critics have noted that the structure of the work becomes part of the means by which the message of the work is conveyed.[27]

One can envision the work as a series of mirrors within mirrors. Art is shown as art, with the Prologue, in Romantic irony, showing the backstage scene. There are, furthermore, two forms of "plays within the play": the mythological opera and the commedia dell'arte performance. The different art forms relativize each other. Moreover, the art forms not only contrast with each other but really interpenetrate. Just as words and music play off of each other and intersect within music-drama as a whole, the two forms of entertainment originally planned within the fiction of the whole opera to occur consecutively take place simultaneously. The work that is finally performed is no simple one, indeed. The play within the play is originally intended as a heroic mythological opera, but it acquires, in the course of being performed, commedia dell'arte interruptions and a happy ending. Thus its heroic mythological nature becomes dubious.

Furthermore, the Romantic irony is also of a specifically hermeneutic nature. The work thematizes both its own performance and its own interpretation, in particular, the interpretation of its mythological subject matter. Thus *Ariadne auf Naxos* does not merely dramatize myth; rather, it primarily thematizes the interpretation of myth. One can describe the work as an exercise in mythological hermeneutics. In this manner, *Ariadne auf Naxos* undoes the heroic Wagnerian mythological music-drama while still being seemingly Wagnerian in places. It thereby thematizes and answers the questions about myth and life that *Elektra* implicitly raised.

In their exchange of letters, both Hofmannsthal and Strauss commented on the lack of plot, action, and external happenings in the work under discussion. Hofmannsthal admitted that the action was thin, simple, as compared to the traditional heroic opera (letter to Strauss of 25 May 1911).[28]

There is, he agreed, no peripeteia, no dramatic turning-point in the work. In another letter to Strauss, Hofmannsthal wrote that the action that transpired between Ariadne and Bacchus was psychological, inner (letter of Hofmannsthal to Strauss of 28 May 1911).[29] That the real drama is internal and psychological is due to the analytic nature of the work. In referring to itself, the work thematizes mythological refabrication. The real action is the exercise in mythological hermeneutics and interpretative intertextuality. Unlike *Elektra*, though, this work turns inward to eventually overcome its own dualities and end happily.

Zerbinetta and her cohorts form a bridge between the two parts, the prologue and the "opera within the opera." Zerbinetta is an ambiguous, protean figure. In the prologue, she is a figure of art, a comic actress; in the opera "Ariadne," she is a figure of life, intruding into the (originally) heroic opera and bringing it down to the level of real-life or history. Critics have noted that Zerbinetta is the only character who does not change name and function in the opera itself.[30] As the Dancing Master says, she is at ease in every situation, for she plays only herself. Thus, Zerbinetta functions to mediate between history and myth. She does this in a hermeneutic way, by interpreting the story of Ariadne and Bacchus.

Furthermore, the different art forms within the fiction of the work as a whole have different musical styles. At the home of the richest man in Vienna, the music is a mixture of styles. One hears disjointed snippets of melody. For instance, the Composer, between declamatory outbursts, conceives melody for his "Ariadne" opera. The Major-Domo even has a speaking role, indicating the opposition between the realistic world that he (along with the richest man in Vienna) represents and the idealistic world of the artist.[31] The characters of (and in) the two kinds of "plays within the play" are characterized by contrasting musical styles. Even a nonmusicologist should be able to discern the different kinds of music in the work. Strauss' score contains distinctively different musical levels.[32] In this manner, different tonal worlds characterize the different art forms, the comical figures and the "opera seria." Ariadne and Bacchus represent the style of the heroic, Wagnerian opera. In contrast, Zerbinetta and her companions, stock figures from the "commedia dell'arte" tradition who represent the world of pleasure and lightheartedness, are characterized by vocal and dance ensembles. Zerbinetta sings coloratura, and her troupe sings strophic songs.

The sound of Zerbinetta's world contrasts with the more formal, intricate, and heroic vocal style of Ariadne's music. Harps, percussion, trumpet, trombone, and harmonium, which were significant elements in Ariadne's scene, do not appear in the scene that follows hers. Rather, the overtly vulgar-sounding piano, an element of Viennese cabaret music, provides the main support of the voices and the orchestra and characterizes them as belonging to a crass, mundane world that exists on the lowest level of triviality. The use of the heroic Wagnerian style for Ariadne and Bacchus is thus deceptive and ironic. To draw the analogy with Wagnerian drama because of the music of Ariadne and Bacchus neglects the fact that this heroic music is relativized by the other tonal world. Furthermore, the mere fact that *Ariadne auf Naxos* comprises various musical and artistic styles makes this work directly opposed to the Wagnerian tradition.[33]

For instance, the opera is written in set pieces (as opposed to the Wagnerian style of endless melody). *Ariadne auf Naxos* contains clearly marked musico-poetical forms of recitative, aria, and various ensembles. Thus, through its structure the music underscores the dramatic contrasts of Hofmannsthal's text. Strauss referred to the "play of forms" ("Formenspiel") and the "architecture garden" ("Architektur-Garten") that he was writing (letter of Strauss to Hofmannsthal of 27 May 1911).[34] The sectional independence of the work requires the almost total rejection of a Wagnerian type of motive system. The opera has only a sparse use of melodic motives. In *Ariadne auf Naxos*, melodic motives occur, but they are limited in overall application.

The music for *Ariadne auf Naxos* represents the turning-away from Wagner and the embracing of a Neoclassical musical language, just as the Classical mythology that supplied the subject matter contrasts with the Germanic folklore that Wagner used as source material for his music-dramas. The orchestra is sized down. The work is scored for a chamber orchestra of Mozartian proportions. With the music of *Ariadne auf Naxos*, Strauss sought a suitable modern imitation of a French Baroque opera orchestra. He did not attempt to imitate a seventeenth-century ensemble. Rather, he discovered in the older musical practice the basis of a very new orchestral sound, one of the early twentieth-century Neoclassical adaptations of the orchestra. It even seems appropriate that Strauss uses the clarinet, celesta, and harmonium, instruments that would have been historically out of place in a seventeenth-century orchestra. The anachronism of certain instruments in a seventeenth-century orchestra can be considered analogous to, or the aural counterpart of, the modern reconstruction of myth that the opera portrays.

Ariadne auf Naxos also contains some of the same themes as does *Elektra*, which facilitates the comparison I am undertaking. With regard to the themes of remembering and forgetting, Ariadne and Zerbinetta resemble Elektra and Chrysothemis respectively. Ariadne, like Elektra, would at first rather not forget her past. In contrast, Zerbinetta, like Chrysothemis, is better adjusted, and can easily adapt to new situations. Forgetting the past comes naturally to them. It is almost as though Elektra were watching her own drama, and talking backstage with Chrysothemis about it. One could say that *Ariadne auf Naxos* has the same themes as *Elektra*, but a different "textuality." If myth explains the world, and *Elektra* explains the individual course of life, showing the dangers of myth, *Ariadne auf Naxos*, I propose, explains *Elektra*. One can picture the earlier drama as being, so to speak, unfolded.

In the "Ariadne Letter" of Hofmannsthal to Strauss, the poet draws an analogy between Elektra and Ariadne, on one hand, and, on the other, Chrysothemis and Zerbinetta.[35] The main theme of the work, Hofmannsthal explains to Strauss, is the problem of fidelity. Elektra and Ariadne hang onto the past; Chrysothemis and Zerbinetta see life as transformation and constant change. Hofmannsthal notes in this letter that at the end of *Ariadne auf Naxos*, the two groups of characters, the gods and the humans, are united by irony. They see the ending of the opera within the opera differently, and thus they fail to understand each other's viewpoint.

Ariadne auf Naxos also takes the thematization of language one step further than did *Elektra*. Whereas the former work, a spoken play, thematized language, *Ariadne auf Naxos* thematizes both language and music. In doing so, however, it shows its own complexity. Furthermore, it explicitly thematizes mythological hermeneutics. For instance, Zerbinetta tries to cheer Ariadne with music. She instructs her clowns, "Versucht es mit Musik!"[36] (Try it with music!). Therefore she advocates the psychologically therapeutic value of music. One of the nymphs is even named "Echo," which just emphasizes that the work explicitly thematizes opera, music, and musical styles. Its thematization of both language and music is not the only way in which *Ariadne auf Naxos* goes beyond *Elektra*. What seems to be a thematization of various communicative mediums becomes rather a discourse on hermeneutics. Nobody would deny that interpretation is essential to understanding. When Zerbinetta sings her long solo, Ariadne receives a lesson in hermeneutics. The work of art as a whole deals with its own performance and interpretation. Zerbinetta is both in a performance and watching a performance. This is one of the ways in which the opera as a whole thematizes its own performance.

That the theme of language is extended to that of understanding and interpretation is made explicit when Zerbinetta, commenting on Ariadne's refusal to listen to her instructive aria, states, "Ja, es scheint, die Dame und ich sprechen verschiedene Sprachen" (Yes, it seems the lady and I speak different languages.) Harlequin agrees, "Es scheint so" (It seems so). They are really not discussing language per se as much as understanding. Zerbinetta answers Harlequin, expressing her wish that Ariadne just finally be able to understand her viewpoint: "Es ist die Frage, ob sie nicht schliesslich lernt, sich in der meinigen auszudrücken" (AN 208) (The question is whether or not she will finally learn to express herself in mine). The two women see and interpret things differently. Thus, *Ariadne auf Naxos* functions, one could say, on a further level of reflection and self-reflection. As though it had mirrors in mirrors, the work thematizes its own performance in various ways. Moreover, the later work shows the process of mythological refabrication in the medium of opera.

The aria that the Composer sings at the end of the prologue is obviously a central point for this ironic reflexivity of the entire opera. This aria seems a simple and beautiful exaltation of music. But this is much more than a praising of the holy powers of music. The Composer extols the unifying powers of music, thus justifying the blend of forms in the opera and, in essence, providing a kind of internal commentary on the work in which he exists. The aria of the Composer deals, in fact, with the relative merits of words and music. He sings, "Die Dichter unterlegen ja recht gute Worte, recht gute" (AN 199) (The poets have good words, really good ones), but music is a holy art. Thus, the work self-referentially says that one of the two primary mediums out of which it is formed is clearly superior to the other.

This is, however, no simple matter indeed; the issue is a complex hermeneutic one. It entails how one interprets the interaction of words and music in the opera, and how this interplay of the various communicative mediums and art forms affects the meaning of the work as a whole. Not only is the work as a whole a mix of music and words that deals explicitly with music and words, but *Ariadne auf Naxos* has a basic (and ironic) contradiction that it, unlike *Elektra*, overcomes within itself. This contradiction has to do with the complex and lopsided (even at times ironic) interaction of words and music in the work. The aria of the Composer extols music over words. The work as a whole, though, undercuts and questions this philosophy, just as the grandiose, heroic work of the Composer is relativized by Zerbinetta and her troupe of comedians.

Critics have discussed Wagner's *Ring* as a myth about the end of myth. The Norns sing, "Zu End ewiges Wissen!" (MD 757) (Eternal Wisdom is at an end!). Carl Dahlhaus, furthermore, writes that in Wagner's *Ring*, myth is restored only to be destroyed.[37] The same can be said, in a very different way, of Hofmannsthal's use of myth in *Ariadne auf Naxos*. Hofmannsthal, however, takes the process one step further and turns it against Wagner himself. With *Ariadne auf Naxos*, Hofmannsthal undoes Wagner's *Ring* and destroys myth in a very different way. Unlike Wagner, Hofmannsthal does not present a huge conflagration that destroys his mythological universe. Instead, he uses the means at his disposal that he was best at using. Being a poet and playwright, that is, most at home with the medium of words, he both glorifies and destroys myth, builds a mythical opera scene, and proceeds in turn to cut it down, despite Strauss' glorious music, through language.

In "Ariadne," as in *Elektra*, the world-view of the protagonist seems to fit, reflect, or even determine the material in which she exists as mythical. Myth is always , it seems, subjective. If one interprets something as mythical, or sees one's world with relation to myth, then myth exists as such. In other words, myth is actually psychology. Ariadne, like Elektra, clearly belongs in mythical material, and for the same literary-psychological reason. Not only is she a conventionally mythical figure, but it fits her state of mind. Her world-view is mythical, for she resists change. The past determines her life and her self-definition, as Elektra's did hers. This has profound interpretative possibilities for this work of art. Myth, one suspects, may very well be more a state of mind than any concrete stage setting. As Strauss and Hofmannsthal realized, the drama is internal, psychological. The real action is the exercise in mythological hermeneutics and interpretative intertextuality. Unlike *Elektra*, though, this work turns inward to overcome its own dualities and end happily.

Zerbinetta, however, lives in the present. She expounds a philosophy of "life," that is, of constant change, metaphorical death and transfiguration. Zerbinetta has a more healthy world-view and mode of existence. Her aria is not really a monologue but, rather, a showpiece in vocal virtuosity, a lesson in romantic transfiguration of the most banal kind, and a display of vocal pyrotechnics, an apotheosis of formal, stylistic devices. Zerbinetta's aria is in the coloratura style, and it contains a recitative, aria (in two parts), and rondo (with variations).[38]

Ariadne's monologue, which is presented in several large sections, tells her private subjective myth, just as Elektra's told hers. Ariadne reflects on her past with Theseus: "Ein Schönes war, hiess Theseus - Ariadne" (It was beautiful, and it was called Theseus-Ariadne). She exclaims, "Warum weiss ich davon? ich will vergessen!" (Why do I still remember it? I want to forget!). However, forgetting is hard for her, as it is for Elektra. Furthermore, like Elektra, Ariadne wants to turn back the clock. She resolves, "Ja, dies muss ich finden: / Das Mädchen, das ich war!" (AN 201) (Yes, I must find the girl that I once was!). Ariadne, like Elektra, evidently has a lesson to learn from the Marschallin. However, Ariadne finally learns it, comically enough, from Zerbinetta.

Like Elektra, Ariadne also has a vision of some kind of redemption, as she projects her story into the future. In her main aria, after she expresses her present abject misery, Ariadne describes her longed-for future, the arrival of Hermes, presenting the story or myth that will be revised by Zerbinetta and the course of the action. The emphasis on how intertwined the names of Ariadne and Theseus were clearly plays off of similar lines in the second act of *Tristan und Isolde*, as well as in the Siegfried-Brünnhilde duet in the prologue of *Götterdämmerung*. The Wagnerian influence in this opera is, however, much more pervasive than this.

Oper und Drama demonstrates the process of mythological explication, as it builds the art-work of the future by telling and interpreting myth, that of Oedipus and Antigone, thus showing the historical relativity of myth and the necessity of refabricating it to comment on history. *Ariadne auf Naxos* seems a parody of *Oper und Drama* and thus of Wagner's aesthetic program that the *Ring* demonstrates. It seems to be humorously demonstrating the narration and interpretation of myth, such as the Oedipus myth, that Wagner presents in this treatise. In doing so, *Ariadne auf Naxos* also thematizes and, in doing so, parodies the notion of mythology as metaphor.

Hofmannsthal seems to agree with Wagner that mythological drama needs music as its only appropriate form of expression, and that such music must sound heroic and grandiose. However, *Ariadne auf Naxos* unworks myth through language. In this opera, myth is reduced to metaphor, both on the level of the entire story and on the minute, linguistic level of the concepts themselves. The Wagner parody that results is comical. In *Ariadne auf Naxos*, because myth is reduced to (linguistic) metaphor, language undercuts the music. When Zerbinetta's commentary has trivialized the story of Ariadne, the music is no longer as grandiose as it may seem when taken alone. The metaphorical nature of myth, as shown in *Ariadne auf Naxos*, trivializes it, being in the mouth of the frivolous Zerbinetta.

Furthermore, *Ariadne auf Naxos* and the *Ring* embody directly opposed relationships between history and myth. In the *Ring*, myth has been refabricated to comment on history. In *Ariadne auf Naxos*, history explains myth. Furthermore, the *Ring* was supposed to affect and revolutionize history. Insofar as Zerbinetta applies the story of Ariadne to real-life, *Ariadne auf Naxos* shows history rewriting, revising, and changing myth. Zerbinetta gives a down-to-earth interpretation of Ariadne's story that applies the myth to a real-life situation. Furthermore, the tragic outcome of the story is somehow averted, and Ariadne follows Zerbinetta's advice and takes Bacchus as her new lover. Wagner wanted to mythicize history. *Ariadne auf Naxos* ends with what one could call "historicized" myth.

Nietzsche saw Wagner's dramas as the rebirth of the tragic myth from the spirit of music. I suggest that in *Ariadne auf Naxos*, Hofmannsthal also parodies and undoes Nietzsche as well as Wagner. One could also conjecture that Hofmannsthal's choice of Bacchus in the text was at least partly due to the role that Nietzsche ascribed to the Dionysian god and thus by extension to music, in *Die Geburt der Tragödie* in the Wagnerian rebirth of tragedy. In this manner, too, *Ariadne auf Naxos* is a Wagnerian parody via Nietzsche's early Wagner reception, as well as a revision of Hofmannsthal's earlier thoughts about myth. Unlike in *Elektra*, where myth was tragic, in *Ariadne auf Naxos*, it's comical. *Ariadne auf Naxos* shows the destruction of the tragic myth by the device of language.

Ariadne auf Naxos shows the process of mythological refabrication in opera. The work, when taken in its entirety, actually evolves itself, just as the prelude to *Rheingold* gradually generates the music that stands for the Rhine out of a single chord. But in *Ariadne auf Naxos*, this process is, in literary-critical terms, one could say reflexive or Romantically ironic. One could say that Hofmannsthal has "aestheticized" tragedy or mythological refabrication. In *Ariadne auf Naxos*, the characters are interpreting and rewriting a work of art. The Prologue deals with the genesis of the performance to be put on. As the Composer, Music Teacher, and Dancing Master tell the story, Zerbinetta interjects her comments, constantly rewriting and revising the story. In showing the genesis of myth, the work shows the characters, on the stage (as backstage), deciding on the opera to be staged in the second part of the work. Mythological reconstruction is followed by mythological deconstruction.

In the second half of the work, the heroic opera is not presented, so to speak, "unbroken." Rather, the fact that Zerbinetta and her cohorts are present onstage disrupting the serious, tragic nature of the mythical opera that is supposedly taking place on the tasteless theatrical barren island, and actually explaining Ariadne's story to her creates an interchange between the levels of high and low art. In doing so, Zerbinetta gives a metaphorical interpretation of Ariadne's story. Thus *Ariadne auf Naxos* thematizes and demonstrates the hermeneutic process, portraying, one could even say, the reception of its own performance, like the Romantic comedies that put an audience on the stage watching a "play within a play." *Ariadne auf Naxos* shows how the same act can be interpreted in opposing ways, depending on the viewpoint of the participant or onlooker.[39]

Furthermore, *Ariadne auf Naxos* parodies the idea of myth as being some kind of a metaphor for history and thus being applicable to real-life. Myth is, by definition, general, symbolic. The Composer insists on the symbolic (i.e., mythical), tragic-heroic, grandiose interpretation of Ariadne's exemplary status. He declares, "Sie ist das Sinnbild der menschlichen Einsamkeit" (AN 194) (She is the symbol of human solitude). As far as the Composer is concerned, it is absolutely essential to the correct meaning of his opera that Ariadne be alone on Naxos. To the thought of her having company on her barren island, he objects, "Nichts um sich als das Meer, die Steine, die Bäume, das fühllose Echo. Sieht sie ein menschliches Gesicht, wird meine Musik sinnlos" (Nothing is around her but the sea, the rocks, the trees, the unfeeling echo. If she sees another human being, my music has no meaning anymore) (AN 194). Thus, the opera thematizes the question of the significance of Ariadne's story. Context certainly determines meaning.

Self-referentiality becomes, in this work by Hofmannsthal and Strauss, hermeneutic intertextuality. Ironically, Zerbinetta's presence explicates the exemplary mythological status of Ariadne. Zerbinetta, however, gives a parody of the Composer's idea of Ariadne being exemplary. She is not a symbol of human solitude but, rather, the quintessential woman. To Zerbinetta, Ariadne is a representative of the female sex. Zerbinetta makes it clear that she is speaking to her as one woman to another, and thus Ariadne becomes for the audience a parody of the exemplary nature of myth. In this way, the work as a whole parodies itself, one could say, as well as Wagner's aesthetic program of mythological refabrication in music-drama.

Furthermore, the notion of myth as metaphor is reduced to the level of language. It consists of word-play and double meanings. Verbal ambiguity can be profound. Thus language can do several things: it can interpret myth, that is, make it applicable to real-life; it can help form myth by participating in the process of myth-making; but it may also trivialize it by reducing real, magical, mythical events to the commonplace level of normal prosaic reality and thereby demythologizing myth.

Matthew Anatole Gurewitsch notes that the two worlds represented by Ariadne and Zerbinetta are joined not only by a common thematic concern but also by a shared language, which, in being mutually misunderstood, expresses their opposing points of view. Gurewitsch points out that the shared language includes the word "Gott" (god) and the verb "verwandeln" (transfigure) together with its substantive form "Verwandlung" (transfiguration).[40] Critics have also noted that Zerbinetta's use of the term "transformation" is a parody of its application to Ariadne. For Zerbinetta, transformation means the mere exchange of one man for another. For Ariadne, however, transformation signifies the actual changes occurring within her.[41]

In her solo that begins "Grossmächtige Prinzessin" (Gracious Princess), Zerbinetta presents a figurative interpretation of Ariadne's story. Zerbinetta establishes the similarity between herself and the prima donna of the mythological opera by explaining, "Ach, solcher wüsten Inseln sind unzäh- lige / Auch mitten unter Menschen, ich—ich selber, / Ich habe ihrer mehrere bewohnt" (Ah, there are countless barren islands, even among other people I myself have inhabited several of them) (AN 206). The barren island suddenly becomes a state of mind. Oddly enough, Zerbinetta now properly belongs in the set where Ariadne is singing her aria. Similarly, Bacchus turns out to be a metaphorical messenger of death ("Todesbote"), for death is figurative when interpreted as transfiguration. The thematic relationship between the music associated with Theseus, Hermes (Death), and Bacchus expresses the parallelism of these figures that exists primarily in Ariadne's mind.[42] In this manner, myth is explicitly interpreted by the figures onstage as more a state of mind than any kind of tangible reality.

Bacchus is, of course, a traditional god, and Ariadne awaits actual transformation. But Zerbinetta's lovers were, in a way, gods to her, too. Zerbinetta sings,

Als ein Gott kam jeder gegangen,
Und sein Schritt schon machte mich stumm,
Küsste er mir Stirn und Wangen,
War ich von dem Gott gefangen,
Und gewandelt um und um! (AN 207)

Each came as a god, and his gait made me speechless. He kissed my forehead and cheek, I was captivated by the god, and fully transformed!

One could say that the libretto contrasts literal and figurative language. In other words, it turns the idea of mythological opera as somehow being metaphorical comically against Wagner himself. What was originally conceived as a heroic version of the tragic myth of Ariadne becomes a complex and intertextual exercise in mythological hermeneutics. Thus, the metaphysical grandeur of the mythological opera within the opera is definitely undercut.

The prologue explicates this literal/figural mythological perspectivism or psychological relativism with Romantic irony, that is, establishing the reflexivity of the text and explicating the work of art. According to the Composer, Ariadne takes Bacchus to be the god of death. "In ihren Augen, in ihrer Seele ist er es, und darum, einzig nur darum—" (In her eyes, in her soul, he is that, and because of that, only because of that—). After Zerbinetta interrupts, he continues, "Einzig nur darum geht sie mit ihm—auf sein Schiff! Sie meint zu sterben! Nein, sie stirbt wirklich" (Only because of that she goes with him—onto his ship! She intends to die! No, she really dies) (AN 196). Though the Composer repeats "Sie stirbt" (She dies), Zerbinetta interprets this metaphorically, as rebirth and transfiguration. In the end, Zerbinetta gets her way. Bacchus is merely a metaphorical messenger of death.

Meaning, it seems, is ultimately subjective. The god of death may just be the god of transfiguration, depending on one's definition of these terms. The issue is really a linguistic one, just as the existence of the gods in *Elektra* was a linguistic one. On the most basic level, it concerns the distinction between the real and the figural, the literal and the metaphorical. The linguistic concept of metaphor can, however, have redemptive value. Ariadne and Bacchus demonstrate the mutual metaphorical transformation that Zerbinetta had described. Death is transfiguration, and thus new life. In *Ariadne auf Naxos*, the double meanings of language, the distinction between the literal and the figural, can interpretatively and hermeneutically smooth out the discrepancies and thus avert tragedy.

Elektra envisioned Agamemnon returning upon the murder of the murderers; instead, Elektra died. In contrast, Ariadne envisions death coming in the guise of Hermes. Instead, Bacchus comes, and metaphorical death represents transfiguration and new life. Thus, Ariadne overcomes Elektra's tragic dichotomy of life and death. Metaphor resolves the tragic contradiction. The gods who were in *Elektra* pathetically absent are in the later work mere metaphors. In speaking lies, Elektra sarcastically told Klytemnestra that she was a god. In *Ariadne auf Naxos*, though, this is not actually a lie, for anybody can be a god, figuratively speaking. Myth has been reduced to metaphor in the most radical way. The verbal contradictions and the clash of myth and history, both of which were tragically fundamental to *Elektra* form, in *Ariadne auf Naxos*, a productive interchange. The horrible Dionysian frenzy with which myth is portrayed in *Elektra* is now conquered by the Apollonian veil of metaphorical language. In this manner, *Ariadne auf Naxos* overcomes the tragedy of *Elektra*.

What seems, then, to be an apotheosis of myth is actually the destruction of myth. One can ask whether such myth is even really myth, or whether it actually violates essential elements of the definition of myth. The story of Ariadne, though outwardly mythological, has been, with Zerbinetta's help, brought down to the level of real-life, of history. Whereas in *Elektra* myth is created by language, in *Ariadne auf Naxos* myth is virtually destroyed by language. For when death and transfiguration are metaphorical, myth is robbed of its essence, its numinosity, despite the mythological trappings, the costumes and props. They are even, in Romantic irony, shown to be such. The opera within the opera depicts what is essentially a theater set. The Prologue makes the audience aware of that.

The heroic, seemingly mythological performance is suffering Zerbinetta's interpretative commentary, Bacchus is in costume, and this version of Naxos is a theatrical set in the house of the richest man in Vienna. Bacchus seems to have learned operatic hermeneutics well. In the love duet, Bacchus builds upon Zerbinetta's metaphorical interpretation of their surroundings and revises the significance of Ariadne's cave. It is "die Höhle deiner Schmerzen" (AN 220) (the cave of your pain), which he will change. Ariadne says, "Du Zauberer, du! Verwandler, du!" (You magician, you! Transformer, you!). Bacchus addresses her, "Du meine Zauberin!" (You, my magician!) (AN 220). The magic is, of course, merely metaphorical, like the transfiguration.

Bacchus even makes the metaphorical nature of his own divinity explicit when he exclaims, after he is (metaphorically) transformed by Ariadne, "Ich bin ein anderer, als ich war! / Der Sinn des Gottes ist wach in mir, / Dein herrlich Wesen ganz zu fassen!" (AN 220) (I am different from what I previously was! The sense of a god is alive in me, to grasp your glorious essence!). When the cave has become the cave of Ariadne's pain, the island is an island of despair, the god only seems a god, and death is new life, with transfiguration being figural, then the mythological theater set seems to dissipate and dematerialize. Myth as metaphor is, after all, no longer really myth. The ends of the two performances, the opera within the opera and the opera as a whole, seem to inevitably converge. A return to the frame would be totally inappropriate. The theater set collapses at the end of the opera within the opera. The curtain falls necessarily when it does.

In a letter to Strauss (13 December 1912), Hofmannsthal said that the composer was called upon to partially "costume" his music and use it as a citation.[43] Accordingly the music participates in the irony of the work. As grandiose as the music in the duet of Ariadne and Bacchus is, it is still in quotation marks. If heard without the drama, it is unquestioningly glorious, that is, without the words and the scenario that are the work of the poet. In the context of the entire drama, though, it recalls the aria of the Composer, also in the grand style, with rising, soaring melodies, and thus the frame is brought to mind, undercutting the illusion and reminding the audience that it is experiencing a work of art. Zerbinetta interrupts the duet with her refrain, the dramatic function of which is now clear.

The end of the story is improvised. Ariadne is the title figure, just as Elektra was. This time, however, Zerbinetta is directing the action. Her hermeneutical commentary, it seems, gives her countercontrol. Ariadne's myth is relativized by the other story and the other kind of music. Significantly enough, the tragic ending that Ariadne and the Composer envisioned is also changed. The explicit interpretation by Zerbinetta of the story of Ariadne and Bacchus somehow undermines its heroic dramatic nature and mythological grandeur, thereby paradoxically trivializing its significance while at the same time giving it more meaning. Thus the music of *Ariadne auf Naxos*, though it seems Wagnerian in places, when understood in its entirety and with reference to the drama as a whole, actually takes issue with the Wagnerian tradition. It contradicts itself. The grandiosity of the seemingly Wagnerian music in *Ariadne auf Naxos* only serves to exaggerate the stylistic discrepancies and parodistic intent of the work as a whole.

Thus the beautiful music is ironic, for one cannot ignore the irony that resides in grandiose music accompanying mythology that has been linguistically relativized and, in this manner, undone. The music is verbally undermined. The Composer did say that if Ariadne saw another human being, the music would have no meaning anymore. Of course, the music that Zerbinetta sings also relativizes Ariadne's music; but it is primarily the language used, the words, the metaphorical language with which Zerbinetta explicates Ariadne's story that go against the music to which Ariadne sings and that accompanies her longing for what seems to her to be her inevitable tragic end. The juxtaposition of Ariadne with Zerbinetta undercuts, accordingly, the heroic nature of the music. It does have meaning, of course, but now it is a parodistic one. The heroic myth, once it is humorously and metaphorically explicated, is no longer quite heroic. Depending on the context in which it is used, heroic music need not be totally serious.

The work thus unworks itself. It consists of an essential contradiction, such as when, at the end of Zerbinetta's aria, she repeatedly sings the word "stumm" (speechless). Hofmannsthal's drama, a main element of which is his use of language, is thus undoing not only Nietzsche's *Die Geburt der Tragödie*, with its emphasis on music creating the mythological tragedy, but also the Wagnerian mythical tradition in which Strauss was at home. The drama undercuts the seriousness and emotional impact of the music, with its lush orchestration and arching melodies. Wagner felt that the music should underscore or complement the drama. In *Ariadne auf Naxos*, the poet attacks the musician. The metaphoricity of language undercuts the grandiosity and mythological nature of the music. The tragic myth is a comedy in the context of *Ariadne auf Naxos*.

As Gurewitsch points out, at Zerbinetta's last appearance, in which she addresses the audience, her refrain has changed from "Kam der neue Gott gegangen, / Hingegeben war ich stumm!" (AN 208) (When the new god came, I surrendered speechlessly!) to "Kommt der neue Gott gegangen, / Hingegeben sind wir stumm!" (AN 221) (When the new god comes, we surrender speechlessly!).[44] The past tense is replaced with the present (which implies the future also), and the audience is now included in the process. The renewal of society that is depicted happens on the individual, personal, psychological level.

Metaphor creates a synthesis that transcends the language skepticism of *Elektra* and resolves the contradiction of mythological music-drama needing to refer to life. The opera as a whole doesn't revert to the frame of the prologue, so the work does have some kind of comical three-stage model. Ironically, the explicit application of the story of Ariadne to real-life, that is, to the plane of the audience, though undercutting the Wagnerian form, just reinforces Wagner's notion of what art should do. Myth ideally becomes historical. Art can change life, and opera can affect history.

Mythological opera helps one live more effectively in the real world by being, ironically enough, demythologized. It is as though *Ariadne auf Naxos* is saying that myth must be historicized and interpreted metaphorically in order to be at all useful for life in the real world. The work, like the *Ring*, demonstrates its aesthetic program. The audience has hopefully learned something about the application of myth to life, just as Ariadne has been instructed by Zerbinetta. In its concluding scene, *Ariadne auf Naxos*, like the *Ring*, opens onto reality. When the performance ends, the audience is supposed to repeat the lesson it has learned in real-life and thus historicize a demythologized mythical pattern.

BRÜNNHILDE ON NAXOS?

Not only does *Ariadne auf Naxos* play off of, and in doing so invert, the aesthetic program and mythological form of the *Ring*. I would also suggest that the *Ring* was a real influence on *Ariadne auf Naxos* in other ways, too. Additional features identify the latter work as what can be understood as a deconstructive parody of the former work. In particular, Brünnhilde's role in the *Ring* clearly indicates that she might very well have served as some kind of prototype or model for Ariadne. More specifically, I propose that *Ariadne auf Naxos* can be understood not only with reference to Wagner's *Ring* but also as a parody of the last part of the cycle, *Götterdämmerung*. As the culmination of the *Ring* cycle, the longest and doubtlessly the most grandiose of the *Ring* dramas, as it contains the final glorious mythological cataclysm, *Götterdämmerung* seems an apt target for the parody of Hofmannsthal and Strauss, and a suitable subject for Zerbinetta to attack and trivialize with her interpretative commentaries.

It is a commonplace that myth displays an entire cosmology. Wagner wrote in a letter to Franz Liszt (11 February 1853) that his *Ring* cycle contained the origin and destruction of the world. *Ariadne auf Naxos* contains what one could call an aesthetic cosmology. As the *Ring* shows the origin of the world, *Ariadne auf Naxos* does the same for the opera within the opera, the new myth. One sees the genesis of art.[45] *Ariadne auf Naxos* is the *Ring* on the level of reflection. Ariadne, awaiting Hermes, resembles Brünnhilde, expecting Siegfried. Both are surprised when the one who arrives is not the expected one. Ariadne even exclaims, "Theseus!" at Bacchus' arrival. Siegfried's death is plotted when Brünnhilde refuses to accept Gunther—she is the woman who will belong to one man only. She suffers from the fault that Zerbinetta hopes to cure Ariadne of. Bacchus grants Ariadne the "magical" gift of forgetting.

Furthermore, the tragedy of the *Ring* follows inevitably from the curse on the ring and the misdeeds of Wotan. The end of the *Ring* has, in fact, even been determined since before *Rheingold*. Erda makes clear to Wotan in *Rheingold* that everything must inevitably end. In the opera "Ariadne," events are improvised, rather than predetermined.[46] The original outcome is changed. The Prologue to *Götterdämmerung* tells what has happened in the past. These past events determine the outcome of the drama. The Norns narrate the story in parts, asking each other, "Weisst du wie das wird?" (MD 754) (Do you know what will happen?), or some variation thereof. The prologue to *Ariadne auf Naxos* tells, in a likewise fragmentary way, the story to come, which is not fixed, but, rather, improvised. The characters debate and argue about how it will be. Whereas Siegfried's forgetting, induced by a real magic potion, has tragic consequences, as it causes him to betray Brünnhilde and thus incur her wrath and Hagen's gladly compliant vengeance, Ariadne learns to forget, which is useful for life, by a figurative magic potion.

Wagner's Zurich writings clearly state that "set pieces," traditional operatic forms such as quartets and duets, have no place in the art-work of the future. Critics point out, however, that he reverted to these in *Götterdämmerung*, for instance, the vengeance trio and the love duet of Siegfried and Brünnhilde. In the awakening duet in the third act of *Siegfried*, main characters, for the first time in the *Ring*, sing in unison, and thus the *Ring* lapses into, some feel, "grand opera." Perhaps this, too, is parodied in the opera within the opera of *Ariadne auf Naxos*. The ensembles of comedians, for instance, the quartet of clowns, in the tragic myth or "opera seria" bring the musical-dramatic phenomenon that I have described to the level of the ridiculous, from the sublime to the absurd. The very presence of clowns onstage while the supposedly tragic myth is being performed does, naturally, itself undo the serious implications and tragic nature of the story that is progressing onstage. The dancing of the clowns can be considered a parody of both Elektra's deadly dance and Wagner's emphasis on the dance in his Zurich writings and the fact that he felt it was essential to tragedy (or its untragic rebirth), the total work of art.

The trio of nymphs that resounds in various ways from time to time is another such device that creates a kind of anti-Wagnerian comic relief.[47] One cannot deny that the duration and amount of the coloratura that the three nymphs produce on insignificant words such as "Ach" (in the first trio) are comically excessive. The nymphs can be interpreted as a parody of (or at least variation on) the Rhinemaidens, if not musically, then at least thematically (as nature spirits). The second trio of the nymphs ("Töne, töne, süsse Stimme") (Sound, sweet voice) forms a sort of background commentary to the love duet. It also thematizes music, like the aria of the Composer.

The nymphs thus show the self-consciousness of art as art, and thus they serve to create Romantic irony, as is, after all, appropriate to their nature as typical Romantic water-sprites. Furthermore, the nymphs can be considered, like the clowns also, a parody of the chorus of Greek tragedy that Nietzsche and Wagner emphasized as essential and theorized has an analogy in the modern orchestra. The nymphs and the clowns comment on the action, the latter in a way that undercuts the seriousness of Ariadne's story. They remind the viewer or listener that the work they are witnessing is not only art, but art within art, and thus art *as* art.

Furthermore, the real work of genius, another mystical transformation, that is, the fusion of two art forms,[48] is really motivated by financial expedients. The evening's show, the play within the play or the opera within the opera, is at the mercy of the richest man in Vienna, who demands that the two forms of art be performed simultaneously, is well able to pay for the entertainment, and thus must be satisfied at the cost of artistic integrity. Mythical timelessness is parodied in the simultaneity of the opera seria and the commedia dell'arte. The composite performance must be over in time for the fireworks display, which one can consider a parody of the Immolation Scene at the end of the *Götterdämmerung*. Art has become commerce and entertainment, a phenomenon that Wagner strongly opposed. Critics discuss the idea of the Composer being a Wagner caricature.[49] But this idea is too simplistic when one considers the broader thematic basis and the formal structure of the work as a whole.

NOTES

1. This survey is based on: Dieter Borchmeyer, *Das Theater Richard Wagners: Idee, Dichtung, Wirkung* (Stuttgart: Reclam, 1982), pp. 334–57 (chapter "Mythos, Mimus, Oper: Hofmannsthals Wagner- und Nietzsche-Rezeption"). More specific references will be given when appropriate. See also: Karl Konrad Polheim, "Hofmannsthal und Richard Wagner," in *Drama und Theater im 20. Jahrhundert*, ed. Hans Dietrich Irmscher and Werner Keller (Göttingen: Vandenhoeck und Ruprecht, 1983), pp. 11–23.

2. On Bayreuth and Salzburg, see: Roger Bauer, "Hofmannsthals Konzeption der Salzburger Festspiele," *Hofmannsthal-Forschungen* 2 (1974): pp. 131–39.

3. On the problem of words and music, see: Johannes Krogoll, "Hofmannsthal-Strauss. Zur Problematik des Wort-Ton Verhältnisses im Musikdrama," *Hofmannsthal-Forschungen* 6 (1981): pp. 81–102. On Hofmannsthal's libretti, see: Hilde D. Cohn, "Hofmannsthals Libretti," *German Quarterly* 35, no. 2 (1962): pp. 149–64; Ursula Scharf, "Hofmannsthal's Libretti," *German Life and Letters* 8, no. 2 (1955): pp. 130–36. For a discussion of the function of music in Hofmannsthal's works, see: Martin E. Schmid, *Symbol und Funktion der Musik im Werk Hugo von Hofmannsthals* (Heidelberg: Carl Winter, 1968).

4. Borchmeyer, *Das Theater Richard Wagners*, pp. 335–42.

5. Borchmeyer, *Das Theater Richard Wagners*, p. 339.

6. Borchmeyer, *Das Theater Richard Wagners*, p. 342.

7. See the letters of Hofmannsthal to Strauss of 2 September 1909 and 6 June 1910. Richard Strauss and Hugo von Hofmannsthal, *Briefwechsel*, ed. Willi Schuh, 4th ed. (Zurich: Atlantis, 1970), pp. 81, 91–92.

8. Borchmeyer, *Das Theater Richard Wagners*, p. 335.

9. I base my commentary on the analysis of Eva-Maria Lenz. For an overview of Hofmannsthal on myth, especially in reference to *Die ägyptische Helena*, see: Eva-Maria Lenz, *Hugo von Hofmannsthals mythologische Oper "Die ägyptische Helena"*, Hermaea, Germanistische Forschungen, Neue Folge, vol. 29 (Tübingen: Max Niemeyer, 1972), pp. 119–43.

10. Hugo von Hofmannsthal, *Reden und Aufsätze III*, ed. Bernd Schoeller and Ingeborg Beyer-Ahlert (Frankfurt am Main: Fischer Taschenbuch Verlag, 1980), p. 358. References to this edition of Hofmannsthal's notebooks will hereafter be given within the text by page numbers, preceded by the abbreviation "A."

11. Hugo von Hofmannsthal, *Briefe 1890–1901* (Berlin: S. Fischer Verlag, 1935), p. 17.

12. Rolf Tarot, *Hugo von Hofmannsthal: Daseinsformen und dichterische Struktur* (Tübingen: Max Niemeyer, 1970), pp. 160–73.

13. Benjamin Bennett, *Hugo von Hofmannsthal: The Theaters of Consciousness* (Cambridge: Cambridge University Press, 1988), pp. 124–26.

14. Martin Stern, "Spätzeitlichkeit und Mythos. Hofmannsthals *Ariadne*," *Hofmannsthal-Forschungen* 8 (1985): pp. 291–312.

15. Karl G. Esselborn, *Hofmannsthal und der antike Mythos* (Munich: Wilhelm Fink, 1969), pp. 36–57. On Hofmannsthal and Nietzsche, see also: H. Jürgen Meyer-Wendt, *Der frühe Hofmannsthal und die Gedankenwelt Nietzsches* (Heidelberg: Quelle und Meyer, 1973).

16. On the influence of *Die Geburt der Tragödie* on the young Hofmannsthal, see: Esselborn, pp. 11, 45–46.

17. On Wagner's theory of language, see: Mary A. Cicora, "From Metonymy to Metaphor: Wagner and Nietzsche on Language," *German Life and Letters* 42, no. 1 (1988): pp. 16–31.

18. Lenz, pp. 126–27. On the early works and the "Chandos crisis," see: Bennett, *Hugo von Hofmannsthal*, pp. 105–28; Manfred Hoppe, *Literatentum, Magie und Mystik im Frühwerk Hugo von Hofmannsthals* (Berlin: Walter de Gruyter, 1968); Karl Pestalozzi, *Sprachskepsis und Sprachmagie im Werk des jungen Hofmannsthal*, Zürcher Beiträge zur deutschen Sprach- und Stilgeschichte, no. 6 (Zurich: Atlantis, 1958);

Richard Brinkmann, "Hofmannsthal und die Sprache," *Deutsche Vierteljahrsschrift für Literaturwissenschaft und Geistesgeschichte* 35, no. 1 (1961): pp. 69–95.

19. Lothar Wittmann, *Sprachthematik und dramatische Form im Werke Hofmannsthals*, Studien zur Poetik und Geschichte der Literatur, vol. 2 (Stuttgart: W. Kohlhammer, 1966), pp. 67–92.

20. Wittmann, pp. 60–66.

21. Hugo von Hofmannsthal, *Dramen II*, ed. Bernd Schoeller (Frankfurt am Main: Fischer Taschenbuch Verlag, 1979), p. 187. References to this edition of *Elektra* will be given within the text by page numbers, preceded by the abbreviation "E."

22. Esselborn, pp. 158–247.

23. Bennett, *Hugo von Hofmannsthal*, pp. 113–17.

24. The work as a whole is cited in italics; the opera within the opera is called "Ariadne," in quote marks.

25. Barbara Könneker, "Die Funktion des Vorspiels in Hofmannsthals *Ariadne auf Naxos*," *Germanisch-Romanische Monatsschrift* 53 / NF 22, no. 2 (1972): pp. 124–41.

26. Bernhard Heimrich, *Fiktion und Fiktionsironie in Theorie und Dichtung der deutschen Romantik* (Tübingen: Max Niemeyer, 1968).

27. Donald G. Daviau and George J. Buelow, *The "Ariadne auf Naxos" of Hugo von Hofmannsthal and Richard Strauss*, University of North Carolina Studies in the Germanic Languages and Literatures, no. 80 (Chapel Hill: University of North Carolina Press, 1975), p. 120.

28. Strauss and Hofmannsthal, *Briefwechsel*, pp. 121–23.

29. Strauss and Hofmannsthal, *Briefwechsel*, pp. 124–26.

30. Könneker, p. 138.

31. Daviau and Buelow, p. 104.

32. Daviau and Buelow, pp. 181–82.

33. In the following, I have consulted: Daviau and Buelow, pp. 158–60.

34. Strauss and Hofmannsthal, *Briefwechsel*, pp. 123–24.

35. See: Letter of Hofmannsthal to Strauss of July 1911. Strauss and Hofmannsthal, *Briefwechsel*, pp. 132–35.

36. Hugo von Hofmannsthal, *Dramen V*, ed. Bernd Schoeller (Frankfurt am Main: Fischer Taschenbuch Verlag, 1979), p. 202. References to the text of *Ariadne auf Naxos* in this edition of Hofmannsthal's opera texts will hereafter be given within the text by page numbers, preceded by the abbreviation "AN."

37. Carl Dahlhaus, *Richard Wagners Musikdramen* (Velber: Friedrich, 1971), p. 111.

38. On Zerbinetta's aria, see: Daviau and Buelow, pp. 183–93.

39. Daviau and Buelow, p. 150.

40. Matthew Anatole Gurewitsch, "The Maker's and the Beholder's Art: Serendipity in *Ariadne auf Naxos*," *Germanic Review* 53, no. 4 (1978): pp. 137–46 (here I am referring to pp. 141–45). See also: Daviau and Buelow, p. 155.

41. Daviau and Buelow, p. 140.

42. See: Daviau and Buelow, pp. 199–202.

43. Strauss and Hofmannsthal, *Briefwechsel*, pp. 205–8.

44. Gurewitsch, p. 144.

45. See Stefan Kunze, "Die ästhetische Rekonstruktion der Oper: Anmerkungen zur 'Ariadne auf Naxos'," *Hofmannsthal-Forschungen* 6 (1981): pp. 103–23.

46. Bennett (*Hugo von Hofmannsthal*, pp. 233–51) calls this "art by accident."

47. On the nymphs, see: Daviau and Buelow, pp. 170–72, 205–6; Karl Dietrich Gräwe, "Sprache, Musik und Szene in 'Ariadne auf Naxos' von Hugo von Hofmannsthal und Richard Strauss," diss., Munich, 1969, pp. 251–55. Daviau and Buelow (p. 172, note 4) take issue with William Mann's likening of the nymphs to the Rhinemaidens.

48. Gurewitsch, p. 141.

49. The idea was proposed by Martin Stern, "Eine heimliche Wagner-Karikatur.—Zum *Ariadne* Vorspiel 1916," in *Neue Zürcher Zeitung*, 26 November 1959. See, for instance, the discussion by Borchmeyer, *Das Theater Richard Wagners*, p. 339.

Chapter 4 ❖

Wagner and Brecht, or, Show Me the Way to Nibelheim, Oh Don't Ask Why, Oh Don't Ask Why

*I*n 1988, Harry Kupfer enraged Bayreuth audiences with a new interpretation of the *Ring*. The phenomenon was by then a familiar one. Kupfer belonged to a group of East German directors, among them Götz Friedrich and Joachim Herz, whose conceptual Wagner productions reflected and commented upon societal problems. Friedrich's Bayreuth *Tannhäuser* production (1972) started this current there. Twelve years earlier than Kupfer's *Ring*, the Frenchman Patrice Chéreau caused a scandal with an Industrial Revolution *Ring*. The trend seemed to be toward undercutting or totally destroying the foggy Romantic illusion and archetypical "mythical" timelessness that the dramas, in the productions of Wieland and Wolfgang Wagner, once had. The mist amply used in Kupfer's *Rheingold*, along with the dreary gray color scheme, emphasized the decadence of the gods.

Even before the premiere, nobody could expect the audience to approve unanimously of Kupfer's *Ring*. This was not the first sample of Kupfer's work that the Bayreuth traditionalists had been presented with. Kupfer had previously staged *Holländer* at Bayreuth. The production, staged on a unit set consisting of a tenement building and a fire escape, depicted Senta's alienation from her domestic milieu. The flickering lights in the third-act chorus scenes, the ghastly white faces of Mary and the spinning women, and a mute double for the Dutchman were all devices that Kupfer used to show the audience that the opera was being depicted from the perspective of an insane Senta. The soprano crouched on the fire escape hugging a picture of the Dutchman, even when the work did not demand her presence onstage. Kupfer's Senta evidently hallucinated his appearance, and at the end of the opera she committed suicide by throwing herself off the fire escape.

Kupfer's *Ring*, likewise varying a basic unit set, this time a long street with a chasm in the middle, addressed environmental issues. Termed by some the "Chernobyl *Ring*," it staged the work after the nuclear holocaust, stressing the humanity of the figures and portraying their interrelationships with powerful acting. The singers climbed over ubiquitous staircases in sets that were supposed to represent the ruins of our own world, such as the remains of a nuclear reactor (in the first and second acts of *Siegfried*) or the spiderlike launch pad of a spaceship (in the second act of *Götterdämmerung*). The Gibichung Hall was flanked by the skyscrapers of New York City. Brünnhilde's rock became a neon cube.

The gods were not dressed as one would imagine conventional gods dressed. They wore trench coats, the color and style of each varying with the dramatic situation. The most fascinating character in the cycle, Wotan was superbly portrayed by John Tomlinson. Sporting instead of the traditional eye patch a pair of sunglasses, he looked like a gangster, a rebel, another Mackie Messer. Already unstable in *Rheingold*, the next evening he was running erratically about, swinging his spear (which, like the sword Nothung and Donner's hammer, was made of Lucite). Dressed in a black vinyl trench coat with fur lapels in *Walküre*, he was powerful but obviously mad. He looked like a renegade from a Hell's Angels band, gesticulating wildly, and lacking all the divine grandeur that conventional productions give him.

In the second scene of *Rheingold*, the gods were a family with its own problems. Fricka, who was portrayed as a "Hausfrau," stroked and caressed her perplexed husband as she lovingly expressed her concern about his fidelity. Meanwhile, Donner and Froh had turned their Lucite suitcases (which they had brought onstage when they entered, as they were moving into Valhalla) upside down, had placed one between them as a table, and had started playing cards to alleviate the boredom. Froh periodically turned his head to spy on the marital discord of the gods. John Rockwell, in his *New York Times* review of the first two installments of the production, commented on the Brechtian resemblance. In discussing Kupfer's *Rheingold*, he wrote, "It is Valhalla as Mahagonny."[1]

Modern stagings of Wagner's works (and other operas, too) in the modern production era that began when the stark mythological and Neoromantic postwar "New Bayreuth" style of Wagner's grandsons Wieland and Wolfgang became passé, and a return to the conventional realism of Wagner's time, represented by the Met *Ring* conducted by James Levine and captured on videotape (1990), was deemed by some to be anachronistic and uninteresting, do seem to be using alienation effects ("Verfremdungseffekte") with the purpose of (in a positive sense) "alienating" the audience, to get them to take a new look at Wagner's (and others') works and see their relevance to modern life and our contemporary world. This "alienation" can often be negative, defeating its purpose when the intent is not made clear and it is misunderstood, or when it is rejected by the audience as a misinterpretation and an unjustified alteration of, or a deadly tampering with, an artistic masterpiece. The audience is then "alienated" in the worst possible way.

I do not intend an exhaustive survey of modern techniques of staging Wagner, or a lengthy debate about the relative merits of updating the *Ring*. One can argue vehemently where artistic license ends and idiocy begins. Issues that ultimately depend on individual, subjective preference can never be settled definitively to everyone's satisfaction, and I will certainly not attempt to tackle this problem here. I have, though, described Kupfer's Bayreuth *Ring* in order to outline the issue that I wish to attack in the present chapter. The production I just discussed can serve, I propose, as a link between Wagner and twentieth-century theater. Kupfer openly acknowledges his debt to Brecht (Berlin Ensemble) and Walter Felsenstein (Komische Oper).[2] Kupfer's Bayreuth *Ring* production tacitly raised an important issue: it posed the question of how justified or appropriate it really is to stage Wagner's works like Brecht's. To answer this question, one must undertake a comparison of the aesthetics, drama theories, political philosophies, and societal standpoints of Wagner and Brecht.

Staging Wagner like Brecht, though, if it provokes a comparative analysis of their works, can indeed be an intellectually profitable enterprise. Though their works may seem radically different, the two men are, beneath the surface, amazingly similar when it comes to their common wish to reform society, and the ensuing similarities and differences seem to line up by themselves when one draws this initial parallel. Brecht's work consistently distorts the Romantic tradition in which the *Ring* belongs. Perhaps this even happens because of the *Ring* and Wagner's philosophy of art and politics, or at least what Brecht saw as Wagner's work and thought. When one explores the philosophical and literary context of the two dramatists, then Kupfer's innovative approach, the whole fascinating production with its trench coats and sunglasses, seems much more than mere directorial excess.

In this chapter, I will concentrate my attention on one of the Brecht-Weill music-dramas or "operatic" projects, *Aufstieg und Fall der Stadt Mahagonny*, and the corresponding essay by Brecht, "Anmerkungen zur Oper *Aufstieg und Fall der Stadt Mahagonny*." Analyzing this selection of texts clearly proves that Brecht's theory and dramas can be understood as a parody of Wagner's. After outlining some basic differences in how Brecht and Wagner relate art and politics and also myth and history, I discuss Brecht's theoretical work about *Mahagonny* with reference to Wagner's *Oper und Drama*. After demonstrating how a theoretical text of Brecht can be read in conjunction with one of Wagner, I then show how the dramas that they were meant to explicate can somehow be understood as inversions of each other, with the later work a parody of the earlier one.

In particular, Brecht plays off of Wagner's political aesthetics of the renewal and the mythicization of modern (historical) society through mythological music-drama. In many ways, Brecht theoretically and dramatically inverts Wagner's dialectics of history and myth. Brecht's parodistic intentions can be seen in his use of history for his subject matter, as opposed to myth, and they are exaggerated by, within this historical subject matter, formal, thematic, and structural parodies. The Brecht/Weill opera inverts Wagner's specific uses of music in the *Ring*, and Brecht's scenario of *Mahagonny* also plays off of specific themes of the *Ring*. The chapter concludes with a comparison of *Mahagonny* with the *Ring*.

WAGNER AND BRECHT, AESTHETICS AND POLITICS, EPIC AND DRAMA

Nothing seems further removed from Wagner's mythological music-drama than Brecht's epic theater. Wagner's Romantic music-drama appeals primarily to the capacity of feeling. The music is grandiose, nineteenth-century, and the subject matter magical and mythological. Brecht's world-view is rationalistic and materialistic. Yet, upon closer examination, much common ground does exist between the dramas of these two men. The divergences between their works, too, are telling to the utmost. The concept of parody implies ambivalence. It means that a later work uses elements of an earlier one without giving them the significance that they had in the previous work. Accordingly, there are similarities and differences, that is, specific distorted correspondences, between the works of the two men.

It is unclear just how much of Wagner's prose Brecht read, how many of Wagner's theories Brecht knew, or even how closely acquainted Brecht was with Wagner's dramas. Hilda M. Brown writes that there is no evidence to suggest that Brecht read Wagner's essays. She feels it is more likely that Brecht's information concerning Wagner's prose and theories came from secondary sources. Brown argues that Brecht's understanding of Wagner's ideas suffered from a kind of reductionism, and she discusses Brecht's separation of the elements as a revolt against the Wagnerian "Gesamtkunstwerk," a term that Brecht uses within quotation marks.[3] The use of specifically this term by Brecht indicates that his perception of Wagner was overgeneralized and came from secondary sources. It is a popular term in the Wagner literature, though Wagner, in fact, never used the term more than a few times. His theories, moreover, concern much more than this issue of the union of the arts.

It is not my intention to prove direct influence or to dogmatically insist that Brecht is consciously working off of specifically Wagnerian prototypes.

Considering the lack of many direct utterances by Brecht about Wagner and his works, or firm facts concerning his knowledge of Wagner, this would remain speculation, though I do not rule out the possibility that such direct influence might indeed exist. The parallels I point to may well indicate a veiled personal quarrel of Brecht with Wagner. However, I wish to show how these parallels and even the differences may be regarded as illustrating evidence of their common ground in the German literary, philosophical, and cultural tradition, and demonstrate how each man can thereby be seen as taking a stance toward larger issues, more general ideas and problems. Conjecture about direct influence is actually beside the point. Influence, after all, need not be direct. Like Wagner, too, Brecht had certain beliefs that somehow found their way into a work of art or a drama. These two men evidently thought about many of the same things.

Brecht is, after all, noted for what is commonly termed "epic theater." Though the association of Brecht's name with this term is standard, an investigation into how this concept is defined actually leads to the unavoidable, though perhaps startling, association of it with Wagner, too. When one considers the distinctive qualities of "epic theater," one must face the realization that Wagner's music-drama, though not usually termed this, as it is commonly considered to be very different from Brecht's type of drama, is actually, in many ways, what one could call "epic theater." Discussions of the tetralogy with reference to the terms "open" and "closed" form of Volker Klotz have shown how it has various elements of "open" form. Wagner's *Ring* does have many "epic" elements. Furthermore, it has, after all, become fashionable, ever since Thomas Mann, to call Wagner's *Ring* "epic" and discuss the use of "epic" narratives in his music-drama.

One often thinks of Wagner's grandiose Romantic dramas, the music of which envelops the listener, to be the direct opposite of Brecht's "epic theater." Of course, the listener or viewer of Wagner's dramas is not supposed to be alienated the way the reader or viewer of Brecht dramas is. Unlike Brecht, Wagner did not want to make the audience take a new look at what was considered familiar, and this was the goal of the "alienation effect" as Brecht intended it. *Oper und Drama* clearly indicates that Wagner wanted the audience to identify with the figures in his dramas. Brecht, though, wanted to prevent the audience from identifying with his figures. In many ways their works are totally different.

For example, whereas Brecht used a narrator to destroy the aesthetic illusion, and he did not want his actors to identify with their roles, Wagner instructed his singers at the Bayreuth Festival to look up or down but never to sing directly to the audience. Furthermore, Brecht strove to separate the various artistic elements and present discrete numbers, whereas Wagner strove to reunite the arts of music, language, and dance, and to create a more or less continuous musical and dramatic texture. However, the various techniques and devices by which Brecht intends to provoke a critical stance in his audience members, and which are subsumed under the basic heading of "alienation effects" ("Verfremdungseffekte" or simply "V-Effekte"), can nevertheless be likened to features of Wagnerian drama. Surprisingly enough, these devices or the equivalents thereof can be found in Wagner's work.

The feeling versus reason dichotomy along which one tends to contrast these two dramatists is also misleading. Brecht's aim is, of course, to make the audience think. However, Wagner did not intend to entirely eliminate the faculty of understanding from the audience reception of his music-dramas, just as Brecht's plays still appeal, in part, to the capacity of feeling. But Brecht's theater is primarily a pedagogical institution. Brecht wanted to appeal mainly to the rational faculties. It is, however, not a strict dichotomy of feeling versus understanding for either of them, just a matter of emphasis. For each of them, the musical and dramatic styles were some kind of means toward the proper audience reception of the works. Furthermore, Brecht, like Wagner, intended to instigate, with the experience of his dramas, a process of bringing something to the consciousness of the audience.

Hilda M. Brown, for example, in the work I cited earlier, challenges the view of Brecht as an antitraditionalist and of modern drama as a complete break with tradition. She proposes a common technique of "perspectivism," whereby image-networks in Brecht's plays fulfill the same function as do "Leitmotive" in Wagner's music-dramas, that is, to provide some kind of authorial commentary upon the drama. The assertion that Wagner's works have "alienation" effects similar to those of Brecht's dramas is startling because one usually never sees them (or hears them) this way, since the audience is very much drawn into the action by the music. It is ironic, then, that the music can, in a way, be considered one such "alienation effect." The "Leitmotiv" is also an "epic" device, for it introduces reflection into the drama. One can, building on Hilda M. Brown's work, consider Wagner's use of the "Leitmotiv," which is, after all, just another kind of repetition, a similar inspiration to link events, analyze situations, and thus interpret the drama, even though Wagner's music is supposed to draw the viewer or listener in rather than alienate him or her.

While Wagner does not introduce a narrator into his dramas the way Brecht does, one can, as Dieter Borchmeyer does, consider the orchestra, in its capacity of commenting on the action of the drama, as some kind of omniscient narrator.[4] The music also comments on the words, showing the fallacy of a character's reasoning or his or her lack of veracity. Sometimes the orchestra expresses to the audience something that the character singing at the moment does not know, just making the character's lack of knowledge blatant. Wagner's music-drama, with the music and verbal text commenting on each other and intertwining, is thus by definition not a totally unified work of art. It contains within itself criticism and reflection.

Reinhold Grimm discusses the alienation effect at length and elaborates upon its various manifestations, extending the definition to all sorts of structural devices and even the rhetorical textual level of the plays.[5] I do not intend a complete survey of these techniques. My point is that there are similar ones in Wagner's dramas. Curiously enough, though the music is intended by Wagner to appeal to the emotions of the listener, it, too, when used in certain ways, can create an "alienation effect" and cause the various mediums of the art-work of the future to diverge from each other, prompting a critical stance in the audience. When the music comments on the words as Wagner often has it do, it conveys to the audience something that the character who is singing either does not know or does not want to admit to himself or herself, let alone to the others onstage.

For instance, Brecht uses contrast for the purpose of alienation. Repetition can also achieve this end. Grimm calls this a kind of "double vision," whereby an event is seen under various aspects. Similarly, Wagner's *Ring* has what one could call a "double vision" that results from the inclusion of "epic" portions, with the narrations of the characters giving varying interpretations of an event, and repeated discourses by the same character presenting not so much an account of the objective event or thing, such as the theft of the gold or the accursed ring, as one's subjective perception of it. To the end of alienation, Brecht also uses the device of the "play within the play." Wagner, similarly, has implicit "play within the play" structures in the *Ring*, with, for instance, characters such as Wotan and Hagen manipulating others for their own devious purposes.

Further similarities between the two dramatists concern the practical purposes that they intended their works of art to achieve. Neither dramatist's work represents art for its own sake. There was a practical purpose for Wagner's appeal to feeling, and Brecht's appeal (conversely) to understanding. Both men believed strongly in the possibility of social change, though Brecht's work is, of course, more directly political than Wagner's. Some of Brecht's plays deal with contemporary political events such as the rise of Fascism in a realistic way, while even Wagner's two "historical" operas, *Meistersinger* and *Rienzi*, place the action at a Romantic distance from normal societal reality. However, both of them saw a close interrelation of aesthetics and politics, and they both expressed it in their works. This interrelation of aesthetics and politics determines, to a certain extent, the form and the content of their works or, one could say, their dramas and the aesthetic theory that underlies and shapes them. Furthermore, because of their views on life and art, each of them revises, in an attempt to overcome, the form of tragedy.

When contending with the topic of Brecht and his drama theory, one also confronts issues and problems similar or analogous to those of Wagner scholarship. Critics discuss how his theory changed over time, and what differences exist between the various versions of his theory as expressed in his various essays. In addition, they question whether, and if so, how, his plays really demonstrate this theory. Perhaps most fundamental to Brecht scholarship, though, are questions about ideology. This topic, with some mixed results, provides an apt point of comparison with Wagner. Some of the names that scholars most often discuss with relation to the political aspects of Brecht's dramas are, after all, not unknown to Wagner scholarship. Gregor-Dellin, for instance, raises the question of what Wagner knew and read of Karl Marx.[6]

Critics treat the differences between Brecht's changing uses of terms such as "entfremden" and "verfremden," record when he first started using each term, and debate about whether he uses it in the same sense as such thinkers as Marx and Hegel.[7] We know when he joined the Communist Party or when his official "conversion" to Marxism was, though it is usually unlikely that the philosophical doctrines of one thinker will enter the aesthetic theories of an artist or writer unchanged. Furthermore, often an acquaintance with a philosopher can just allow an artist to conceptualize something that was already present in his works from the beginning of his career. Having noted these problems and having voiced these cautionary remarks, I would venture to say that most agree that basic to Brecht's work, in many ways, is his political engagement.

Both dramatists under discussion are, to some extent, politically oriented. My task is to show how this is reflected in the dramas that I am analyzing in this chapter. Some of Wagner's works, of course, have little or nothing to do with politics, such as *Lohengrin, Holländer,* or *Tristan und Isolde.* It is hard to discuss the *Ring,* though, without in some way dealing with politics and exploring what values it opposes to those of gold and capitalism. The *Ring* tetralogy shows the ills of modern society, and it actually proposes a way to repair them. One must remember that the *Ring* is only indirectly political. But one cannot deny that *Oper und Drama* outlines a theory of revolutionary drama based on the aesthetic program of changing society.

One dare not, of course, seek too firm a connection between the political beliefs of Wagner and Brecht, nor is this really necessary. Brecht's drama is firmly rooted in, specifically, Marxism. Wagner's politics were unconventional and unique. He propounded a sort of Idealistic-Romantic utopian politics of organizing society around and by his own music-drama and theater. But one can say that Brecht's works arose from the basic conviction that the world can and should be changed, and that his plays could help bring this change about. Wagner, though his political beliefs were different from Brecht's, was also occupied with these same concerns when he wrote the *Ring.* Not only were their political beliefs different, but the relation of art and politics was, in some ways, the reverse for each of these dramatists. Their priorities were different.

Critics such as Andrea Mork have noted how Wagner, in his theoretical writings, has a tendency to treat politics in aesthetic terms.[8] Brecht, one could say, treats art (drama) with concepts such as dialectic, which are probably more appropriate to his political philosophy. Wagner subsumed politics under art, as he was, after all, a revolutionary for the sake of his art. A new society would enable him to realize his artistic ideal, and he felt that the decadence of his contemporary world was evident in the way it had debased art. In contrast, writing plays and aesthetic treatises was, for Brecht, a kind of politicizing. Art was to serve the cause of, that is, help bring about, a revolution, a Marxist overthrow of society.

According to Wagner, the novel depicted individuals in their social and political milieu, and thus only the novel could be directly political. It showed the individual as a product of his or her environment. In contrast, drama, he felt, could portray the free individual, "das Reinmenschliche" (the purely human). For these reasons, I would argue, the *Ring* is only indirectly political, just as, in *Oper und Drama*, Wagner illustrates his drama theory of reworking Greek tragedy and thus causing the overthrow of the "state" by retelling the myth of Oedipus and Antigone. Wagner felt that social drama was not real drama. But he just might have approved of Brecht's aims. Whether the ends would have justified the means for him is another question.

In contrast to Wagner, Brecht wanted to depict human beings in their social and political milieu.[9] While Wagner's *Ring* represents, in many ways, a revolt against the modern scientific age in which he found himself, with its basic fragmentation and dehumanization, Brecht strove to create a kind of theater commensurate to the modern scientific age, with its corresponding world-view. For Brecht, epic theater was the only adequate expression of the modern world. In discussing how and why Brecht achieves this, one is also treating the form of tragedy and questioning the possibility of tragedy in the twentieth century.

Brecht's purpose was to make the audience aware that change was both possible and necessary. To this end, Brecht used a behavioristic, pragmatic philosophy. For Brecht, epic theater was an instrument for social change. He felt that no other drama techniques but non-Aristotelian or epic ones were appropriate to his Marxist social philosophy and revolutionary intentions. For instance, Brecht is not concerned with showing unity of character. By demonstrating the decisive effect of external factors on a figure, he depicts the figure not as a constant but, rather, as a product of the environment. In order to get the audience to think about the interaction of a character and a situation, or question why an individual acts the way he or she does in a particular instance, Brecht makes the contradictions of the character evident.[10]

The political concerns of each of these men and the different means that they used toward achieving them are expressed by their differing stances toward history and myth. In other words, their stances are reflected by their choice of raw material. Each chooses his raw material, specifically, whether it should be historical or mythical, because of his specific political concerns and his resultant drama theory; that is, he chooses his type of subject matter to fit his concerns, persuasion, and drama theory. One could say that both valued human autonomy, but they extol it in different ways. One uses history, and the other, myth.

Wagner, functioning within the Romantic tradition, chooses mythological music-drama; he defines his revision of tragedy as a specifically mythological product. Strange as it may seem, for Wagner, mythological music-drama was a means to social change. He felt that only myth could portray "das Reinmenschliche." Brecht did not envision a mythical-historical utopia such as Wagner wished to bring about. Brecht opted for depicting the real world and dealing with history rather than myth. Wagner wants to transcend tragedy through myth; Brecht negates tragedy. In Brecht's work, history denies and defies myth. Later I demonstrate this with the Brecht-Weill *Mahagonny* in particular.

Critics usually see Aristotelian and non-Aristotelian (or epic) drama as reflecting different stances toward the world and different world-views. Critics usually see the form of non-Aristotelian drama as reflecting a challenge to, and denial of, mankind's autonomy. It supposedly showed that the individual had become a passive object of outside forces. Non-Aristotelian drama presents a more comprehensive world-view and a kind of objectivity more appropriate to the form of epic than to that of drama. In traditional drama, the individual is the subject of his or her world; a character of epic is, in contrast, the object of his or her surroundings, for he or she lacks autonomy and is at odds with his or her environment. With the increasing weight that history assumed in the nineteenth century, and thus the societal determinism that writers and artists became more and more aware of, the hero became passive, and drama became nondramatic.

Tragedy implies fate, which, in turn, means an inability to change one's miserable objective circumstances or a corrupt external world. Tragedy portrays a fatalistic world-view. It depicts the clash of free will and destiny, the volition of the tragic hero and the fate that has power over him. Tragedy is a dramatic, not an epic, form. It portrays a confrontation of mankind with the gods, fate, or circumstances. Though he is tragically doomed to failure, the protagonist of a tragedy does have free will. The tragic hero has freedom to act, and though his demise is not totally his own doing, he falls of his own accord. For this reason, he is tragic.

When one analyzes the drama theory of Wagner and Brecht, though, it seems somehow ironic that epic theater, in which the dramas of both can be classified, is usually considered, in its world-view, a denial of the autonomy of mankind. The ultimate aim of both Wagner and Brecht is to affirm human autonomy and thereby change the world. One wonders, however, if Wagner, in a kind of indirect way, undoes tragedy because of his non-Aristotelian world-view. Because he saw the world as being overtaken by determinism and the mechanism of an inhuman society, he decided to reaffirm human autonomy through a mythological musical-dramatic renewal of the world.

This is, one could say, demonstrated by the *Ring*. The aim of the whole aesthetic program of the *Ring* was to overcome tragedy onstage, showing the Romantic transcendence of tragedy in the universal redemption at the close of *Götterdämmerung*, and to thereby cause a redemption of tragedy in reality by inducing in the audience, through the experience of the *Ring*, some kind of revolutionary consciousness. Myth and tragedy (or the revision and transcendence thereof), for Wagner, imply each other. Both Wagner and Brecht are revising tragedy for the age in which they lived. But the twentieth-century negation of tragedy differs immeasurably from the nineteenth-century Romantic revision of tragedy. Brecht's drama theory totally obviates the possibility of tragedy in the modern world.

Brecht intends the transcendence (if this term, which has metaphysical implications, can be used for realistic social change such as that which Brecht envisioned) to take place in the real world. It is, for this purpose, noticeably absent from his stage picture. His plays end, significantly enough, nowhere. They do not contain anything comparable to the universal redemption that sounds at the end of the *Ring* cycle. Brecht's denial of tragedy is very different from Wagner's transcendence of tragedy. Societal renewal is markedly absent from Brecht's finales. George Steiner writes that Marxism, like Christianity, means an avoidance of the tragic.[11] Ronald Gray points out that Brecht was not a fatalist, and that he regarded a tragic outcome of plays as fatalism. "Man must be shown as capable of avoiding tragedy," writes Gray.[12] Brecht was not alone in doubting the viability of tragedy at the time in which he lived. Friedrich Dürrenmatt, for instance, wrote about the impossibility of tragedy in the twentieth century. The age, he felt, was more suited to comedy.[13]

In his *Messingkauf*, Brecht wrote that the fate of mankind is mankind, and that tragedy should be used to eliminate those situations in which people feel fear of each other and must feel pity for, or compassion with, each other. The causes of tragedy, he felt, cannot be outside the power of those who suffer them. They only seem to be beyond the control of people. It is almost as though Brecht were translating Wagner's psychological interpretation of the Greek concept of fate into direct political action. Thus Brecht has completely unworked tragedy. There is no central conflict in his plays; no catastrophe, and no reconciliation. Because they leave so many questions unanswered, as the aim of these plays is to provoke questioning, Brecht's plays deliberately fail to fulfill the standard requirement that tragedy needs to depict the world as having some sort of Absolute or to show a belief in some kind of transcendence. Brecht undermines rigid belief systems. In the light of my later analysis, it will also seem no coincidence that Brecht's *Messingkauf* is divided into four evenings, just like the *Ring.*

The differences in how Wagner and Brecht relate aesthetics and politics become obvious through a comparison of their versions of the Antigone myth. To illustrate his revolutionary theory of tragedy or his utopian unworking of Greek tragedy in the second part of *Oper und Drama,* Wagner retells and thereby interprets the story of Oedipus. For Wagner, this myth portrays world-history, in other words the conflict between custom and free self-determination that is, according to Wagner, the basic dichotomy in Greek tragedy, and that therefore is central to his modern German unworking and transcendence of tragedy. Antigone, Wagner writes, acts with purely human motives. In Wagner's interpretation, she indirectly causes the destruction of the state by attempting to bury her subversive brother, for, according to Wagner, the state is destroyed when the ruler Creon, at the sight of the corpse of his son, who killed himself out of love for Antigone, becomes a father. According to Wagner, the Antigone myth gives a symbolic or mythical account of world-history. It portrays a veiled historical progression.

Brecht, like Wagner, formulated a reworking of the Antigone story that reveals his basic concerns and political orientation.[14] Brecht's interpretation is, predictably enough, much more directly political than that of Wagner. According to Brecht, the story portrays a totalitarian regime and the forces opposing it, and questions the use of power by a head of state. Brecht interprets and reworks the play to show the overthrow of tyranny and the move to democracy. Brecht was a more rational human being than Wagner. Unlike Brecht, Wagner deals in abstractions; that is, he uses myth instead of history. For Brecht, Antigone represents the "Volk" that is drawn by a ruler to ruin. Polynices is a rabble-rouser, a rebel who opposes the totalitarian regime.

In some respects, the interpretations of these two men are similar. For Brecht, as for Wagner, Antigone acts with purely human motives, and thus both feel she demonstrates what Wagner called "das Reinmenschliche." But Brecht uses this myth to depict an individual historical case or a specific historical event. He does not deal solely in mythical terms or abstract patterns. The parallels are obvious: Hitler is Creon, and the war against Argos is that of Germany against the Soviet Union. Creon is, for Brecht, merely an inhuman tyrant. Brecht has no interest in mythology per se or recombining mythological elements or motives.

Furthermore, Brecht, like Wagner, rejects the idea of an inherited family curse. In *Oper und Drama,* Wagner theorizes that the curse of Greek tragedy was the projection or fiction of a conservative society, which it used to psychologically coerce a nonconformist into behavior that was more acceptable from the standpont of society. According to Wagner, then, "fate" is nothing metaphysical. Thus Wagner dematerializes the traditional tragic curse. Similarly, Brecht did not see fate as something unchangeable and impersonal, but, rather, he felt that fate was something that human beings really made for themselves. It does not arise from magical and mysterious curses or other supernatural powers. Antigone represents, in Brecht's version of this myth, anti-Fascist opposition. Brecht is concerned with the conflict of classes, and he feels that a regime that does not address the problem of class differences and conflicts cannot survive in the long run.

In the final section of this chapter, I undertake a comparison of two works that, unlike these two reworkings of the Antigone story, do not really seem to be analogous. To compare one of Brecht's dramas with four of Wagner's, one can refer all of them (in two sets, of course) to a basic set of concepts. To find Marxist ideas and theories in Brecht's plays is circular and tautological. It is far more interesting to link these basic ideas to how they were used (in a Marxist or non-Marxist way) in the previous German tradition. Wagner was also dissatisfied with his contemporary world, and, like Brecht, he wrote dramas to solve societal problems, believing that political change could be brought about by aesthetic means, and that the world could be bettered from the inside out.[15] Is he, then, a forerunner of Brecht?

HISTORY VERSUS MYTH

To investigate the possible influence of Wagner on Brecht, or to demonstrate parallels between their works and contrast a pair of their dramas, I propose that the political concerns of each dramatist and the different means that each man uses to achieve them are expressed by the way each views the functions of history and myth, and the relative merits (or lack thereof) that each dramatist attributes to them. In his theoretical writings, Wagner presents a dialectic of history and myth, and I have repeatedly pointed to how the *Ring* represents this. I would generalize that history occupies, for Brecht, the same position that myth does for Wagner. Furthermore, the relationship of history and myth was, for the two men, opposite. Accordingly, I show, in the final section of this chapter, how Brecht, with the text and the plot of *Mahagonny*, parodistically reverses the mythical-historical program represented by Wagner's *Ring*.

Two concepts that are used by scholars when discussing Brecht's drama theory will prove particularly applicable to my comparison of Brecht with Wagner. The terms that correspond to history and myth for Brecht scholarship are historicization and parable. In this section, I define these concepts of Brecht scholarship to the aim of constructing some kind of Brechtian equivalent of Wagner's theoretical dichotomy and interrelationship of history and myth. Defining the first of these, "historicization" ("Historisierung"),[16] means discussing how Brecht's plays are, in various ways, historical, or outlining the ways in which they historicize reality. Wagner, of course, felt that history had no place in drama. In contrast, Brecht's plays are basically "historical" in several different (but not totally unrelated) ways.

First, most simply and fundamentally, the action of "epic theater" takes place in the past. This is by definition; it occurs automatically; and it is intrinsic to his drama theory. Epic theater depicts the action that it is presenting as having happened already; that is, it historicizes the action. Alienation, because it means placing something at a distance, is in itself historicization, and vice versa. When historical subject matter is chosen, there is yet another level of historicization. Furthermore, epic theater is supposed to make the viewer aware of its historicity. Conditions are depicted by the drama as changeable, and thus the present is relativized. This can be considered a kind of temporal alienation.

The contrast with Wagner's theory is obvious. Wagner wanted to portray "das Reinmenschliche," and he stressed myth as something timeless. Myth, he felt, had a kind of immediacy. As it represented a compressed worldview, it could be easily grasped by the capacity of feeling. For Brecht, however, the historicity of reality should be brought to the consciousness of the spectator. The audience should, in some way, be taken out of the present, and thus made to take a critical stance toward it. Whereas for Brecht there is a close connection between historicization and alienation, Wagner stressed the opposing pair of concepts. Wagner felt that myth appealed to the feeling, and that it had a sensual immediacy; that is, that it was fully present, and that it spoke to the present. According to Wagner, myth, even mythical music-drama, which is synthetic myth and thus not strictly "mythical," was supposed to overcome the alienation of the modern world.

Klaus-Detlef Müller points out that Marxism is essentially a philosophy of history, as it deals with the dialectic of society, that is, of the historical reality. Furthermore, Müller points out that the Brechtian drama shows the forces at work in history, in other words, that it demonstrates the laws of historical development. Brecht felt that these laws should not be illustrated in a purely abstract way but, rather, that they should be depicted at work in individual instances. For Brecht, the individual is a function of events, not vice versa. The base determines the superstructure, as is consistent with the tenets of Marxism. Klaus-Detlef Müller argues that history is a formal dimension of Brecht's plays. A concrete reality is alienated in a way that will show its structure or its laws. Historicization is thus the depiction of the historical rules at work in concrete reality. History is actualized, and the actual is historicized.

Because of the very historicity of the typical Brecht play, the work is a parable.[17] This may seem to be contradictory—Wagner would certainly have thought so, and he would have denied the possibility of reconciling the two concepts, much as this synthesis or dialectic of history and myth seems intrinsic to his theory of societal critique through mythological refabrication. However, in a paradoxical way, pairing these concepts dialectically makes perfect sense within Brecht's theory and system. A parable is a story that is told for some specific purpose. It answers a question or solves a problem. The parable, too, is an alienation effect. It is a pedagogical instrument, and it is intended to bring the audience to some kind of realization. It has sense only when one assumes that knowledge can change reality. To help parallel the systems of Wagner and Brecht, "parable," I would argue, is the Brechtian equivalent of myth, as it implies "mythical," timeless laws. Brecht's "parable" is a Brechtian version of what Wagner called "das Reinmenschliche."

The Brechtian play is a parable because it is a scenic presentation of the historical process and the laws by which society functions. Brecht sees reality not as substance but as process. One can consider the Brecht drama a kind of skeleton or X-ray. The parable is an analogy. The theater shows a model of reality. The assumption is that history operates according to laws. Insofar as the historical presentation is alienated, it becomes a parable. Because it is a parable, though, the play, as regards content, is historicized, for the given reality is, so to speak, made transparent so as to reveal the historical laws that determine the structure of reality. The parable is an "alienated" presentation of reality that shows the historical laws of reality. Through the process of historicization emerges a model of reality.

Brecht's work thus unites two important trends of postwar drama, two ways of reacting to historical and political conditions. It shows both a turn toward history, that is, an emphasis on external reality, and an abstraction from this reality to form an allegory or parable. One could say that these two extremes correspond to history and myth. Postwar dramatists either criticized society directly, such as in the documentary theater, or withdrew into the form of the allegory or parable.[18] These are two basic ways of dealing with history: one can either historicize or mythicize. These options, however, are by no means mutually exclusive. Like that of the other dramatists I have been discussing, Brecht's output shows the interrelationship of history and myth.

In Brecht's work, the process of historicization and the form of the parable imply each other reciprocally, just as there is, in Wagner's theory, an interrelationship of history and myth. Discussing the theory of Brecht and its interrelationship of mythical and historical drama reminds us that Wagner's myths lack all mythical timelessness, and these stories, which may seem to be eternally valid, were written from the perspective of a nineteenth-century artist. Wagner's works are essentially timely reflections on timelessness, in other words synthetic, what might be called second-order, myths. One could say that Wagner historicizes myth. Not only does he want to realize it in the real world, with myth being the beginning and end of history in his three-stage teleology, but onstage he also portrays a myth that is somehow historical. His gods are human and mortal. Though their situations and concerns are vastly different from ours, in other ways they have many of the same problems as normal people.

The relationship between history and myth was, however, the reverse for these two men. Despite the similarities of their theories, one cannot deny that Brecht inverts Wagner's priorities. Brecht is saying that historical drama can somehow be mythical. Wagner felt the opposite way. According to Wagner, only mythical drama was an appropriate portrayal of, and comment on, history. One could even say that history fulfills for Brecht the function that myth does for Wagner. The two systems seem to complement each other. Characteristically, Brecht's ideas turn Wagner's right around. Then, also typically, he demolishes them completely.

Brecht's dramaturgy thus seems to be a negative version of Wagner's theory. The double negative might make a positive for Brecht. One can see historicized history as forming, in Brecht's work, a kind of myth. For Wagner, myth comments on history. In doing so, it can also change history. For Brecht, though, history forms a myth; it can become a parable. In this manner, Brecht establishes an identity of two things that Wagner felt were dissimilar and could be reconciled only in a great cataclysm, a mythical-historical musical-dramatic renewal of society. When *Mahagonny* is discussed with reference to Wagner's *Ring*, it shows this mythical-historical inversion drastically.

The aesthetic project of Wagner's *Ring* is based on the productive interchange between history and myth. This, in turn, is possible only when one acknowledges the basic dichotomy of the two. Wagner states that myth is the beginning and end of history. By writing the *Ring* and thus mythicizing history, that is, by forming a myth that tells the story of history, Wagner hoped, via the audience reception of this work, to historicize myth and usher in a new Golden Age. Brecht, however, completely collapses the dichotomy of history and myth that Wagner saw as some kind of dialectic interchange. In Brecht's work, history is a myth. Thus, mythical patterns such as those that the *Ring* is based on are in Brecht's work not viable, and for these reasons they appear in *Mahagonny* only in a distorted and debased way. The musical texture changes the Wagnerian style in a like manner. It sounds appropriate to the work at hand. This is the basic comparison that I pursue in more detail, in both a theoretical and a literary-critical way, in the remainder of this chapter.

The concepts of historicization and parable provide the link between Brecht's thought and the aesthetic program of Wagner's *Oper und Drama*, a parallel that I will, in the next section, pursue in more detail. The divergent views of Wagner and Brecht on history and myth in drama can be illustrated by a comparison of the *Ring* with *Mahagonny*. I am not the first to investigate the affinities and divergences between the works of Wagner and Brecht. Vera Stegmann, for instance, has argued that Brecht's work can be understood with reference to Wagner's.[19] I wish to take some of her ideas further and demonstrate the notion of Brecht's work being a parody of Wagner's with close analysis of a selection of specific texts and particular issues.

In the final sections of this chapter, I show how *Mahagonny* is not only a parody of the form of opera, among which Brecht obviously saw Wagner's works, counter to the explicit wishes of the composer, but also a parody of the *Ring* as a particular mythological music-drama (or set of dramas). I argue that the Brecht-Weill *Mahagonny* parodies, specifically, the mythological elements of the *Ring*. Thus, it is a parody of the Wagnerian unworking and transcendence of tragedy, as Wagner defined tragedy (or his transcendence thereof) as a mythological work of art. Furthermore, as Wagner felt that myth needed music as its vehicle and that tragedy was a synthesis of various art-forms, a total work of art, the Brecht-Weill *Mahagonny* parodies Wagner's reunion of the arts as well.

THE QUESTION OF GENRE: OPERA, MUSIC-DRAMA, AND EPIC THEATER

Each of the two dramas that I will discuss, *Mahagonny* and the *Ring* cycle, has a theoretical work that somehow, either explicitly or implicitly, accompanies it. The theoretical treatise serves to define to one's contemporaries (and the author's opponents especially) the genre of the dramatic work and thus ground the work within musical and dramatic history. These two treatises, as the theoretical groundings of the works under discussion, tell us some important things about them. They serve to define the works and identify their genre. Already it is clear that they stand in an inverse relationship to each other. Even the essay that Brecht wrote about *Mahagonny* identifies this dramatic work as a Wagner parody, for Brecht's ideas stand in inverse relations to Wagner's in ways that go far beyond the obvious.

In this essay Brecht is not, it is true, discussing primarily Wagner. Rather, the essay is directed against Weill and those who felt that the form of "opera" could be revived and renewed.[20] For Weill, the music was more important than the text, and this angered Brecht. Weill and Busoni proposed innovation and reform of opera by means of purely musical reforms. For Weill, opera was a musical form. Brecht answered Weill's emphasis on the musical side of the matter with the essay on *Mahagonny*, thus focusing on the social function of music and art. Brecht doubted that the art of opera could be renovated. He judged music not by its form but by its effect and reception, its function in society. The essay under discussion, one could say, is a twentieth-century counterpart or, one could also say, a Brechtian version of *Oper und Drama*.

Though both Brecht and Weill opposed Wagner, the collaborators on *Mahagonny* thought differently about music and opera. Wagner can, of course, be considered as a background influence (or deterrent) to Brecht. Others have noted this connection. For instance, Vera Stegmann suggests that Brecht was rebelling against Wagner, and that his work should be understood within the context of European anti-Wagnerism, a trend to which also belonged the jazz movement, Ferruccio Busoni, the French group of composers "Les Six" (with whom Jean Cocteau and Eric Satie were associated), and Igor Stravinsky. Brecht understood his theater, Stegmann argues, in opposition to that of Wagner. Under the influence of his teacher Busoni and possibly Brecht, Weill also rejected Wagner's subject matter and his form of music-drama.

Vera Stegmann, among others, has noted the way the treatise under discussion reverses Wagner's reunion of the various arts in the "Gesamt-kunstwerk." This is an obvious allusion. Other features seem to clearly identify the essay as an unworking of Wagner's theory. It is hard to imagine Brecht's use of such words as "Magie" (magic) and "Hypnotisierversuche" (attempts at hypnotism) as not being directed specifically against Wagner's art. Furthermore, the Nietzschean connotations of the word "Rausch" (intoxication), recalling as it does *Die Geburt der Tragödie*, make it seem likely that this essay was also influenced by Nietzsche's late anti-Wagner writings, which Stegmann mentions that Brecht knew (AzM 79).[21] Certain passages of the essay, indeed, seem to clearly place it in the German tradition of describing the dangers of Wagner's art.

The essay even mentions Wagner directly. Brecht admits that some traditional operas (such as *Zauberflöte*, *The Marriage of Figaro*, and *Fidelio*) arose from ideological principles, but these ideas have become lost with time, and the function of opera as entertainment has eclipsed them. Wagner's opera, Brecht says, was still basically culinary. The Wagnerians are content with knowing that these works were once ideologically deter-mined, but these meanings have become lost with time. His main point seems to be that Wagner's art wound up being precisely what Wagner revolted against and insisted that his art was not. The parallel and parody, however, go much deeper than these points. In identifying his own work as an "opera," Brecht implicitly pulls the rug out from under Wagner.

Despite the fact that Brecht was a dramatist and Wagner a composer, too, their theories do have some similarities. Both theoretical treatises under discussion arose from the same polemical intention. Brecht, like Wagner, was opposing his contemporaries. Furthermore, both are objecting to the kind of "opera" that was fashionable at the time. Even though Brecht is not intending the essay to be directed specifically against Wagner, the essay under discussion reads, in many ways, like a parody of Wagner's aesthetics. In particular, it seems to be parodying the aesthetic system that Wagner presents in *Oper und Drama*. The essay by Brecht serves to ground the musical-dramatic work that it explicates according to genre. In other words, this theoretical work deals with defining the genres of music, opera, and drama. The reversals and distorted parallels between the two systems of Wagner and Brecht blatantly illustrate the different outlooks and philoso-phies of Wagner and Brecht.

Because of its anti-opera polemical intent, Brecht's essay closely resembles *Oper und Drama*. Both Wagner and Brecht have different ways of objecting to the emphasis on the purely musical element in opera. To Brecht's chagrin, Weill, like those "opera" composers so anathema to Wagner, stressed the music. Wagner felt that the main problem of contemporary opera was that the music, which should be a means to the greater end of the drama, had been made into an end in itself. Brecht was also interested in more than mere entertainment. He felt that the function of the music for society was more important than its use as mere entertainment. According to Brecht, the form of "opera" encouraged a passive stance toward (or away from) the outside world, and thus he, like Wagner, objected to the current emphasis on the musical side of it. *Mahagonny* was therefore not intended to be a renewal of "opera" but, rather, a work that demonstrated the problems of opera, in other words, a sociological experiment.

Furthermore, the Brecht essay has many other surface similarities to the Zurich writings, besides an attack on "opera," with a discussion of the term. For example, it takes a standpoint on the synthesis of the various art-forms; it voices an opposition to mere entertainment; and it presents a discussion of the function of art, in particular "opera," in society. The artistic circumstances under which it was written were comparable to those that gave rise to *Oper und Drama*. Its polemical purpose is comparable. But upon closer analysis, without necessarily being intended as such, Brecht's essay seems a spoof or parody of *Oper und Drama*. When the two theoretical works are read together, the Brecht essay definitely comes across as ironic or tongue-in-cheek.

It is generally acknowledged that *Oper und Drama* is the theoretical counterpart of the *Ring* cycle. Not only does it "ground" the *Ring* in the teleology of musical-dramatic history, but in this treatise, Wagner uses a three-stage model that the tetralogy also contains, and he discourses at length on the relation of words and music, with the correspondence to the *Ring*, the "Leitmotiv" system, for example, clear and easy to establish. Wagner did not want the works that constituted the *Ring* termed "operas" or received within the category of "opera." This is one of the main points, if not the very basis, of *Oper und Drama*. He felt that he wrote the latter, not the former, type of work. The treatise is based on the opposition of his brand of art to traditional "opera," which he ruthlessly criticizes. Similarly, Bayreuth was founded in opposition to the big-city commercialization of art, in particular, opera.

Oper und Drama presents a theory of mythological refabrication and reconstruction on a modern level of self-consciousness. It sketches a theory of mythological music-drama on the stage of reflection. The treatise by Brecht that I discuss here can be understood as *Oper und Drama* on the stage of reflection. One could say that it reads like a reflection on *Oper und Drama*. The two theoretical writings relate to each other like a negative to a positive.

Wagner criticizes opera, proposing music-drama instead. His treatise advocates a synthesis of the arts, which in the course of time had become separated. Brecht does the opposite of what Wagner does. He destroys the total work of art to replace it with, ironically, opera.

Like the first of the Zurich writings, "Die Kunst und die Revolution," the first part of Brecht's treatise discusses the interrelationship of art and society. Wagner objected to the modern commercialization of art, feeling that art was being debased when it was used as mere entertainment. Brecht, too, describes the evils of the modern commercialized artistic apparatus, but his stance is, to a large extent, ironic and ambivalent. He does not object to this commercialization of art the way Wagner does. He is writing a work similar to those he is opposing, an anti-opera to oppose an opera, and his opposition to the apparatus is only apparent because he knows this effort is, in the last result, basically futile. Thereby he surrenders blithely to a pursuit that he categorically opposes. The apparatus, he resigns, cannot really be opposed.

Reforms are, he seems to be saying, futile. If a reform succeeds, it is because it did not really threaten the entertainment function of the artistic apparatus, and it did not intend to change society. Art is a ware, and the apparatus functions to provide entertainment for the evening. Brecht ends the first section of his essay with a statement concerning the use of the term "Oper." The problem is simple. "Eine Oper kann man nur für die Oper machen" (AzM 76) (One can write an opera only for the opera house). Wagner's works are, after all, performed in "opera houses." They are, Brecht seems to be saying, despite Wagner's efforts and protests to the contrary, "operas." One suspects that Brecht wants to parody Wagner by writing what he jokingly acknowledges as an opera. Wagner's undertaking, Brecht might very well have felt, was futile.

Furthermore, Wagner's Bayreuth project arose in direct and explicit opposition to the big-city commercialization of art. Some, and probably Brecht was among them, feel that it was impossible to decommercialize music-drama. Brecht states, simply enough, "Kunst ist Ware—ohne Produktionsmittel (Apparate) nicht herzustellen!" (AzM 76) (Art is a ware, and cannot be produced without the apparatus as a means of production). When the *Ring* is considered with these basic definitions in mind, Brecht is essentially labeling Wagner's art as what he describes as an aquatic creature that has been invented by Böcklin, in other words, a nonentity. Brecht writes, "Selbst wenn man die Oper als solche (ihre Funktion!) zur Diskussion stellen wollte, müsste man eine Oper machen" (AzM 76) (Even if one wanted to pose the function of opera for discussion, one would still have to write an opera). The dilemma is circular, the art form inescapable.

In the second section of the essay, Brecht discusses the current state of opera. His use of the term "culinary opera" recalls how Wagner, in *Oper und Drama*, categorizes opera into the types of "serious" ("ernst") or "frivolous" ("frivol"). The present-day opera is, Brecht writes, "culinary opera." Brecht further defines his terms with the use of other key concepts. It was a means of pleasure before it became a ware. Brecht writes that *Mahagonny* has the basic attitude of opera, that is, the culinary. It approaches its topic with a stance of pleasure. Furthermore, it is an experience. The content of this opera, not its form, is pleasure. It offers enjoyment as a ware. In a footnote Brecht writes that Romanticism is also used as a ware; it is a content, not a form. I would argue, accordingly, that *Mahagonny* thematizes Romanticism, or, in particular, it discourses upon Wagner's *Ring* tetralogy. In the next section, I will point out various parodies of the Romantic tradition in this opera.

The term "culinary opera" would have been redundant to Wagner. As far as Wagner was concerned, all works that deserve the genre designation "opera" exist for mere entertainment and use music for the idle pleasure of an end in itself, whereas he felt that music is more properly a means of expression to the end of what is therefore not opera but, rather, drama. By identifying his work as an "opera," Brecht is doing the direct opposite of what Wagner did, with Brecht's jocular attitude in the process making a mockery of Wagner and the Bayreuth Festival. Whereas Wagner writes in total opposition to opera, Brecht opposes opera by writing an opera. In doing so, he thus opposes, in a roundabout way, Wagner.

Brecht explicitly points out that the opera *Mahagonny* paradoxically shows the contradictions of opera. Brecht writes, "Die Oper 'Mahagonny' wird dem Unvernünftigen der Kunstgattung Oper bewusst gerecht" (AzM 76)[22] (The opera *Mahagonny* consciously does justice to all that is unreasonable in the artistic genre of opera). One could even call it an anti-opera, or an opera parody. It does not take itself seriously. Insofar as *Mahagonny* thematizes opera and is itself an opera, the work is self-referential, just as Romantic literature was, though in a far different way. Insofar as it is an opera, it thematizes itself. The comment that it makes about itself is a parodistic one. The work itself is thus, in its basic contradiction, a kind of nonentity, perhaps in that regard even comparable to an aquatic creature that has been invented by Böcklin. Brecht states, " 'Mahagonny' ist ein Spass" (AzM 76). ("Mahagonny" is a joke.) Ironically, in another way it takes itself very seriously, apparently poking fun mostly at Wagner.

Brecht continues to explain just why "opera" is so unreasonable. He writes, "Dieses Unvernünftige der Oper liegt darin, dass hier rationelle Elemente benutzt werden, Plastik und Realität angestrebt, aber zugleich alles durch die Musik wieder aufgehoben wird" (AzM 76) (The irrationality of opera lies in rational elements being used and plasticity and reality being striven for, but everything then being negated by the music). Brecht writes that the amount of pleasure that opera provides exists in direct proportion to its unreality. (Brecht was mainly concerned with history, and Wagner, with myth.) Whereas Wagner felt that music-drama could be a means toward the revolution of modern society, such a project, Brecht feels, is not only aesthetically unpleasing, but more important, it is societally unproductive and even dangerous.

The essence of *Mahagonny* as an operatic parody, in particular, a parody of the *Ring*, expresses what he thus describes as this futility of the genre. With *Mahagonny*, Brecht laughs at Wagner's music-drama. That Brecht felt the *Ring* cycle fit into the genre of opera and therefore parodied it in writing *Mahagonny* may well be evidence of the irony of artistic influence as well as the parodistic intent of Brecht. The music of *Mahagonny* is not grandiose and Wagnerian, and the Romantic elements and associations of the work that form parallels with the *Ring* are, by Brecht, accordingly deromanticized. In writing *Mahagonny*, Brecht and Weill bring the *Ring* down to the level of harsh reality. They are saying, perhaps, that it is precisely what it says it is not.

It may not be coincidental that some of Brecht's reasons for disapproving of "opera" distinctly recall Wagner's works. Brecht writes, "Ein sterbender Mann ist real. Wenn er zugleich singt, ist die Sphäre der Unvernunft erreicht" (AzM 76–77) (A dying man is real. When he sings at the same time, the height of unreason has been reached). When reading this, one cannot help but think of the dying Siegfried, who sings his last praise of Brünnhilde after he has been fatally wounded by Hagen's spear. Brecht's use of the term "conscious" ("bewusst") in his statement of how *Mahagonny* shows the shortcomings of the operatic form is important. He seems to be saying that Wagner's works are still unintentionally operatic. In *Mahagonny*, Brecht presents a conscious parody of both, opera and Wagnerian music-drama (which he sees, ironically enough, as identical). Furthermore, it is also no coincidence that the example that Brecht uses, that of a man singing as he is dying, is from Wagner's *Ring*, in particular, *Götterdämmerung*.

After Wagner discusses opera in the first part of *Oper und Drama*, he then treats drama in the second, reuniting these two forms in the third section, where he builds his own kind of music-drama or "art-work of the future." Whereas Wagner takes special care to set his music-drama apart from the traditional form of opera, such differentiations are less useful for Brecht. His opera is an opera. He deals only with the difference between traditional theater and "epic" drama. His essay has nevertheless a dual structure similar to that of *Oper und Drama*, as it contains a section about opera and a part about innovations. With his use of the two concepts "Oper" and "Neuerungen," which he finally unites to form the theory of "epic theater," which he opposes to traditional dramatic theater, Brecht's treatise seems a mockery of the dual terminological structure or tripartite thinking expressed in the title and basic argument of *Oper und Drama*.

Just as in the third section of *Oper und Drama*, Wagner treats the new genre and plans his innovations, Brecht, too, has ideas of his own that he wants to put into practice, and he therefore writes a section on "Neuerungen" (innovations) in the essay under discussion. With these innovations Brecht hopes to bring opera up to the technical standards of the modern theater, the epic theater. But Brecht's innovations are, significantly enough, the opposite of Wagner's. Calling them "innovations" is in itself ironic, and probably intentionally so. Brecht advocates a separation of the elements that Wagner strove so hard to theoretically and dramatically reunite. In that respect, Brecht's ideas are not innovational but, rather, reactionary. Just as Brecht separates the elements theoretically, he undoes the *Ring* with the plot of *Mahagonny*.

Brecht's introduction of this idea in his essay seems to parodistically or sarcastically answer Wagner's dilemma and that age-old problem of opera since its inception. The topic of words and music, Brecht essentially says, is a silly one. For him the issue is not even important. Brecht writes,

Der grosse Primatkampf zwischen Wort, Musik und Darstellung (wobei immer die Frage gestellt wird, wer wessen Anlass sein soll—die Musik der Anlass des Bühnenvorgangs, oder der Bühnenvorgang der Anlass der Musik usw.) kann einfach beigelegt werden durch die radikale Trennung der Elemente. (AzM 79)

The great fight for primacy between words, music, and presentation, which constantly poses the question of which one should be the occasion for the other, the music the excuse for the scenic presentation, or the scenic presentation the occasion for the music etc., can be simply dismissed by the radical separation of the elements.

Thus Brecht does, of course, obviate the entire issue and effectively end all debate about the primacy of one medium over the other. But he does so in a way that seems to obliterate the entire sense of Wagner's theoretical production and musical-dramatic undertaking. One can argue that Wagner's Golden Age, utopian thinking is regressive. But Brecht is being reactionary only insofar as he is reacting to, and undoing, Wagner's theory and dramas. In this manner Brecht's essay unworks Wagner's *Oper und Drama*. Brecht's innovations are retrogressive insofar as they dismantle the Wagnerian music-drama.

The term "Gesamtkunstwerk" is a blatant reference to Wagner. "Gesamtkunstwerk," Brecht writes, means "dass das Gesamte ein Aufwaschen ist, solange also Künste 'verschmelzt' werden sollen, müssen die einzelnen Elemente alle gleichermassen degradiert werden, indem jedes nur Stichwortbringer für das andere sein kann" (AzM 79) (that the whole thing is a mess, as long as the arts are fused together, the separate elements are each equally degraded, insofar as each is an excuse for the other). Thus, Brecht can totally dismiss the value of Wagner's union of the arts. Brecht deems Wagner's union of the arts a worthless and incoherent mass of art forms. One need not debate the primacy of the art forms in the total work of art because, according to Brecht, none of them really has any value anymore.

I propose that the correspondences between these two theoretical works that define the reciprocal genres to which the musical-dramatic works under discussion belong, just invite a comparison of the two dramatic (or nondramatic, as the case may be) works that these treatises accompany. I undertake such a comparison in the next section and demonstrate that the later work is an inversion of the former in certain important respects. The Brecht/Weill *Mahagonny* puts into practice the theory that this essay presents. Just as Brecht dismantles the Wagnerian theory in this essay, *Mahagonny* accordingly deconstructs Wagner's mythological tetralogy. Wagner's *Ring* represents the Romantic unworking of tragedy. Brecht, in turn, unworks Wagner's *Ring* with *Mahagonny*.

MAHAGONNY: A PARODY OF WAGNER'S *RING*

Critics have often commented upon Brecht's fondness for parody. One of his alienation effects consists in citation. By creating a tension between the original context of a citation and the new use to which the citation is put, Brecht encourages the audience to take a new look at familiar works. Scholars are fond of quoting Brecht's statement that the Bible was his favorite reading material, and they have shown that Biblical quotations can be found in his works. Parody, one could say, is a kind of indirect citation. It is a way of modeling one work upon another, and thus significantly changing a basic pattern or structure. This concept of parody, I argue, establishes the vital link between *Mahagonny* and the *Ring*.

Gunter G. Sehm has analyzed *Mahagonny* as a Biblical parody.[23] Sehm proposes that Brecht is evoking, in this work, specifically Biblical mythology. For instance, Sehm parallels the events of the plot with Biblical events. He suggests that the Widow Begbick may be modeled after the Old Testament God; that her prohibitions can be seen as a parody of the Ten Commandments; and that Paul Ackermann (the woodcutter from Alaska) can be considered a Christ-figure. Brecht's Bible parody, Sehm explains, demonstrates what the dramatist considers an essential contradiction in the Christian doctrine of salvation.

This is not the only kind of parody that has been found in Brecht's plays. Critics have also analyzed his plays with reference to various classic works of German literature. Hans Mayer, for instance, has argued that citations, in Brecht's plays, that Brecht has taken from the classic works of German literature function to comically transpose pathos into situations where it is totally inappropriate and thus turns ludicrous, showing the discrepancy between the original classical text and the Brechtian one.[24] I would like to explore parodies of the Romantic tradition, more particularly Wagner parodies, in *Mahagonny*.

It is, after all, common knowledge that Brecht opposed the Romantic tradition. Wilhelm Vosskamp, for instance, has discussed Brecht's relation to, and use of, the tradition of utopian thought and imagery.[25] Brecht was, he says, critical of such utopian thinking. His use of such motives is, accordingly, satirical. Brecht, Vosskamp shows, plays with traditional imagery and appeals to archetypical images and associations. Dümling points out how *Mahagonny* plays off of utopian and Romantic imagery and thinking.[26] Brecht's play represents a critique of mythological music-drama as well as (or even thus through it) a critique of utopian thinking. I argue that it exercises this critique through the concept of parody. In particular, it parodies these themes via the *Ring*.

Brecht's plays have also been analyzed as playing off of the traditional structure and themes of tragedy. Although he does not explicate *Mahagonny* in this context, Arnold Heidsieck discusses what he considers the travesty of tragedy in twentieth-century drama.[27] He demonstrates this phenomenon with specific pairs of texts. In his essay Heidsieck treats two plays of Brecht that he considers parodies of Classical models. He analyzes *Die heilige Johanna der Schlachthöfe* as a parody of Schiller's *Die Jungfrau von Orleans*, and he argues that *Der aufhaltsame Aufstieg des Arturo Ui* plays off of Goethe's *Faust* and Shakespeare's *Macbeth* and *Richard III*. I further apply this idea to the works at hand in this chapter. I propose that *Mahagonny* can be seen and heard as a parody of Wagner's utopian unworking of tragedy in the *Ring*.

Mahagonny certainly contains musical parodies of general operatic conventions. It blatantly opposes the "high," heroic, continuous Wagnerian style. In this manner, the music of *Mahagonny* reflects or echoes the drama theory represented by the opera.[28] While Richard Strauss was still working within the Wagnerian tradition even while parodying and thus relativizing it, with the mythological opera "Ariadne" represented by the heroic, Wagnerian continuous musical form (which is then ironically broken), the music of *Mahagonny* is a complete break with the Wagnerian tradition. *Mahagonny* is a total reversion to "numbers." It is not continuous. As is appropriate for the "epic" manner of depicting distinct episodes, the work is clearly separated into discrete numbers. The Wagnerian "Leitmotiv" system is an elaborate system of musical repetition. In the *Ring*, musical phrases assume complex psychological significance and present the critic with vast hermeneutical dilemmas. In *Mahagonny*, what are repeated are banal refrains, such as "Oh! Moon of Alabama / We now must say good-bye" (scenes 2 and 11); "Denn wie man sich bettet, so liegt man" (Because one must lie in the bed that one has made) (sung in scenes 11 and 16); and "Erstens, vergesst nicht, kommt das Fressen" (Do not forget that first one must eat), which recurs in scenes 13–16.[29]

Furthermore, Gottfried Wagner points out that Weill's music in the Brecht/Weill stage works has two levels.[30] Weill uses elements of both serious music (associated with such forms as opera and traditionally associated with the aristocracy) and "lower" music ("Unterhaltungsmusik"), intended for the bourgeoisie and the proletariat. One could parallel these two forms of "high" and "low" art with the two kinds of opera that Wagner discusses in *Oper und Drama*, "ernst" and "frivol," or the two styles of the heroic opera and the commedia dell'arte that meet and intermingle in *Ariadne auf Naxos*. However, whereas the Strauss opera outwardly and explicitly establishes the two separate forms as distinct and then mixes them, Weill wants to call into question clichés that link musical form or style and class differences. Weill uses elements of different kinds of music to alienate them from their original context and cause the audience to think critically.

The formal structures that Weill uses from the tradition of opera include the recitative, arioso, opera finale, and the "Leitmotiv" technique. The elements of less serious music include trite rhythm and catchy, tuneful (though trite) melody. The song form also falls into this latter category, a prime example of which is Jenny's "Alabama Song." The score for *Mahagonny* includes features of jazz and blues, for instance. The two musical levels are no longer separated, within the fiction, into different works of art that eventually meet onstage—rather, they run into each other in the same opera (which has no explicit frame or "work within the work" structure). In *Mahagonny*, (supposedly) serious music (opera) itself has elements of lower and less serious forms. The heroic opera style of "Ariadne" is totally absent. Furthermore, Gottfried Wagner explains that in the orchestra, Weill mixes, among the typical inhabitants of the nineteenth-century orchestra, instruments of twentieth-century music, such as the saxophone, banjo, and zither.[31]

In the work under discussion, Brecht and Weill parody not only traditional musical forms, but also the operatic plot-elements that they imply. Albrecht Dümling and Gottfried Wagner, for instance, have discussed how Weill's score contains musical citations and parodies.[32] Weill uses traditional forms that have certain associations, but gives them a new and incongruous function. Conventional operatic forms thereby become alienated, just as Ariadne's heroic aria is not meant to have a totally serious purpose by Strauss. Incongruity resides in anarchy and hedonism being represented by strict musical form. Dümling points out that the numbers of the second act, all variations on the theme of pleasure and consumption, form a rondo.[33]

To cite another instance, the approach of the hurricane is heralded by a fugue and a chorale. The traditional, archaic, Baroque-sounding form of the chorale, and the fact that the fugue is the utmost expression of musical order, are totally inappropriate to the dramatic situation. The gravity of the chorale creates an ironic effect, for it is too exaggerated an expression for the situation at hand. That the hurricane eventually takes a different course and misses the city just exaggerates the incongruity of the music with the action, and in this manner the work laughs at itself. The hurricane has been acknowledged as an obvious parody of impossible operatic events and the music that usually accompanies them. The fact that the hurricane misses the city by taking an absurd unnatural course has been taken to be a parody of the "deus ex machina" that miraculously saves the day in traditional opera. The discrepancy between what is happening onstage with the fugue and the chorale that musically express it creates parody.[34] Alienation results from the incongruity of the musical citation or musical form or convention with the present dramatic situation.

That the plot of *Mahagonny* can be understood as a parody of the content of Wagner's *Ring* as well as the aesthetic theory that the tetralogy embodies does not seem at all unlikely, especially considering that critics have also found specific parodies of other serious operatic music (by Weber, Mozart, or Wagner) in the Brecht/Weill *Mahagonny*. The most famous example is the "green moon of Alabama," a textual and melodic parody of the green bridal wreath chorus from Weber's *Freischütz*. There are, however, others. Paul Ackermann curses the day, like Tristan.[35] The chorus (scene 11)—"Haltet euch aufrecht, fürchtet euch nicht" (M 355–61) (Stay upright, do not be afraid)—plays off of a similar chorus in Mozart's *Zauberflöte*.[36]

Critics have, furthermore, found specific Wagner parodies in Brecht's work. Stegmann points to the "Ride of the Valkyries" in *Trommeln in der Nacht*, and notes that the final scene of *Mahagonny* is a parody of the final scene of *Parsifal*.[37] I would like to take the idea of Wagner parody in Brecht's work further and apply it to the texts under discussion here. Brecht, in the theoretical treatise that explicates *Mahagonny*, undoes the aesthetic program upon which the *Ring* is based. This theoretical contrast provides the foundation for a difference in the works themselves. Not only is *Mahagonny* an admittedly "culinary" opera, thus openly opposing Wagner's aesthetics, but I would like to demonstrate a deeper and more extensive transposition of the *Ring* in *Mahagonny*. The later work can, I propose, be identified as a parody of the former in other ways as well.

Many of the plays of Brecht that have been discussed as parodies of texts from the "standard" or classical canon of German literature are outwardly similar to their prototypes. *Die heilige Johanna der Schlachthöfe*, for instance, explicitly plays off of Schiller's *Jungfrau von Orleans*. Despite (or even because of) outward dissimilarity, I propose *Mahagonny* as a parody of the *Ring*. The dissimilarities are also significant. Both the *Ring* and *Mahagonny* demonstrate their own aesthetic programs. *Mahagonny* does this by, appropriately enough, parodistically turning the *Ring* inside-out.

What does *Mahagonny* have to do with the *Ring*? Both works take some kind of a stance toward the genre designation "opera," both represent an opposition to capitalistic society, and both are revisions of traditional theories of tragedy. Furthermore, each uses the same elements of the Romantic tradition, including the myth of the "Golden Age" or utopian thinking.[38] Both works can also be discussed with reference to my main topic, myth and history. When these two works are analyzed in conjunction with each other, the correspondences between them are striking. I propose that *Mahagonny* can be understood as Brecht's version of the *Ring*. This implies that it is, characteristically, a parody of the *Ring*.

The work has, in addition, elements that seem to be Wagner parodies, and that seem to be playing off, specifically, Wagner's *Ring*. As both works somehow represent their own aesthetic programs, these establish the later work as one that inverts the entire philosophical and aesthetic system that the earlier work stands for. The Brecht/Weill *Mahagonny* is not just a parody of the synthesis of the arts, but of Wagner's whole aesthetic program, to which this is a means to an end, and which is represented by the Romantic content, the cyclical plot, and the mythological subject matter of the *Ring*. The *Ring* represents its own aesthetic program through its regressive and progressive tendencies, and the cyclical plot structure of the "fall" from nature and the loss of a primal unity and the eventual re-establishment of that unity. *Mahagonny* is Brecht's version of, or Brecht's answer to, Wagner's *Ring* tetralogy. It is his mythical/historical analysis of, and solution to, the problems of modern society. Significantly enough, it proposes no explicit solution.

The *Ring* shows its Romantic self-conscious reflexivity in several ways. The Zurich writings present a three-stage model of the "fall" of modern society from nature. The art-work of the future, the union of the arts, was not only to represent a third stage in this model, but also to repair the decadence. Furthermore, the theme of the cycle is also the fall from nature. Thus, the *Ring* expresses, in several ways, Wagner's world-view and philosophy of art. It thematizes, one could say, its own social and artistic presuppositions. Furthermore, it is a myth (an artificial, idiosyncratic, synthetic, and modern myth) about myth. It shows the characters telling stories to try to explain the world in which they find themselves. In doing so, they show the work as thematizing the hermeneutic process. One can also see the tetralogy as somehow thematizing its own mythical raw material. It is as though it were, in some way, discussing the genre designation of tragedy. Wotan and Fricka, in discoursing and debating in the second act of *Walküre* on the relation of the gods to mankind, and the dichotomy of free will and fate, seem to be defining the work in which they exist vis-à-vis traditional tragedy theory.

Similarly, *Mahagonny* demonstrates its own aesthetic program and thematizes the idea of the "culinary." It portrays all of those things that Brecht felt distinguished the genre of opera—pleasure, enjoyment, leisure activity, and escape from reality. The city of Mahagonny was founded in opposition to the bourgeois, capitalist reality of big cities. It might not be going too far to extend this notion of thematizing the genre of opera and suggest that, by extension, Brecht's *Mahagonny* is thematizing the *Ring* and the Bayreuth Festival, perhaps in the same way that *Ariadne auf Naxos* seems to be discussing or "unfolding" *Elektra*. In each instance, the earlier work is presented on yet a further level of reflection.

Furthermore, *Mahagonny* clearly establishes itself as a parody of the Romantic tradition by using Romantic motives in a characteristically Brechtian way. The "green moon of Alabama" is clearly a parody of nature Romanticism. According to Albrecht Dümling, the moon of Alabama represents Romantic illusions. Accordingly, it is green. This passage is generally recognized as a parody, in particular, of Weber's "Jungfraukranz" melody from *Freischütz*. What is taken from the early Romantic opera is in Brecht's work inverted. The bridal wreath is outdated, stale.[39] *Mahagonny*, accordingly, in its very structure and its various textual and musical elements, pokes fun at the Romantic tradition. The exaggeratedly sentimental farewell to the green moon of Alabama can be considered an image of the work as a whole, more specifically, its relation to Wagner's *Ring* tetralogy. *Mahagonny* abandons, through inversion and parody, the Romantic tradition in particular.

In addition, *Mahagonny* even has some of the same themes that the *Ring* does. For instance, it presents a collection of vices that one could consider a parody of those of the *Ring*—lust, murder, or magic potions. Wotan, for instance, fathers the Volsungs and the Valkyries in love affairs that Fricka reproaches him for. Brecht deromanticizes the vices portrayed in *Mahagonny*, though. He presents the evils of eating and drinking, for instance, and boxing matches rather than Germanic battles. In scene 11, Jacob advises, to assuage the ennui, "Am besten wird es sein / Du bleibst sitzen / Und wartest / Auf das Ende" (M 356) (It is best to just sit around and wait for the end), thus recalling Wotan's behavior toward the end of the cycle, reported by Waltraute to Brünnhilde in the *Götterdämmerung*. In addition, *Mahagonny* thematizes law, just as the *Ring* does. Certain elements of *Mahagonny* certainly seem to be playing off of the *Ring*. The correspondences are, however, much deeper. *Mahagonny* represents an inversion of the entire aesthetic program upon which the *Ring* is based.

Furthermore, *Mahagonny* deals with money, just as the *Ring* shows the evils of capitalism by writing a myth about the Rhinegold under a river (which is then stolen from the original thief by a god). Gold is, after all, the central symbol and the title object of the *Ring*. Valhalla also seems to have been a model for Mahagonny, in anticipation of Kupfer's *Rheingold* staging. The city Mahagonny was founded (perhaps in parody of the *Ring*) by those seeking gold. Thus, the work opens with an "originary" act, as does *Rheingold*. The prelude to the first of the *Ring* dramas also portrays what is considered the musical evolution of a mythical cosmos from a simple chord, although, as reported in the Norns' Scene of *Götterdämmerung*, Wotan has already violated the World Ash Tree for his spear. The *Ring* thus starts with what is already a false origin, a "fallen" secondarity.

The opening scene of *Mahagonny* clearly seems to establish the work as a parody of the *Ring*. Begbick, in explaining that gold was found on the coast, says:

Seht, alle Leute, die von dort herunterkamen, sagten, dass die Flüsse das Gold sehr ungern hergeben. Es ist eine schlimme Arbeit, und wir können nicht arbeiten. Aber ich habe diese Leute gesehen, und ich sage euch, sie geben das Gold her! Ihr bekommt leichter das Gold von Männern als von Flüssen! (M 336)

Look, everyone who came from there said that it is hard to get gold from the rivers. It is hard work, and we can't work. But I've seen these people, and I tell you, they'll give over the gold! You can get the gold more easily from people than you can from rivers!

The talk of gold being obtained from rivers can be understood as a veiled parody of *Rheingold*. The title object of *Rheingold* is, after all, a lump of gold that is under the Rhine, and then stolen by Alberich and then from Alberich. The plot surrounding the ring holds the whole work together through three more evenings. That Begbick speaks negatively of getting gold from rivers, choosing rather to con it from people instead, clearly places the opera in an implicit opposition to the *Ring*. Money, so it seems, can cynically enough buy everything and anything in the world depicted in *Mahagonny*. Wealth is glorified by Brecht in an ironically critical and deromanticized way.

Valhalla has become "der Hotel zum Reichen Mann" (Hotel of the Rich Man), which is reminiscent of the house of the richest man in Vienna. Brecht's play, like Wagner's tetralogy, is a parable of modern society. Mahagonny stands for the world of capitalism.[40] Albrecht Dümling calls the work a "Parabel einer politisch-ökonomischen Entwicklung"[41] (parable of a political-economic development). The "loose maids of Alabama" can be considered parodies of the Rhinemaidens, or perhaps of the Flower Maidens of *Parsifal*. They are not, however, the naive and flirtatious nature spirits that the Romantics were so fond of but, rather, depraved prostitutes. The correspondences go far deeper than these isolated features. These isolated parallels hint at a deeper affinity of the two works. *Mahagonny* is an inversion of the entire aesthetic program upon which the *Ring* is based.

Mahagonny can, like Wagner's *Ring*, be analyzed with regard to the traditional form of tragedy. Insofar as Paul Ackermann can be considered a parody of the traditional tragic hero, *Mahagonny* can also be considered a travesty of the tragic form. Like the typical tragic hero, Paul Ackermann is a victim. The affinity of this play with Wagner's unworking of tragedy, however, goes far deeper. Wagner defined his deconstruction of Greek tragedy as a modern-day mythological drama that comments on history. Paul Ackermann is also a parody of a mythical and (as Wagner would put it, "purely human") figure, for he is representative. His exemplary status (which qualifies him to be, in a way, "mythological") is made clear by the explanatory heading of the fifth scene, in which it is related that specifically his story will be told (M 341).

Furthermore, myth was essential to Wagner's theory of revolution through music-drama. Wagner's aesthetic program is an elaborate theory of societal change by means of mythological refabrication. That Brecht's subject matter or raw material is historical rather than mythical makes the parody of Wagner all the more blatant. Brecht's reversal or denial of Wagner's theoretical history/myth dichotomy that I discussed earlier in this chapter is exemplified by a comparison of the *Ring* with *Mahagonny*. Brecht's choice of subject matter is itself telling to the utmost. Brecht not only writes a parody of Wagner's *Ring* but, in doing so, performs a parodistic transposition of mythological motives into historical subject matter.

In this manner the Brecht/Weill *Mahagonny* seems a reverse of Wagner's *Ring* with regard to the forms of history and myth. For Wagner, myth is a metaphor for history. For Brecht, history is a metaphor for myth. Wagner's music-drama is mythical; the subtext is history. Brecht's drama is historical; it has a mythical subtext. Wagner explicates and proposes to change the course of history with a set of mythical music-dramas; for Wagner, myth explains history. Brecht historicizes a mythological pattern.

One of the utopian themes that the *Ring* represents and that Brecht inverts in *Mahagonny* is that of the "Golden Age" or the utopia, the paradise of the Romantics. It doesn't matter, really, whether Brecht's play is working directly off of Wagner's work, or whether he is just spoofing the whole German Romantic tradition within which Wagner was functioning. The city of Mahagonny, in opposition to the world of work and (alienated) production or labor, is some kind of utopia (or at least it is considered such and perceived to be this). Within the play, the (oxymoronic) term "Paradiesstadt" (paradise-city) is used to refer to it. The people move into it carrying suitcases, just as the demythologized modern gods moved into Kupfer's Valhalla carrying Lucite suitcases in his *Rheingold* staging.

The originary act of founding the city can be understood as a parody of the start of *Rheingold* and the evolution of the entire cosmology from a single sustained chord. The city Mahagonny is supposed to be some kind of paradise on earth, but even this doesn't prove true, just as the gods of the *Ring* are corrupt and must end. It is hardly a paradise. The act of grounding the city is a negative one: "Aber dieses ganze Mahagonny / Ist nur, weil alles so schlecht ist" (M 337) (This whole Mahagonny project was begun because everything else is so bad). It is no utopia; it was founded because everything else is worse. It seems good only in comparison to worse places. It promises everything, every kind of imaginable pleasure—in exchange for money, of course. It is, however, so peaceful as to be boring. Such tranquillity, Brecht seems to be saying, is not a realistic goal. Perhaps it even suspiciously resembles the complacency that one settles into when one sits down for a Wagnerian drama. In a reversal of traditional imagery, Paul

Ackermann spent seven years, the traditional time that one spends in a magical land, a utopia, or a paradise, in Alaska before coming to Mahagonny.

A structural comparison of *Mahagonny* with the *Ring*, a contrastive discussion of how each of them uses the idea of utopia or the myth of the "Golden Age," further highlights Brecht's parodistic intent. Brecht's play unworks the model that the *Ring* is built on. Wagner's *Ring* uses the three-stage model of a unity with nature, a violation of this "natural" state, and an apocalyptic ending that is, at the same time, the start of a new era. Brecht's play distorts this structure, turning it inside-out. Brecht does not present a complete mythological Wagnerian cosmology that encompasses the beginning and end of the world. He deals with history, not myth. Accordingly, he shows the founding of the city, the approach of a hurricane, then the leaving of the city. The story that he presents is, one could say, a deromanticized historical three-stage model. Thus *Mahagonny* parodies the utopian thinking upon which the *Ring* is based.

At the start of *Mahagonny*, far from being a state of nature or some kind of primal unity, a "paradiesiacal" city (!) is (secondarily) founded. That Mahagonny is a city can be considered a parody of the important role that nature played in the *Ring* and in Romanticism in general. Wagner denigrated the big-city commercialization of art, choosing to place his own theater in a small town. Perhaps Mahagonny is really Brecht's dramatic portrayal, in the style of a historical parable, of course, of Bayreuth. The city is "fern vom Getriebe der Welt" (M 338) (far from the busy world), which is just the feature of Bayreuth that qualified it for Wagner as the proper home for his festival. The hurricane, which may be considered some kind of parody of apocalyptic imagery, comes at the middle of the play, not at the end. The play ultimately resolves nothing. Volker Klotz points out that the intention is destructive, not constructive.[42] The end does revert to the beginning, but in a negative way. They leave the utopia.

This work thus contains a distorted kind of cyclical structure, a modern realistic kind of big-city "cosmology." The structure can be considered a parody of the three-stage model of the Romantics and perhaps of Hegelian historical dialectic also. Wagner's *Ring* depicts a regression that is, at the same time, a progression. It seems typically Brechtian that *Mahagonny* shows absolutely nothing having been accomplished. The work fails to portray a renewal of society. Things are so bad in Mahagonny that the dramatic characters who founded the city at the beginning of the work finally have to leave the city. *Mahagonny* has no redemption at the end, thus directly opposing the Romantic tradition that Wagner represents.

Wagner's *Ring* represents a Romantic transcendence of tragedy. It shows conflicts and disasters galore, but it is basically an optimistic work. It overcomes tragedy in the cataclysmic glorification of the ideals that Brünnhilde champions as the corrupt Valhalla burns and, hopefully, in the societal revolution from within that the resultant, emotionally induced wisdom of the audience will cause. There is hope for a future utopia. The cycle ends with a new beginning. In contrast, Brecht's world-view in *Mahagonny* is pessimistic and cynical. Begbick states, in scene 11, "Schlimm ist der Hurrikan / Schlimmer ist der Taifun / Doch am schlimmsten ist der Mensch" (M 357) (The hurricane is bad, even worse is the typhoon, but the worst is mankind). The inner causes of the catastrophe overshadow the outer ones. There is no hope that the world depicted in *Mahagonny* can ever be bettered. In contrast, of course, the real world should be improved, and the opera was supposed to instill through its performance an awareness in the audience that society could and should be improved.

Thus, *Mahagonny* shows no transcendent values, no real Absolutes, only the cynical conviction that greed for money reigns supreme. In scene 16, Jenny quotes some advice she has been given, "Das Grösste auf Erden ist Liebe" (M 374) (The greatest thing on earth is love). But this is relativized in what could thus be considered a parody of the *Ring*. Brecht and Weill, in this opera, show materialism and carnal pleasures as ruling the world. The plot of Wagner's *Ring* functions on the dichotomy of love and power, which the stipulation that one must renounce love in order to attain the magic power of the ring clearly establishes. It is obvious which of the two Wagner romanticizes and glorifies. Brecht, however, has completely collapsed the Wagnerian love/power dichotomy. He pairs love with power. His fictional universe shows his cynicism. The latter cannot be overcome in the city of Mahagonny, and the former is base pleasure. In the *Ring*, idealized love ("Minne") must be renounced in order to gain power, symbolized by the gold ring. In *Mahagonny*, love (which is, in this cosmos, merely base sensuality) can be bought for money.

The concluding scene of the Brecht/Weill work shows Mahagonny burning, like Valhalla. In the final scene, the people demonstrate with the burning city in the background. Perhaps this is a spoofing of Wagner's revolution through opera. The text states, "Und in zunehmender Verwirrung, Teuerung und Feindschaft aller gegen alle demonstrierten in den letzten Wochen der Netzestadt die noch nicht Erledigten für ihre Ideale— unbelehrt" (M 386) (And in mounting confusion and enmity of all against all demonstrated, for their ideals, in the last weeks of the city those who had learned nothing). This is, I would argue, the Brechtian version of Brünnhilde's Immolation Scene. It parodies the finale of the *Ring*.

Wagner's drama was supposed to make one wise through feeling. Because one had thus attained a kind of consciousness, the outer reform of society would inevitably follow from this inner change. This is the aesthetic program of *Oper und Drama*. Brecht's finale shows people who have learned nothing. The futility depicted is blatantly conveyed by the term "unbelehrt." Furthermore, they demonstrate for their ideals precisely because they have learned nothing. There is not peace, but, rather, enmity abounds.

Thus, Brecht totally reverses the notion of the Wagnerian revolution through art that is at the basis of the *Ring* project.

The final chorus (scene 20) "Können einem toten Mann nicht helfen" (M 388–89) (A dead man cannot be helped) is generally acknowledged as a parody of Titurel's funeral procession in the third act of *Parsifal*. The blatant reference has wide ramifications for the rest of the work. The parody points toward a deeper negative correspondence between the two works and thus, by extension, the aesthetic and political thought of the two dramatists. Wagner's last drama has an ultimate redemption at the end. Parsifal has cured Amfortas' wound and regenerated the Grail Realm, which stands, of course, in some way for the future regeneration of modern society. *Mahagonny* lacks any kind of redemption at the end. Thus, Brecht and Weill brutally destroy Wagner's Romantic transcendence of tragedy.

The essence of Wagner's use of the three-stage model of the Romantics in *Oper und Drama* and the *Ring* is that a mythical version of history can, in turn, affect history. One of the ways he states the three-stage model in *Oper und Drama* is that myth is the beginning and end of history. He mythicizes history; that is, he writes a myth about it, to the purpose of, through the performance of this myth, mythicizing history, in other words, introducing a new Golden Age or utopia. In contrast, Brecht's opera vehemently denies any dialectical interchange between myth and history. *Mahagonny* is basically historical. Within Brecht's play, myth is beneath the surface. In fact, one could say that myth is beneath Brecht's text, as history is beneath the *Ring*. But for Brecht, myth has no societal reality, and it really never can.

Furthermore, a comparison of Brecht's and Wagner's stances toward the genre of tragedy, both theoretically and as reflected in these works under discussion, proves instructive and revealing. Wagner felt that myth was essential to tragedy, and thus myth was the raw material that he used for his new version of tragedy, which was, though, actually an unworking of tragedy, a Romantic transcendence of tragedy in which the duality of existence would be completely eradicated. In fact, Wagner defines the form of tragedy by its mythological content or raw material. It seems appropriate to his transcendence of tragedy that he introduces myth to, however, destroy it. The mythological musical-dramatic cosmos that he evolves in the prelude to *Rheingold* is destroyed in the cataclysm at the end of *Götterdämmerung*, in which the gods of nineteenth-century music-drama inevitably end. Wagner unworks and transcends tragedy by using and unworking myth; Brecht denies tragedy by parodying myth.

NOTES

1. John Rockwell, "Bayreuth 'Ring' Has Brechtian Flavor," in *New York Times*, 30 July 1988, p. 14.

2. See: Hans Mayer, "Theaterarbeit und Neue Zuschaukunst. Zur Erinnerung an Bertolt Brecht und Walter Felsenstein," in *Harry Kupfer*, by Michael Lewin (Vienna and Zurich: Europaverlag, 1988), pp. 11–15.

3. Hilda Meldrum Brown, *Leitmotiv and Drama: Wagner, Brecht, and the Limits of "Epic" Theatre* (Oxford: Oxford University Press, 1991), pp. 68–107 (chapter 3, "Brecht: Modes of Perspective in 'Epic' Theatre").

4. Dieter Borchmeyer, *Das Theater Richard Wagners: Idee, Dichtung, Wirkung* (Stuttgart: Reclam, 1982), p. 135.

5. Reinhold Grimm, *Bertolt Brecht. Die Struktur seines Werkes*, 2d ed., Erlanger Beiträge zur Sprach- und Kunstwissenschaft, vol. 5 (Nuremberg: Verlag Hans Carl, 1960).

6. Martin Gregor-Dellin, *Richard Wagner: Sein Leben, Sein Werk, Sein Jahrhundert* (Munich: Piper, 1980), pp. 290–91. See also: Martin Gregor-Dellin, "Beziehungen zum Sozialismus" in *Richard Wagner—die Revolution als Oper*, Reihe Hanser 129 (Munich: Carl Hanser, 1973), pp. 20–41.

7. See: the discussion under the entry "Verfremdung" in: Jan Knopf, *Brecht-Handbuch. Theater. Eine Ästhetik der Widersprüche* (Stuttgart: Metzler, 1980), pp. 378–402.

8. See: Andrea Mork, *Richard Wagner als politischer Schriftsteller: Weltanschauung und Wirkungsgeschichte* (Frankfurt am Main and New York: Campus, 1990), here cited from p. 199.

9. See: the entry "Negation des Allgemein-Menschlichen" in: Knopf, *Brecht-Handbuch*, pp. 402–4.

10. On the theory of the "epic theater," see: Ronald Gray, *Brecht* (Edinburgh and London: Oliver and Boyd, 1961), pp. 60–75; Marianne Kesting, *Das epische Theater. Zur Struktur des modernen Dramas*, 2d ed., Urban-Bücher 36 (Stuttgart: W. Kohlhammer, 1959), pp. 57–88; Helmut Jendreiek, *Bertolt Brecht: Drama der Veränderung* (Düsseldorf: August Bagel, 1969), pp. 31–93; Walter H. Sokel, "Figur—Handlung—Perspektive. Die Dramentheorie Bertolt Brechts," in *Deutsche Dramentheorien. Beiträge zu einer historischen Poetik des Dramas in Deutschland*, ed. Reinhold Grimm, vol. 2 (Frankfurt am Main: Athenäum, 1971), pp. 548–77; Gerhard Zwerenz, *Aristotelische und Brechtsche Dramatik. Versuch einer ästhetischen Wertung* (Rudolstadt: Greifenverlag, 1956); Otto Mann, pp. 593–97, 610–15; Martin Esslin, *Brecht: A Choice of Evils* (London: Eyre and Spottiswoode, 1959), pp. 106–29. This is only a sampling of some general information I have used; the literature is, of course, enormous.

11. George Steiner, *The Death of Tragedy* (New York: Alfred A. Knopf, 1961), p. 324.

12. Ronald Gray, *Brecht* (Edinburgh and London: Oliver and Boyd, 1961), p. 63.

13. Friedrich Dürrenmatt, "Theaterprobleme," in *Theater: Essays, Gedichte und Reden*, vol. 24 of *Werkausgabe*, ed. Thomas Bodmer (Zurich: Verlag der Arche, 1980), pp. 31–72.

14. On Brecht's *Antigone*, see: Knopf, *Brecht-Handbuch*, pp. 271–80; Werner Mittenzwei, *Brechts Verhältnis zur Tradition* (Berlin: Akademie-Verlag, 1972), pp. 221–29.

15. For a comparative study of Wagner and Brecht on this topic, see: Jürgen Söring, "Wagner und Brecht: Zur Bestimmung des Musik-Theaters," in *Richard Wagner 1883–1983. Die Rezeption im 19. und 20. Jahrhundert*, ed. Ulrich Müller, Stuttgarter Arbeiten zur Germanistik, no. 129 (Stuttgart: Akademischer Verlag Hans-Dieter Heinz, 1984), pp. 451–73.

16. On "historicization," see: Knopf, *Brecht-Handbuch,* pp. 386–87; and, more extensively: Klaus-Detlef Müller, *Die Funktion der Geschichte im Werk Bertolt Brechts. Studien zum Verhältnis von Marxismus und Ästhetik* (Tübingen: Max Niemeyer, 1967).

17. On the parable, see: Knopf, *Brecht-Handbuch,* pp. 404–12 (entry "Geschichtsdrama und Parabeltyp"); Klaus-Detlef Müller, pp. 146–218.

18. See the survey of German drama after 1945 in: Manfred Durzak, *Dürrenmatt, Frisch, Weiss. Deutsches Drama der Gegenwart zwischen Kritik und Utopie* (Stuttgart: Reclam, 1972), pp. 9–30.

19. Vera Stegmann, "Brecht contra Wagner: The Evolution of the Epic Music Theater," in *A Bertolt Brecht Reference Companion,* ed. Siegfried Mews (Westport, CT: Greenwood Press, 1997), pp. 238–60.

20. On the theories of Brecht and Weill, see: Albrecht Dümling, *Lasst euch nicht verführen. Brecht und die Musik* (Munich: Kindler, 1985), pp. 211–24; Gottfried Wagner, *Weill und Brecht. Das musikalische Zeittheater* (Munich: Kindler, 1977), pp. 61–81. See also: Thomas R. Nadar, "Brecht and His Musical Collaborators," in *A Bertolt Brecht Reference Companion,* ed. Siegfried Mews (Westport, CT: Greenwood Press, 1997), pp. 261–77.

21. I am citing from: Bertolt Brecht, *Schriften 4. Texte zu Stücken,* vol. 24 of *Werke,* Grosse kommentierte Berliner und Frankfurter Ausgabe, ed. Werner Hecht, Jan Knopf, Werner Mittenzwei, and Klaus-Detlef Müller (Berlin and Weimar: Aufbau-Verlag, and Frankfurt am Main: Suhrkamp Verlag, 1991), p. 79. Citations to this edition of the essay will be given in my text by page numbers, preceded by the abbreviation "AzM." On the Wagner and Nietzsche influence, see: Stegmann, pp. 246–47.

22. In the edition that I am quoting from, this line is all in emphasis.

23. Gunter G. Sehm, "Moses, Christus und Paul Ackermann. Brechts *Aufstieg und Fall der Stadt Mahagonny,*" *Brecht-Jahrbuch* (1976): pp. 83–100.

24. See also: Hans Mayer, *Bertolt Brecht und die Tradition* (Pfullingen: Günther Neske, 1961), here cited from p. 54.

25. Wilhelm Vosskamp, "Zwischen Utopie und Apokalypse: Die Diskussion utopischer Glücksphantasien in Brechts *Aufstieg und Fall der Stadt Mahagonny,*" in *Drama und Theater im 20. Jahrhundert,* ed. Hans Dietrich Irmscher und Werner Keller (Göttingen: Vandenhoeck und Ruprecht, 1983), pp. 157–68.

26. Dümling, p. 168.

27. Arnold Heidsieck, "Die Travestie des Tragischen im deutschen Drama," in *Tragik und Tragödie,* ed. Volkmar Sander, Wege der Forschung, vol. 108 (Darmstadt: Wissenschaftliche Buchgesellschaft, 1971), pp. 456–81.

28. On the music of *Mahagonny,* see: Gottfried Wagner, *Weill und Brecht,* pp. 182–212; Dümling, pp. 136–224. I am basing my discussion on these two works.

29. See: Bertolt Brecht, *Stücke 2,* vol. 2 of *Werke,* Grosse kommentierte Berliner und Frankfurter Ausgabe, ed. Werner Hecht, Jan Knopf, Werner Mittenzwei, und Klaus-Detlef Müller (Berlin and Weimar: Aufbau-Verlag, and Frankfurt am Main: Suhrkamp Verlag, 1988), pp. 337–38, 355; 360, 374; 362, 365, 368, 375. Subsequent references to this edition of *Mahagonny* will be given by page numbers within my text, preceded by the abbreviation "M."

30. The following discussion of the musical levels is based on: Gottfried Wagner, *Weill und Brecht,* pp. 85–154.

31. On instrumentation in the Brecht/Weill works, see: Gottfried Wagner, *Weill und Brecht*, pp. 121–27.

32. Dümling, pp. 164–72; Gottfried Wagner, *Weill und Brecht*, pp. 89–121.

33. Dümling, p. 168.

34. Gottfried Wagner, *Weill und Brecht*, pp. 199–203.

35. Gottfried Wagner, *Weill und Brecht*, pp. 194–95.

36. Dümling, p. 169.

37. Stegmann, p. 246. Dümling (p. 169) also notes the citations from *Zauberflöte* and *Parsifal*.

38. I am basing the following analysis, to a large extent, on ideas from the discussion of *Mahagonny* under that entry in: Knopf, *Brecht-Handbuch*, pp. 64–71. Other references will be given as necessary.

39. Dümling, pp. 146–47. See also: Gottfried Wagner, *Weill und Brecht*, pp. 194–95.

40. Grimm also notes this; see: Grimm, *Bertolt Brecht. Die Struktur seines Werkes*, p. 69. Grimm interprets *Mahagonny* as a parable. See also: Dümling, p. 161.

41. Dümling, p. 162.

42. Volker Klotz, *Bertolt Brecht. Versuch über das Werk* (Bad Homburg v.d.H.: Hermann Gentner, 1957), pp. 41–42.

Conclusions: History or Myth?

*A*rtistic inspiration, the anxiety of influence, and basic differences in the stances of selected individuals toward reality in its various facets can all manifest themselves in subtle and indirect ways. Often they are shown by the manner in which one reflects upon history and thus forms myths about it. History and myth are opposites, but they are also interrelated. History refers to what is objectively there; myth declares what is subjectively somehow true. Myth and history are often not totally distinct from each other. There is, on the contrary, a basic interrelation between history and myth. This is both more fundamental and more profound than simply stating that, for instance, Wallenstein was a general in the Thirty Years' War, or that Elektra is a Greek (or perhaps German) mythological character. Schiller's Wallenstein is not identical with his historical counterpart, and Elektra has a modern nonmythical psychic depth. Her dialogue with her mother shows that she has read up on Freud's interpretation of dreams, and that she is quite good at it, too.

Affinities and differences between pairs of dramatic works can be subtle, as I have shown. Literary critics often have to dig beneath the surface to uncover them. Even the choice of subject matter can be deceptive. What seems an outwardly mythological drama can have a profound relation to history and can thus, in actuality, be understood as a historical work. Conversely, a historical drama can be analyzed as taking an implicit or explicit stance toward myth. Critical comparisons can become very complex. To say, for instance, that the *Ring* and *Elektra* are both mythological is a drastic oversimplification that fails to specify how and why each is mythological; how myth functions in each work, and why it does so in this manner; in what way each of them is historical; and finally how they are mythical to the broader aim of being historical.

It seems that the boundaries between history and myth will always inevitably blur. The basic choice of a certain type of subject matter immediately establishes a fictional use of what was once historical, or a synthetic and anachronistic (if I may use a temporal term for an atemporal phenomenon) reconstitution of what was once strictly mythical, or any combination of these possibilities, anything, that is, in between the extremes. History is no longer really historical once it is made into fiction. A modern use of mythology, moreover, is usually a timely, temporal reworking of what is by definition an atemporal kind of material. I have shown how all of the works under consideration reflect these various ways in which history and myth interact with each other.

Scholars would be quick to tell you that literary analysis is a much more complex procedure than one of simply labeling what exists in a work of art, or finding things that a dramatist put there. A simple hunt for mythological prototypes or literary reflections of historical figures or events would indeed be a poor excuse for textual analysis and literary criticism. Drama theory is a reflection of the world-view of a dramatist and, by extension, of a certain age, the historically conditioned age in which the dramatist lived. It is, furthermore, reflective of some kind of stance toward myth and history. The thematic study that I have undertaken is, I feel, more satisfying and enlightening than a simple comparison of how each dramatist uses formal elements and the statement that some dramas use music, and others do not.

Therefore, the crucial question I have asked is not simply whether one uses myth or history for raw material, but, rather, how one uses myth or history. I have attempted to analyze, more deeply, the function of these in each work and with regard to each other. The aim of undertaking these analyses is not just the single thematic comparison I have pursued but, rather, a more general literary-historical one of suggesting a way in which Wagner's works can be discussed with regard to the history of German drama. Hopefully these studies that I have presented will contribute to a still better appreciation of Wagner's works, further the understanding of their influence on German literature, and vice versa, and help place them within the tradition and within the history of the genre in which they belong.

Selected Bibliography

Anders, Hans-Joachim. "Zum tragischen Idealismus bei Friedrich Hebbel." In *Deutsche Dramentheorien. Beiträge zu einer historischen Poetik des Dramas in Deutschland*, vol. 2, edited by Reinhold Grimm, pp. 323–44. Frankfurt am Main: Athenäum, 1971.

Baker, George M. "Hofmannsthal and Greek Tragedy." *The Journal of English and Germanic Philology* 12 (1913): pp. 383–406.

Barthes, Roland. *Mythologies*. Translated by Annette Lavers. New York: Hill and Wang, 1972.

Bauer, Roger. "Hofmannsthals Konzeption der Salzburger Festspiele." *Hofmannsthal-Forschungen* 2 (1974): pp. 131–39.

Bennett, Benjamin. *Modern Drama and German Classicism: Renaissance from Lessing to Brecht*. Ithaca, NY, and London: Cornell University Press, 1979.

Bennett, Benjamin. *Hugo von Hofmannsthal: The Theaters of Consciousness*. Cambridge: Cambridge University Press, 1988.

Berghahn, Klaus L. " ' Das Pathetischerhabene.' Schillers Dramentheorie." In *Deutsche Dramentheorien. Beiträge zu einer historischen Poetik des Dramas in Deutschland*, vol. 1, edited by Reinhold Grimm, pp. 214–44. Frankfurt am Main: Athenäum, 1971.

Berghahn, Klaus L. *Schiller: Ansichten eines Idealisten*. Frankfurt am Main: Athenäum, 1986.

Bermbach, Udo, ed. *In den Trümmern der eignen Welt: Richard Wagners "Der Ring des Nibelungen"*. Hamburger Beiträge zur öffentlichen Wissenschaft, vol. 7. Berlin: Dietrich Reimer, 1989. Includes: Udo Bermbach, "Die Destruktion der Institutionen. Zum politischen Gehalt des 'Ring'," pp. 111–44; Herbert Schnädelbach, " 'Ring' und Mythos," pp. 145–61.

Bohrer, Karl Heinz, ed. *Mythos und Moderne. Begriff und Bild einer Rekonstruktion*. Edition Suhrkamp, Neue Folge, vol. 144. Frankfurt am Main: Suhrkamp,

1983. Includes: Wolfgang Lange, "Tod ist bei Göttern immer nur ein Vorurteil. Zum Komplex des Mythos bei Nietzsche," pp. 111–37.

Bönig, Alois. "Hebbel und das Drama der Griechen—Zur Funktion des Mythos und der Geschichte in der Tragödie." *Hebbel-Jahrbuch* (1974): pp. 44–68.

Borchmeyer, Dieter. *Das Theater Richard Wagners: Idee, Dichtung, Wirkung*. Stuttgart: Reclam, 1982.

Borchmeyer, Dieter. "Richard Wagner und Nietzsche." In *Richard-Wagner-Handbuch*, edited by Ulrich Müller and Peter Wapnewski, pp. 114–36. Stuttgart: Alfred Kröner.

Borchmeyer, Dieter, ed. *Wege des Mythos in der Moderne. Richard Wagner, "Der Ring des Nibelungen"*. Munich: Deutscher Taschenbuch Verlag, 1987. Includes: Dieter Borchmeyer, " ' Faust' und 'Der Ring des Nibelungen'. Der Mythos des 19. Jahrhunderts in zwiefacher Gestalt," pp. 133–58; Wolfgang Frühwald, "Wandlungen eines Nationalmythos. Der Weg der Nibelungen ins 19. Jahrhundert," pp. 17–40; Dieter Bremer, "Vom Mythos zum Musikdrama. Wagner, Nietzsche und die griechische Tragödie," pp. 41–63.

Borchmeyer, Dieter. "Vom Anfang und Ende der Geschichte. Richard Wagners mythisches Drama. Idee und Inszenierung." In *Macht des Mythos—Ohnmacht der Vernunft?*, edited by Peter Kemper, pp. 176–200. Frankfurt am Main: Fischer, 1989.

Bradley, A. C. *Oxford Lectures on Poetry*. London: Macmillan, 1909; 2d ed., 1909. Includes: "Hegel's Theory of Tragedy," pp. 69–95.

Brecht, Bertolt. *Stücke 2*. Vol. 2 of *Werke*, Grosse kommentierte Berliner und Frankfurter Ausgabe, edited by Werner Hecht, Jan Knopf, Werner Mittenzwei, and Klaus-Detlef Müller. Berlin and Weimar: Aufbau-Verlag; Frankfurt am Main: Suhrkamp Verlag, 1988.

Brecht, Bertolt. *Schriften 4. Texte zu Stücken*. Vol. 24 of *Werke*, Grosse kommentierte Berliner und Frankfurter Ausgabe, edited by Werner Hecht, Jan Knopf, Werner Mittenzwei, and Klaus-Detlef Müller. Berlin and Weimar: Aufbau-Verlag; Frankfurt am Main: Suhrkamp Verlag, 1991.

Bremer, Dieter. "Vom Mythos zum Musikdrama. Wagner, Nietzsche und die griechische Tragödie." In *Wege des Mythos in der Moderne. Richard Wagner, "Der Ring des Nibelungen"*, edited by Dieter Borchmeyer, pp. 41–63. Munich: Deutscher Taschenbuch Verlag, 1987.

Brinkmann, Reinhold. "Szenische Epik. Marginalien zu Wagners Dramenkonzeption im *Ring des Nibelungen*." In *Richard Wagner: Werk und Wirkung*, edited by Carl Dahlhaus, pp. 85–96. Studien zur Musikgeschichte des 19. Jahrhunderts, vol. 26. Regensburg: Gustav Bosse, 1971.

Brinkmann, Richard. "Hofmannsthal und die Sprache." *Deutsche Vierteljahrsschrift für Literaturwissenschaft und Geistesgeschichte* 35, no. 1 (1961): pp. 69–95.

Brown, Hilda M. *Leitmotiv and Drama: Wagner, Brecht, and the Limits of "Epic" Theatre*. Oxford: Oxford University Press, 1991.

Butler, Eliza Marian. *The Tyranny of Greece over Germany*. Boston: Beacon Press, 1958. (First published in 1935 by Cambridge University Press.)

Cicora, Mary A. " 'Eva im Paradies': An Approach to Wagner's *Meistersinger*." *German Studies Review* 10, no. 2 (1987): pp. 321–33.

Cicora, Mary A. *"Parsifal" Reception in the "Bayreuther Blätter"*. American University Studies, 55. New York: Peter Lang, 1987.

Cicora, Mary A. "From Metonymy to Metaphor: Wagner and Nietzsche on Language." *German Life and Letters* 42, no. 1 (1988): pp. 16–31.

Cicora, Mary A. "Wagner Parody in *Doktor Faustus.*" *Germanic Review* 63, no. 3 (1988): pp. 133–39.

Cicora, Mary A. "Beethoven, Shakespeare, and Wagner: Visual Music in *Doktor Faustus.*" *Deutsche Vierteljahrsschrift für Literaturwissenschaft und Geistesgeschichte* 63, no. 2 (1989): pp. 267–81.

Cicora, Mary A. "Aesthetics and Politics at the Song Contest in Wagner's *Tannhäuser.*" *Germanic Review* 67, no. 2 (1992): pp. 50–58.

Cicora, Mary A. *From History to Myth: Wagner's "Tannhäuser" and its Literary Sources.* Germanic Studies in America, 63. Bern: Peter Lang, 1992.

Cicora, Mary A. "Music, Myth, and Metaphysics: Wagner Reception in Günter Grass' *Hundejahre.*" *German Studies Review* 16, no. 1 (1993): pp. 49–60.

Cicora, Mary A. *Mythology as Metaphor: Romantic Irony, Critical Theory, and Wagner's Ring.* Westport, CT: Greenwood Press, 1998.

Cicora, Mary A. *Modern Myths and Wagnerian Deconstructions: Literary-Critical Approaches to Wagner's Music-Dramas.* Westport, CT: Greenwood Press, forthcoming.

Clément, Catherine. *Opera, or the Undoing of Women.* Translated by Betsy Wing. Minneapolis: University of Minnesota Press, 1988.

Cohn, Hilde D. "Hofmannsthals Libretti." *German Quarterly* 35, no. 2 (1962): pp. 149–64.

Cooke, Deryck. *I Saw the World End: A Study of Wagner's "Ring".* London: Oxford University Press, 1979.

Corse, Sandra. *Wagner and the New Consciousness: Language and Love in the "Ring".* Madison, NJ: Fairleigh Dickinson University Press, 1990.

Cowen, Roy C. *Das deutsche Drama im 19. Jahrhundert.* Sammlung Metzler, vol. 247. Stuttgart: Metzler, 1988.

Crumbach, Franz Hubert. *Die Struktur des Epischen Theaters. Dramaturgie der Kontraste.* Schriftenreihe der Pädagogischen Hochschule Braunschweig, Heft 8. Braunschweig: Waisenhaus-Buchdruckerei und Verlag, 1960.

Dahlhaus, Carl. *Richard Wagners Musikdramen.* Velber: Friedrich, 1971.

Dahlhaus, Carl. *Wagners Konzeption des musikalischen Dramas.* Regensburg: Gustav Bosse, 1971.

Dahlhaus, Carl, ed. *Das Drama Richard Wagners als musikalisches Kunstwerk.* Studien zur Musikgeschichte des 19. Jahrhunderts, vol. 23. Regensburg: Gustav Bosse, 1970. Includes: Carl Dahlhaus, "Das unterbrochene Hauptwerk. Zu Wagners *Siegfried,*" pp. 235–38; Tibor Kneif, "Wagner: eine Rekapitulation. Mythos und Geschichte im *Ring des Nibelungen,*" pp. 213–21.

Dahlhaus, Carl, ed. *Richard Wagner: Werk und Wirkung.* Studien zur Musikgeschichte des 19. Jahrhunderts, vol. 26. Regensburg: Gustav Bosse, 1971. Includes: Dietrich Mack, "Zur Dramaturgie des *Ring,*" pp. 53–63; Reinhold Brinkmann, "Szenische Epik. Marginalien zu Wagners Dramenkonzeption im *Ring des Nibelungen,*" pp. 85–96; Carl Dahlhaus, "Über den Schluss der *Götterdämmerung,*" pp. 97–115.

Daviau, Donald G., and George J. Buelow. *The "Ariadne auf Naxos" of Hugo von Hofmannsthal and Richard Strauss.* University of North Carolina Studies in the

Germanic Languages and Literatures, no. 80. Chapel Hill: University of North Carolina Press, 1975.

deBoor, Helmut, ed. *Friedrich Hebbel: Die Nibelungen. Dichtung und Wirklichkeit.* Frankfurt am Main and Berlin: Ullstein, 1966.

Demetz, Peter, ed. *Brecht: A Collection of Critical Essays.* Englewood Cliffs, NJ: Prentice-Hall, 1962.

Denkler, Horst. "Politische Dramaturgie. Zur Theorie des Dramas und des Theaters zwischen den Revolutionen von 1830 und 1848." In *Deutsche Dramentheorien. Beiträge zu einer historischen Poetik des Dramas in Deutschland*, vol. 2, edited by Reinhold Grimm, pp. 345–73. Frankfurt am Main: Athenäum, 1971.

Denkler, Horst. *Restauration und Revolution: Politische Tendenzen im deutschen Drama zwischen Wiener Kongress und Märzrevolution.* Munich: Wilhelm Fink, 1973.

Dümling, Albrecht. *Lasst euch nicht verführen. Brecht und die Musik.* Munich: Kindler, 1985.

Dürrenmatt, Friedrich. "Theaterprobleme." In *Theater: Essays, Gedichte und Reden.* Vol. 24 of *Werkausgabe*, edited by Thomas Bodmer, pp. 31–72. Zurich: Verlag der Arche, 1980.

Durzak, Manfred. *Dürrenmatt, Frisch, Weiss. Deutsches Drama der Gegenwart zwischen Kritik und Utopie.* Stuttgart: Reclam, 1972.

Ehrismann, Otfrid. "Siegfried. Studie über Heldentum, Liebe und Tod. Mittelalterliche Nibelungen, Hebbel, Wagner." *Hebbel-Jahrbuch* (1981): pp. 11–48.

Emrich, Wilhelm. *Geist und Widergeist. Wahrheit und Lüge der Literatur. Studien.* Frankfurt am Main: Athenäum, 1965. Includes: "Friedrich Hebbels Vorwegnahme und Überwindung des Nihilismus," pp. 147–62.

Emrich, Wilhelm. "Hebbels *Nibelungen*—Götzen und Götter der Moderne." In *Friedrich Hebbel*, edited by Helmut Kreuzer and Roland Koch, pp. 305–26. Wege der Forschung, vol. 642. Darmstadt: Wissenschaftliche Buchgesellschaft, 1989.

Esselborn, Karl G. *Hofmannsthal und der antike Mythos.* Munich: Wilhelm Fink, 1969.

Esslin, Martin. *Brecht: A Choice of Evils. A Critical Study of the Man, His Work and His Opinions.* London: Eyre and Spottiswoode, 1959.

Ewans, Michael. *Wagner and Aeschylus: The "Ring" and the "Oresteia".* New York: Cambridge University Press, 1982.

Fähnrich, Hermann. *Schillers Musikalität und Musikanschauung.* Hildesheim: Gerstenberg, 1977.

Fenner, Birgit. *Friedrich Hebbel zwischen Hegel und Freud.* Stuttgart: Klett-Cotta, 1979.

Frank, Manfred. *Der kommende Gott. Vorlesungen über die Neue Mythologie.* Edition Suhrkamp 1142. Frankfurt am Main: Suhrkamp, 1982.

Franke, Rainer. *Richard Wagners Zürcher Kunstschriften: Politische und ästhetische Entwürfe auf seinem Weg zum "Ring des Nibelungen".* Hamburger Beiträge zur Musikwissenschaft, vol. 26. Hamburg: Verlag der Musikalienhandlung Karl Dieter Wagner, 1983.

Fries, Othmar. *Richard Wagner und die deutsche Romantik: Versuch einer Einordnung.* Zurich: Atlantis, 1952.

Frühwald, Wolfgang. "Wandlungen eines Nationalmythos. Der Weg der Nibelungen ins 19. Jahrhundert." In *Wege des Mythos in der Moderne. Richard Wagner, "Der Ring des Nibelungen"*, edited by Dieter Borchmeyer, pp. 17–40. Munich: Deutscher Taschenbuch Verlag, 1987.

Glaser, Horst Albert. "Ein deutsches Trauerspiel: Friedrich Hebbels *Nibelungen*." In *Die Nibelungen. Ein deutscher Wahn, ein deutscher Alptraum. Studien und Dokumente zur Rezeption des Nibelungenstoffs im 19. und 20. Jahrhundert*, edited by Joachim Heinzle and Anneliese Waldschmidt, pp. 333–50. Suhrkamp Taschenbuch 2110. Frankfurt am Main: Suhrkamp, 1991.

Gockel, Heinz. "Mythologie als Ontologie: Zum Mythosbegriff im 19. Jahrhundert." In *Mythos und Mythologie in der Literatur des 19. Jahrhunderts*, edited by Helmut Koopmann, pp. 25–58. Studien zur Philosophie und Literatur des neunzehnten Jahrhunderts, vol. 36. Frankfurt am Main: Vittorio Klostermann, 1979.

Graevenitz, Gerhard von. *Mythos: Zur Geschichte einer Denkgewohnheit*. Stuttgart: Metzler, 1987.

Gräwe, Karl Dietrich. "Sprache, Musik und Szene in 'Ariadne auf Naxos' von Hugo von Hofmannsthal und Richard Strauss." Diss., Munich, 1969.

Gray, Ronald. *Brecht*. Edinburgh and London: Oliver and Boyd, 1961.

Gray, Ronald. *Brecht, the Dramatist*. Cambridge: Cambridge University Press, 1976.

Gregor-Dellin, Martin. *Richard Wagner—die Revolution als Oper*. Reihe Hanser, 129. Munich: Carl Hanser, 1973.

Gregor-Dellin, Martin. *Richard Wagner: Sein Leben, Sein Werk, Sein Jahrhundert*. Munich: Piper, 1980.

Grimm, Reinhold. *Bertolt Brecht: Die Struktur seines Werkes*. Erlanger Beiträge zur Sprach- und Kunstwissenschaft, vol. 5. Nuremberg: Verlag Hans Carl, 1960.

Grimm, Reinhold. *Bertolt Brecht*. 2d ed. Stuttgart: Metzler, 1961, 1963.

Grimm, Reinhold. "Notizen zu Brecht, Freud und Nietzsche." *Brecht-Jahrbuch* (1974): pp. 34–52.

Grimm, Reinhold. *Brecht und Nietzsche oder Geständnisse eines Dichters. Fünf Essays und ein Bruchstück*. Frankfurt am Main: Suhrkamp, 1979.

Grimm, Reinhold, ed. *Episches Theater*. Cologne and Berlin: Kiepenheuer und Witsch, 1966.

Grimm, Reinhold, ed. *Deutsche Dramentheorien. Beiträge zu einer historischen Poetik des Dramas in Deutschland*. 2 vols. Frankfurt am Main: Athenäum, 1971. Includes: Klaus L. Berghahn, " 'Das Pathetischerhabene.' Schillers Dramentheorie," vol. 1, pp. 214–44; Peter Schmidt, "Romantisches Drama: Zur Theorie eines Paradoxons," vol. 1, pp. 245–69; Horst Denkler, "Politische Dramaturgie. Zur Theorie des Dramas und des Theaters zwischen den Revolutionen von 1830 und 1848," vol. 2, pp. 345–73; Hans-Joachim Anders, "Zum tragischen Idealismus bei Friedrich Hebbel," vol. 2, pp. 323–44; Jost Hermand, "Depravierter Idealismus. Dramentheorien um die Jahrhundertwende," vol. 2, pp. 429–50; Dieter Kimpel, "Hugo von Hofmannsthal: Dramaturgie und Geschichtsverständnis," vol. 2, pp. 451–81; Walter H. Sokel, "Figur—Handlung—Perspektive. Die Dramentheorie Bertolt Brechts," vol. 2, pp. 548–77.

Grundmann, Hilmar, ed. *Friedrich Hebbel: Neue Studien zu Werk und Wirkung*. Steinburger Studien, vol. 3. Heide: Westholsteinische Verlagsanstalt Boyens, 1982. Includes: Otfrid Ehrismann, "Philosophie, Mythologie und Poesie. Hebbels Schellingrezeption in den 'Nibelungen' ", pp. 85–102; Klaus Harro Hilzinger, "Hebbels 'Nibelungen'—Mythos und Nationalgeschichte," pp. 103–16.

Gurewitsch, Matthew Anatole. "The Maker's and the Beholder's Art: Serendipity in *Ariadne auf Naxos.*" *Germanic Review* 53, no. 4 (1978): pp. 137–46.

Guthke, Karl. S. *Wege zur Literatur. Studien zur deutschen Dichtungs- und Geistesgeschichte.* Bern and Munich: Francke, 1967. Includes: "Struktur und Charakter in Schillers *Wallenstein,*" pp. 72–91.

Hatfield, Henry. *Clashing Myths in German Literature.* Cambridge: Harvard University Press, 1974.

Hebbel, Friedrich. *Sämtliche Werke.* Historisch-kritische Ausgabe. Edited by Richard Maria Werner. *Tagebücher,* vol. 2 (1840–1844). Berlin: B. Behr's Verlag, 1903.

Hebbel, Friedrich. *Sämtliche Werke.* Historisch-kritische Ausgabe. Edited by Richard Maria Werner. *Tagebücher,* vol. 3 (1845–1854). Berlin: B. Behr's Verlag, 1905.

Hebbel, Friedrich. *Sämtliche Werke.* Historisch-kritische Ausgabe. Edited by Richard Maria Werner. *Tagebücher,* vol. 4 (1854–1863). Berlin: B. Behr's Verlag, 1905.

Hebbel, Friedrich. *Sämtliche Werke.* Historisch-kritische Ausgabe. Edited by Richard Maria Werner. *Briefe,* vol. 5 (1852–1856). Berlin: B. Behr's Verlag, 1906.

Hebbel, Friedrich. *Die Nibelungen.* Edited by Helmut deBoor. Frankfurt am Main and Berlin: Ullstein, 1966.

Heidsieck, Arnold. "Die Travestie des Tragischen im deutschen Drama." In *Tragik und Tragödie,* edited by Volkmar Sander, pp. 456–81. Wege der Forschung, vol. 108. Darmstadt: Wissenschaftliche Buchgesellschaft, 1971.

Heimrich, Bernhard. *Fiktion und Fiktionsironie in Theorie und Dichtung der deutschen Romantik.* Studien zur deutschen Literatur, vol. 9. Tübingen: Max Niemeyer, 1968.

Heinzle, Joachim, and Anneliese Waldschmidt, eds. *Die Nibelungen. Ein deutscher Wahn, ein deutscher Alptraum. Studien und Dokumente zur Rezeption des Nibelungenstoffs im 19. und 20. Jahrhundert.* Suhrkamp Taschenbuch 2110. Frankfurt am Main: Suhrkamp, 1991. Includes: Klaus von See, "Das Nibelungenlied—ein Nationalepos?", pp. 43–110; Horst Albert Glaser, "Ein deutsches Trauerspiel: Friedrich Hebbels *Nibelungen,*" pp. 333–50.

Hermand, Jost. "Depravierter Idealismus. Dramentheorien um die Jahrhundertwende." In *Deutsche Dramentheorien. Beiträge zu einer historischen Poetik des Dramas in Deutschland,* vol. 2, edited by Reinhold Grimm, pp. 429–50. Frankfurt am Main: Athenäum, 1971.

Heuer, Fritz, and Werner Keller, eds. *Schillers Wallenstein.* Wege der Forschung, vol. 420. Darmstadt: Wissenschaftliche Buchgesellschaft, 1977.

Hinck, Walter, ed. *Handbuch des deutschen Dramas.* Düsseldorf: August Bagel, 1980. Includes: Gerhard Kluge, "Das romantische Drama," pp. 186–99.

Hinderer, Walter, ed. *Schillers Dramen. Neue Interpretationen.* Stuttgart: Reclam, 1979. Includes: "Wallenstein," pp. 126–73.

Hofmannsthal, Hugo von. *Briefe 1890–1901.* Berlin: S. Fischer Verlag, 1935.

Hofmannsthal, Hugo von. *Dramen II.* Edited by Bernd Schoeller. Frankfurt am Main: Fischer Taschenbuch Verlag, 1979.

Hofmannsthal, Hugo von. *Dramen V.* Edited by Bernd Schoeller. Frankfurt am Main: Fischer Taschenbuch Verlag, 1979.

Hofmannsthal, Hugo von. *Reden und Aufsätze III.* Edited by Bernd Schoeller and Ingeborg Beyer-Ahlert. Frankfurt am Main: Fischer Taschenbuch Verlag, 1980.

Hollenbach, Eugen. "Die Hagen-Gestalt bei Hebbel und im Nibelungenlied." *Hebbel-Jahrbuch* (1969): pp. 144–77.

Hoppe, Manfred. *Literatentum, Magie und Mystik im Frühwerk Hugo von Hofmannsthals.* Berlin: Walter de Gruyter, 1968.

Hübner, Kurt. *Die Wahrheit des Mythos.* Munich: C. H. Beck, 1985.

Ingenhoff, Anette. *Drama oder Epos? Richard Wagners Gattungstheorie des musikalischen Dramas.* Untersuchungen zur deutschen Literaturgeschichte, vol. 41. Tübingen: Max Niemeyer, 1987.

Ingenschay-Goch, Dagmar. *Richard Wagners neu erfundener Mythos: Zur Rezeption und Reproduktion des germanischen Mythos in seinen Operntexten.* Abhandlungen zur Kunst-, Musik- und Literaturwissenschaft, vol. 311. Bonn: Bouvier Verlag Herbert Grundmann, 1982.

Irmscher, Hans Dietrich, and Werner Keller, eds. *Drama und Theater im 20. Jahrhundert.* Göttingen: Vandenhoeck und Ruprecht, 1983. Includes: Karl Konrad Polheim, "Hofmannsthal und Richard Wagner," pp. 11–23; Wilhelm Vosskamp, "Zwischen Utopie und Apokalypse: Die Diskussion utopischer Glücksphantasien in Brechts *Aufstieg und Fall der Stadt Mahagonny*," pp. 157–68.

Jendreiek, Helmut. *Bertolt Brecht: Drama der Veränderung.* Düsseldorf: August Bagel, 1969.

Kafitz, Dieter. *Grundzüge einer Geschichte des deutschen Dramas von Lessing bis zum Naturalismus.* Vol. 1. Königstein/Ts.: Athenäum, 1982.

Kaiser, Herbert. *Friedrich Hebbel: Geschichtliche Interpretationen des dramatischen Werks.* Munich: Wilhelm Fink, 1983.

Kayser, Otto. "Die Nibelungensage bei Hebbel und Wagner." *Hebbel-Jahrbuch* (1962): pp. 143–59.

Keller, Werner, ed. *Beiträge zur Poetik des Dramas.* Darmstadt: Wissenschaftliche Buchgesellschaft, 1976.

Kemper, Peter, ed. *Macht des Mythos—Ohnmacht der Vernunft?* Frankfurt am Main: Fischer, 1989. Includes: Dieter Borchmeyer, "Vom Anfang und Ende der Geschichte. Richard Wagners mythisches Drama. Idee und Inszenierung," pp. 176–200; Norbert Bolz, "Entzauberung der Welt und Dialektik der Aufklärung," pp. 223–41; Philipp Rippel, "Nietzsches Utopie des dionysischen Menschen," pp. 201–22.

Kesting, Marianne. *Das epische Theater. Zur Struktur des modernen Dramas.* 2d ed. Urban-Bücher, 36. Stuttgart: W. Kohlhammer, 1959.

Kimpel, Dieter. "Hugo von Hofmannsthal: Dramaturgie und Geschichtsverständnis." In *Deutsche Dramentheorien. Beiträge zu einer historischen Poetik des Dramas in Deutschland,* vol. 2, edited by Reinhold Grimm, pp. 451–81. Frankfurt am Main: Athenäum, 1971.

Klotz, Volker. *Bertolt Brecht. Versuch über das Werk.* Bad Homburg v.d.H.: Hermann Gentner, 1957.

Klotz, Volker. *Geschlossene und offene Form im Drama.* 4th ed. Munich: Carl Hanser, 1969.

Kluckhohn, Paul. "Die Arten des Dramas." *Deutsche Vierteljahrsschrift für Literaturwissenschaft und Geistesgeschichte* 19, no. 3 (1941): pp. 241–68.

Kneif, Tibor. "Wagner: eine Rekapitulation. Mythos und Geschichte im *Ring des Nibelungen.*" In *Das Drama Richard Wagners als musikalisches Kunstwerk,* edited by Carl Dahlhaus, pp. 213–21. Studien zur Musikgeschichte des 19. Jahrhunderts, vol. 23. Regensburg: Gustav Bosse, 1970.

Knopf, Jan. *Brecht-Handbuch. Theater. Eine Ästhetik der Widersprüche.* Stuttgart: Metzler, 1980.

Kommerell, Max. *Geist und Buchstabe der Dichtung: Goethe, Schiller, Kleist, Hölderlin.* 3d ed. Frankfurt am Main: Vittorio Klostermann, 1944. Includes: "Schiller als Gestalter des handelnden Menschen," pp. 132–74.

Könneker, Barbara. "Die Funktion des Vorspiels in Hofmannsthals *Ariadne auf Naxos.*" *Germanisch-Romanische Monatsschrift* 53 / NF 22, no. 2 (1972): pp. 124–41.

Koopmann, Helmut, ed. *Mythos und Mythologie in der Literatur des 19. Jahrhunderts.* Studien zur Philosophie und Literatur des neunzehnten Jahrhunderts, vol. 36. Frankfurt am Main: Vittorio Klostermann, 1979. Includes: Heinz Gockel, "Mythologie als Ontologie: Zum Mythosbegriff im 19. Jahrhundert," pp. 25–58; Peter Pütz, "Der Mythos bei Nietzsche," pp. 251–62.

Koppen, Erwin. *Dekadenter Wagnerismus. Studien zur europäischen Literatur des Fin de siècle.* Komparatistische Studien, vol. 2. Berlin and New York: Walter de Gruyter, 1973.

Korff, H. A. *Geist der Goethezeit. Versuch einer ideellen Entwicklung der klassisch-romantischen Literaturgeschichte.* Vol. 2: *Klassik.* Leipzig: Verlagsbuchhandlung von J. J. Weber, 1930.

Kraft, Herbert. *Poesie der Idee: Die tragische Dichtung Friedrich Hebbels.* Tübingen: Max Niemeyer, 1971.

Kreuzer, Helmut, and Roland Koch, eds. *Friedrich Hebbel.* Wege der Forschung, vol. 642. Darmstadt: Wissenschaftliche Buchgesellschaft, 1989. Includes: Wilhelm Emrich, "Hebbels *Nibelungen*—Götzen und Götter der Moderne," pp. 305–26.

Krogoll, Johannes. "Hofmannsthal-Strauss. Zur Problematik des Wort-Ton Verhältnisses im Musikdrama." *Hofmannsthal-Forschungen* 6 (1981): pp. 81–102.

Kröplin, Eckart. *Richard Wagner: Theatralisches Leben und lebendiges Theater.* Leipzig: VEB Deutscher Verlag für Musik, 1989.

Kunze, Stefan. "Die ästhetische Rekonstruktion der Oper: Anmerkungen zur 'Ariadne auf Naxos'." *Hofmannsthal-Forschungen* 6 (1981): pp. 103–23.

Kunze, Stefan. *Der Kunstbegriff Richard Wagners: Voraussetzungen und Folgerungen.* Regensburg: Gustav Bosse, 1983.

Lange, Wolfgang. "Tod ist bei Göttern immer nur ein Vorurteil. Zum Komplex des Mythos bei Nietzsche." In *Mythos und Moderne. Begriff und Bild einer Rekonstruktion,* edited by Karl Heinz Bohrer, pp. 111–37. Edition Suhrkamp, Neue Folge, vol. 144. Frankfurt am Main: Suhrkamp, 1983.

Lenz, Eva-Maria. *Hugo von Hofmannsthals mythologische Oper "Die ägyptische Helena".* Hermaea, Germanistische Forschungen, Neue Folge, vol. 29. Tübingen: Max Niemeyer, 1972.

Lewin, Michael. *Harry Kupfer.* Vienna and Zurich: Europaverlag, 1988. Contains: an Introduction by Hans Mayer, "Theaterarbeit und Neue Zuschaukunst. Zur Erinnerung an Bertolt Brecht und Walter Felsenstein," pp. 11–15.

Loos, Paul Arthur. *Richard Wagner: Vollendung und Tragik der deutschen Romantik.* Munich: Leo Lehnen, 1952.

Lütkehaus, Ludger. "Hebbel: Drama—Geschichte—'gegenwärtiger Welt-Zustand'." *Hebbel-Jahrbuch* (1978): pp. 130–36.

McInnes, Edward. "Lessing's 'Hamburgische Dramaturgie' and the Theory of the Drama in the Nineteenth Century." *Orbis Litterarum* 28, no. 4 (1973): pp. 293–318.

McInnes, Edward. *Das deutsche Drama des 19. Jahrhunderts.* Grundlagen der Germanistik, 26. Berlin: Erich Schmidt, 1983.

Mack, Dietrich. *Ansichten zum Tragischen und zur Tragödie. Ein Kompendium der deutschen Theorie im 20. Jahrhundert.* Munich: Wilhelm Fink, 1970.

Mack, Dietrich. "Zur Dramaturgie des *Ring.*" In *Richard Wagner: Werk und Wirkung,* edited by Carl Dahlhaus, pp. 53–63. Studien zur Musikgeschichte des 19. Jahrhunderts, vol. 26. Regensburg: Gustav Bosse, 1971.

Magee, Bryan. *Aspects of Wagner.* Rev. ed. Oxford: Oxford University Press, 1988.

Magee, Elizabeth. *Richard Wagner and the Nibelungs.* New York: Oxford University Press, 1990.

Mann, Otto. *Geschichte des deutschen Dramas.* 3d ed. Kröners Taschenausgabe, vol. 296. Stuttgart: Alfred Kröner, 1969.

Martini, Fritz. *Deutsche Literatur im bürgerlichen Realismus 1848–1898.* 4th ed. Stuttgart: Metzler, 1981.

Martini, Fritz. "Drama und Roman im 19. Jahrhundert: Perspektiven auf ein Thema der Formgeschichte." In *Literarische Form und Geschichte: Aufsätze zu Gattungstheorie und Gattungsentwicklung vom Sturm und Drang bis zum Erzählen heute,* pp. 48–80. Stuttgart: Metzler, 1984.

Mayer, Hans. *Bertolt Brecht und die Tradition.* Pfullingen: Günther Neske, 1961.

Mayer, Hans. *Anmerkungen zu Richard Wagner.* Edition Suhrkamp 189. Frankfurt am Main: Suhrkamp, 1966. 2d ed., 1977. Includes: "Zerstörung und Selbstzerstörung im 'Ring des Nibelungen'," pp. 91–99; "Wagners 'Ring' als bürgerliches Parabelspiel," pp. 100–111.

Mayer, Hans. *Richard Wagner: Mitwelt und Nachwelt.* Stuttgart: Belser, 1978. Includes: "Der 'Ring' und die Zweideutigkeit des Wissens," pp. 230–35; "Siegfrieds Trauermarsch," pp. 236–41.

Mayer, Hans. "Theaterarbeit und Neue Zuschaukunst. Zur Erinnerung an Bertolt Brecht und Walter Felsenstein." In *Harry Kupfer,* by Michael Lewin, pp. 11–15. Vienna and Zurich: Europaverlag, 1988.

Meetz, Anni. *Friedrich Hebbel.* 3d ed. Stuttgart: Metzler, 1973.

Meier, Helmut G. "Orte neuer Mythen. Von der Universalpoesie zum Gesamtkunstwerk." In *Philosophie und Mythos. Ein Kolloquium,* edited by Hans Poser, pp. 154–73. Berlin and New York: Walter de Gruyter, 1979.

Mews, Siegfried, ed. *A Bertolt Brecht Reference Companion.* Westport, CT: Greenwood Press, 1997. Includes: Vera Stegmann, "Brecht contra Wagner: The Evolution of the Epic Music Theater," pp. 238–60; Thomas R. Nadar, "Brecht and His Musical Collaborators," pp. 261–77.

Meyer-Wendt, H. Jürgen. *Der frühe Hofmannsthal und die Gedankenwelt Nietzsches.* Heidelberg: Quelle und Meyer, 1973.

Michel, Laurence, and Sewall, Richard B., eds. *Tragedy: Modern Essays in Criticism.* Englewood Cliffs, NJ: Prentice-Hall, 1963.

Mittenzwei, Werner. *Brechts Verhältnis zur Tradition.* Berlin: Akademie-Verlag, 1972.

Mork, Andrea. *Richard Wagner als politischer Schriftsteller: Weltanschauung und Wirkungsgeschichte.* Frankfurt and New York: Campus, 1990.

Moutoux, Eugene. "Wallenstein: Guilty and Innocent." *Germanic Review* 57, no. 1 (1982): pp. 23–27.

Müller, Klaus-Detlef. *Die Funktion der Geschichte im Werk Bertolt Brechts. Studien zum Verhältnis von Marxismus und Ästhetik.* Tübingen: Max Niemeyer, 1967.

Müller, Ulrich, and Peter Wapnewski, eds. *Richard-Wagner-Handbuch.* Stuttgart: Alfred Kröner, 1986. Includes: Peter Wapnewski, "Die Oper Richard Wagners als Dichtung," pp. 223–352; Dieter Borchmeyer, "Richard Wagner und Nietzsche," pp. 114–36; Ulrich Müller, "Richard Wagner und die Antike," pp. 7–18.

Müller-Seidel, Walter. *Die Geschichtlichkeit der deutschen Klassik. Literatur und Denkformen um 1800.* Stuttgart: Metzler, 1983. Includes: "Die Idee des neuen Lebens in Schillers *Wallenstein*," pp. 127–39; "Episches im Theater der deutschen Klassik. Eine Betrachtung über Schillers *Wallenstein*," pp. 140–72.

Nadar, Thomas R. "Brecht and His Musical Collaborators." In *A Bertolt Brecht Reference Companion,* edited by Siegfried Mews, pp. 261–77. Westport, CT: Greenwood Press, 1997.

Nadler, Käte. "Die Idee des Tragischen bei Hegel." *Deutsche Vierteljahrsschrift für Literaturwissenschaft und Geistesgeschichte* 19, no. 3 (1941): pp. 354–68.

Nattiez, Jean-Jacques. *Wagner Androgyne.* Translated by Stewart Spencer. Princeton, NJ: Princeton University Press, 1993.

Nehring, Wolfgang. *Die Tat bei Hofmannsthal. Eine Untersuchung zu Hofmannsthals grossen Dramen.* Germanistische Abhandlungen 16. Stuttgart: Metzler, 1966.

Neubauer, John. "The Idea of History in Schiller's *Wallenstein*." *Neophilologus* 56, no. 4 (1972): pp. 451–63.

Neubuhr, Elfriede, ed. *Geschichtsdrama.* Wege der Forschung, vol. 485. Darmstadt: Wissenschaftliche Buchgesellschaft, 1980.

Das Nibelungenlied. Edited and translated by Ulrich Pretzel. Stuttgart: S. Hirzel Verlag, 1973.

Nölle, Volker. "Schwert und 'Bettlerstab'. Zur Semantik des Epischen in Hebbels 'Nibelungen.' " *Hebbel-Jahrbuch* (1990): pp. 113–27.

Oster, Otto. "Der Nibelungen-Stoff bei Richard Wagner und Friedrich Hebbel." *"Die Walküre": Programmhefte der Bayreuther Festspiele* (1966): pp. 37–44.

Pestalozzi, Karl. *Sprachskepsis und Sprachmagie im Werk des jungen Hofmannsthal.* Zürcher Beiträge zur deutschen Sprach- und Stilgeschichte, no. 6. Zurich: Atlantis, 1958.

Polheim, Karl Konrad. "Hofmannsthal und Richard Wagner." In *Drama und Theater im 20. Jahrhundert,* edited by Hans Dietrich Irmscher and Werner Keller, pp. 11–23. Göttingen: Vandenhoeck und Ruprecht, 1983.

Poser, Hans, ed. *Philosophie und Mythos. Ein Kolloquium.* Berlin and New York: Walter de Gruyter, 1979. Includes: Helmut G. Meier, "Orte neuer Mythen. Von der Universalpoesie zum Gesamtkunstwerk," pp. 154–73; Jörg Salaquarda, "Mythos bei Nietzsche," pp. 174–98.

Pütz, Peter. "Der Mythos bei Nietzsche." In *Mythos und Mythologie in der Literatur des 19. Jahrhunderts,* edited by Helmut Koopmann, pp. 251–62. Studien zur Philosophie und Literatur des neunzehnten Jahrhunderts, vol. 36. Frankfurt am Main: Vittorio Klostermann, 1979.

Reinhardt, Hartmut. *Apologie der Tragödie. Studien zur Dramatik Friedrich Hebbels.* Studien zur deutschen Literatur, vol. 104. Tübingen: Max Niemeyer, 1989.

Rippel, Philipp. "Nietzsches Utopie des dionysischen Menschen." In *Macht des Mythos—Ohnmacht der Vernunft?*, edited by Peter Kemper, pp. 201–22. Frankfurt am Main: Fischer, 1989.

Rockwell, John. "Bayreuth 'Ring' Has Brechtian Flavor." *New York Times*, 30 July 1988, p. 14.

Salaquarda, Jörg. "Mythos bei Nietzsche." In *Philosophie und Mythos. Ein Kolloquium*, edited by Hans Poser, pp. 174–98. Berlin and New York: Walter de Gruyter, 1979.

Sander, Volkmar, ed. *Tragik und Tragödie.* Wege der Forschung, vol. 108. Darmstadt: Wissenschaftliche Buchgesellschaft, 1971. Includes: Arnold Heidsieck, "Die Travestie des Tragischen im deutschen Drama," pp. 456–81.

Sautermeister, Gert. *Idyllik und Dramatik im Werk Friedrich Schillers: Zum geschichtlichen Ort seiner klassischen Dramen.* Studien zur Poetik und Geschichte der Literatur, vol. 17. Stuttgart: W. Kohlhammer, 1971.

Schadewaldt, Wolfgang. "Richard Wagner und die Griechen." In *Richard Wagner und das neue Bayreuth*, edited by Wieland Wagner, pp. 149–74. Munich: Paul List, 1962.

Schadewaldt, Wolfgang. *Antike und Gegenwart. Über die Tragödie.* Munich: Deutscher Taschenbuch Verlag, 1966.

Schanze, Helmut. *Drama im Bürgerlichen Realismus (1850–1890): Theorie und Praxis.* Studien zur Philosophie und Literatur des neunzehnten Jahrhunderts, vol. 21. Frankfurt am Main: Vittorio Klostermann, 1973.

Scharf, Ursula. "Hofmannsthal's Libretti." *German Life and Letters* 8, no. 2 (1955): pp. 130–36.

Schiller, Friedrich von. *Wallenstein.* Vol. 8 of *Schillers Werke*, Nationalausgabe. Edited by Hermann Schneider and Lieselotte Blumenthal. Weimar: Hermann Böhlaus Nachfolger, 1949.

Schiller, Friedrich von. *Philosophische Schriften. Erster Teil.* Vol. 20 of *Schillers Werke*, Nationalausgabe. Edited by Benno von Wiese and Helmut Koopmann. Weimar: Hermann Böhlaus Nachfolger, 1962.

Schiller, Friedrich von. *Philosophische Schriften, Zweiter Teil.* Vol. 21 of *Schillers Werke*, Nationalausgabe. Edited by Benno von Wiese and Helmut Koopmann. Weimar: Hermann Böhlaus Nachfolger, 1963.

Schmid, Martin E. *Symbol und Funktion der Musik im Werk Hugo von Hofmannsthals.* Heidelberg: Carl Winter, 1968.

Schmidt, Peter. "Romantisches Drama: Zur Theorie eines Paradoxons." In *Deutsche Dramentheorien. Beiträge zu einer historischen Poetik des Dramas in Deutschland*, vol. 1, edited by Reinhold Grimm, pp. 245–69. Frankfurt am Main: Athenäum, 1971.

Schnädelbach, Herbert. " 'Ring' und Mythos." In *In den Trümmern der eignen Welt: Richard Wagners "Der Ring des Nibelungen"*, edited by Udo Bermbach, pp. 145–61. Hamburger Beiträge zur öffentlichen Wissenschaft, vol. 7. Berlin: Dietrich Reimer, 1989.

Schneider, Rolf. "Der fortgeschriebene Mythos." *"Die Walküre": Programmhefte der Bayreuther Festspiele* (1989): pp. 17–27.

See, Klaus von. "Das Nibelungenlied—ein Nationalepos?" In *Die Nibelungen. Ein deutscher Wahn, ein deutscher Alptraum. Studien und Dokumente zur Rezeption des Nibelungenstoffs im 19. und 20. Jahrhundert*, edited by Joachim Heinzle and Anneliese Waldschmidt, pp. 43–110. Suhrkamp Taschenbuch 2110. Frankfurt am Main: Suhrkamp, 1991.

Sehm, Gunter G. "Moses, Christus und Paul Ackermann. Brechts *Aufstieg und Fall der Stadt Mahagonny.*" *Brecht-Jahrbuch* (1976): pp. 83–100.

Sengle, Friedrich. "Vom Absoluten in der Tragödie." *Deutsche Vierteljahrsschrift für Literaturwissenschaft und Geistesgeschichte* 20, no. 3 (1942): pp. 265–72.

Sengle, Friedrich. *Das historische Drama in Deutschland. Geschichte eines literarischen Mythos.* 2d ed. Stuttgart: Metzler, 1969.

Skrodzki, Karl Jürgen. *Mythopoetik. Das Weltbild des antiken Mythos und die Struktur des nachnaturalistischen Dramas.* Bonner Arbeiten zur deutschen Literatur, vol. 44. Bonn: Bouvier Verlag Herbert Grundmann, 1986.

Smith, Martin E. "Das Gegensätzliche als Darstellungsprinzip in Hebbels 'Nibelungen'-Trilogie." *Hebbel-Jahrbuch* (1978): pp. 91–129.

Sokel, Walter H. "Figur—Handlung—Perspektive. Die Dramentheorie Bertolt Brechts." In *Deutsche Dramentheorien. Beiträge zu einer historischen Poetik des Dramas in Deutschland*, vol. 2, edited by Reinhold Grimm, pp. 548–77. Frankfurt am Main: Athenäum, 1971.

Söring, Jürgen. "Wagner und Brecht: Zur Bestimmung des Musik-Theaters." In *Richard Wagner 1883–1983. Die Rezeption im 19. und 20. Jahrhundert. Gesammelte Beiträge des Salzburger Symposions*, edited by Ulrich Müller, pp. 451–73. Stuttgarter Arbeiten zur Germanistik, no. 129. Stuttgart: Akademischer Verlag Hans-Dieter Heinz, 1984.

Stegmann, Vera. "Brecht contra Wagner: The Evolution of the Epic Music Theater." In *A Bertolt Brecht Reference Companion*, edited by Siegfried Mews, pp. 238–60. Westport, CT: Greenwood Press, 1997.

Steiner, George. *The Death of Tragedy.* New York: Alfred A. Knopf, 1961.

Stern, Martin. "Spätzeitlichkeit und Mythos. Hofmannsthals *Ariadne.*" *Hofmannsthal-Forschungen* 8 (1985): pp. 291–312.

Strässner, Matthias. *Analytisches Drama.* Munich: Wilhelm Fink, 1980.

Strauss, Richard, and Hugo von Hofmannsthal. *Briefwechsel.* 4th ed. Edited by Willi Schuh. Zurich: Atlantis, 1970.

Szondi, Peter. *Schriften I.* Edited by Wolfgang Fietkau. Frankfurt am Main: Suhrkamp, 1978. Includes: "Versuch über das Tragische," pp. 151–260; "Theorie des modernen Dramas 1880–1950," pp. 11–148.

Tarot, Rolf. *Hugo von Hofmannsthal: Daseinsformen und dichterische Struktur.* Tübingen: Max Niemeyer, 1970.

Vosskamp, Wilhelm. "Zwischen Utopie und Apokalypse: Die Diskussion utopischer Glücksphantasien in Brechts *Aufstieg und Fall der Stadt Mahagonny.*" In *Drama und Theater im 20. Jahrhundert*, edited by Hans Dietrich Irmscher and Werner Keller, pp. 157–68. Göttingen: Vandenhoeck und Ruprecht, 1983.

Wagner, Cosima. *Die Tagebücher.* 4 vols. 2d ed. Edited by Martin Gregor-Dellin and Dietrich Mack. Munich: Piper, 1976, 1982. English translation by Geoffrey Skelton. *Diaries.* 2 vols. New York and London: Harcourt Brace Jovanovich, 1978/80.

Wagner, Gottfried. *Weill und Brecht. Das musikalische Zeittheater.* Munich: Kindler, 1977.

Wagner, Richard. *Gesammelte Schriften und Dichtungen.* 10 vols. Leipzig: E. W. Fritzsch, 1887–88. Rpt. Steiger, 1976.

Wagner, Richard. *Sämtliche Briefe.* Vol. 4: *Briefe der Jahre 1851–1852.* Edited by Gertrud Strobel and Werner Wolf. Leipzig: VEB Deutscher Verlag für Musik, 1979.

Wagner, Richard. *Sämtliche Briefe.* Vol. 5: *September 1852–Januar 1854.* Edited by Gertrud Strobel and Werner Wolf. Leipzig: Deutscher Verlag für Musik, 1993.

Wagner, Richard. *Sämtliche Briefe.* Vol. 6: *Januar 1854–Februar 1855.* Edited by Hans-Joachim Bauer and Johannes Forner. Leipzig: VEB Deutscher Verlag für Musik, 1986.

Wagner, Richard. *Die Musikdramen.* Edited by Joachim Kaiser. Hamburg: Hoffmann und Campe, 1971; Munich: Deutscher Taschenbuch Verlag, 1978, 1981.

Wagner, Richard. *Mein Leben.* Edited by Martin Gregor-Dellin. Munich: Paul List, 1963; Goldmann, 1983.

Wagner, Richard. *Oper und Drama.* Edited by Klaus Kropfinger. Stuttgart: Reclam, 1984.

Wapnewski, Peter. *Der traurige Gott: Richard Wagner in seinen Helden.* Munich: C. H. Beck, 1978; Deutscher Taschenbuch Verlag, 1982.

Wapnewski, Peter. "Der Ring und sein Kreislauf. Überlegungen zum Textverständnis der 'Götterdämmerung'." *"Götterdämmerung": Programmhefte der Bayreuther Festspiele* (1984): pp. 25–50.

Wapnewkski, Peter. "Die Oper Richard Wagners als Dichtung." In *Richard-Wagner-Handbuch,* edited by Ulrich Müller and Peter Wapnewski, pp. 223–352. Stuttgart: Alfred Kröner, 1986.

Westernhagen, Curt von. *Richard Wagners Dresdener Bibliothek 1842 bis 1849. Neue Dokumente zur Geschichte seines Schaffens.* Wiesbaden: F. A. Brockhaus, 1966.

Wiese, Benno von. "Geschichte und Drama." *Deutsche Vierteljahrsschrift für Literaturwissenschaft und Geistesgeschichte* 20, no. 4 (1942): pp. 412–34. Rpt. in: *Geschichtsdrama,* edited by Elfriede Neubuhr, pp. 381–403. Wege der Forschung, vol. 485. Darmstadt: Wissenschaftliche Buchgesellschaft, 1980.

Wiese, Benno von. "Probleme der deutschen Tragödie im 19. Jahrhundert." *Wirkendes Wort* 1 (1950/51): pp. 32–38.

Wiese, Benno von. "Schiller und die deutsche Tragödie des 19. Jahrhunderts." *Deutsche Vierteljahrsschrift für Literaturwissenschaft und Geistesgeschichte* 25, no. 2 (1951): pp. 199–213.

Wiese, Benno von. *Friedrich Schiller.* 3d ed. Stuttgart: Metzler, 1963.

Wiese, Benno von, ed. *Das deutsche Drama vom Barock bis zur Gegenwart.* Vol. I, Interpretationen. Düsseldorf: August Bagel, 1964. Includes: Benno von Wiese, "Wallenstein," pp. 271–306.

Wiese, Benno von. *Die Deutsche Tragödie von Lessing bis Hebbel.* Hamburg: Hoffmann und Campe, 1948. 6th ed., 1964.

Wiese, Benno von. *Von Lessing bis Grabbe: Studien zur deutschen Klassik und Romantik.* Düsseldorf: August Bagel, 1968. Includes: "Schiller als Geschichtsphilosoph und Geschichtsschreiber," pp. 41–57; "Das Problem der ästhetischen Versöhnung bei Schiller und Hegel," pp. 138–61; "Das verlorene und wieder zu findende Paradies. Eine Studie über den Begriff der Anmut bei Goethe, Kleist und Schiller," pp. 162–90.

Wittmann, Lothar. *Sprachthematik und dramatische Form im Werke Hofmannsthals.* Studien zur Poetik und Geschichte der Literatur, vol. 2. Stuttgart: W. Kohlhammer, 1966.

Ziegler, Klaus. *Mensch und Welt in der Tragödie Friedrich Hebbels.* Berlin, 1938. Rpt. Darmstadt: Wissenschaftliche Buchgesellschaft, 1966.

Zwerenz, Gerhard. *Aristotelische und Brechtsche Dramatik. Versuch einer ästhetischen Wertung.* Wir diskutieren, 5. Rudolstadt: Greifenverlag, 1956.

Index

About the Author

MARY A. CICORA has published many articles on Wagner and German literature. She is also the author of *Mythology as Metaphor: Romantic Irony, Critical Theory, and Wagner's* Ring (Greenwood, 1998). After completing her undergraduate work at Yale, she received her doctorate degree in German literature from Cornell.

ISBN 0-313-30529-3

90000>

EAN

9 780313 305290

HARDCOVER BAR CODE